# I THOUGHT MY FATHER WAS GOD

*And Other True Tales from NPR's*

National Story Project

EDITED AND INTRODUCED BY
## PAUL AUSTER

NELLY REIFLER, ASSISTANT EDITOR

**G.K. Hall & Co. • Waterville, Maine**

Published in 2002 by arrangement with Henry Holt
and Company, LLC.

G.K. Hall Large Print Nonfiction Series.

The text of this Large Print edition is unabridged.
Other aspects of the book may vary from the original edition.

Set in 16 pt. Plantin.

Printed in the United States on permanent paper.

**Library of Congress Cataloging-in-Publication Data**

I thought my father was God, and other true tales from NPR's
National Story Project / edited and introduced by Paul Auster.
    p. cm.
  Includes index.
  ISBN 0-7838-9765-0 (lg. print : hc : alk. paper)
  1. United States — Social life and customs — 20th century —
Anecdotes.  2. United States — Social conditions — 1945 —
Anecdotes.  3. United States — Biography — Anecdotes.
4. Oral history.  5. Large type books.  I. Auster, Paul, 1947–
II. National Story Project (U.S.)
E169.02 .I22 2002
973.91—dc21                                 2001051771

# EDITOR'S NOTE

Grateful thanks to the following people for their help and support: Daniel Zwerdling, Jacki Lyden, Rebecca Davis, Davar Ardalan, Walter Ray Watson, Kitty Eisele, Marta Haywood, and Hannah Misol — all of *Weekend All Things Considered* — as well as to Carol Mann, Jennifer Barth, and — first, last, and always — Siri Hustvedt.

P. A.

5/02

# CONTENTS

## FAMILIES

SLAPSTICK

## STRANGERS

## WAR

## DEATH

# INTRODUCTION

I never intended to do this. The *National Story Project* came about by accident, and if not for a remark my wife made at the dinner table sixteen months ago, most of the pieces in this book never would have been written. It was May 1999, perhaps June, and earlier that day I had been interviewed on National Public Radio about my most recent novel. After we finished our conversation, Daniel Zwerdling, the host of *Weekend All Things Considered*, had asked me if I would be interested in becoming a regular contributor to the program. I couldn't even see his face when he asked the question. I was in the NPR studio on Second Avenue in New York, and he was in Washington, D.C., and for the past twenty or thirty minutes we had been talking to each other through microphones and headsets, aided by a technological marvel known as fiber optics. I asked him what he had in mind, and he said that he wasn't sure. Maybe I could come on the air every month or so and tell stories.

I wasn't interested. Doing my own work was difficult enough, and taking on a job that would force me to crank out stories on command was the last thing I needed. Just to be polite, however, I said that I would go home and think about it.

It was my wife, Siri, who turned the proposition on its head. That night, when I told her about NPR's curious offer, she immediately came up

15

with a proposal that reversed the direction of my thoughts. In a matter of thirty seconds, no had become yes.

You don't have to write the stories yourself, she said. Get people to sit down and write their own stories. They could send them in to you, and then you could read the best ones on the radio. If enough people wrote in, it could turn into something extraordinary.

That was how the *National Story Project* was born. It was Siri's idea, and then I picked it up and started to run with it.

Sometime in late September, Zwerdling came to my house in Brooklyn with Rebecca Davis, one of the producers of *Weekend All Things Considered*, and we launched the idea of the project in the form of another interview. I told the listeners that I was looking for stories. The stories had to be true, and they had to be short, but there would be no restrictions as to subject matter or style. What interested me most, I said, were stories that defied our expectations about the world, anecdotes that revealed the mysterious and unknowable forces at work in our lives, in our family histories, in our minds and bodies, in our souls. In other words, true stories that sounded like fiction. I was talking about big things and small things, tragic things and comic things, any experience that felt important enough to set down on paper. They shouldn't worry if they had never written a story, I said. Everyone was bound to know some good ones, and if enough people answered the call to participate, we would inevitably begin to learn some surpris-

16

ing things about ourselves and each other. The spirit of the project was entirely democratic. All listeners were welcome to contribute, and I promised to read every story that came in. People would be exploring their own lives and experiences, but at the same time they would be part of a collective effort, something bigger than just themselves. With their help, I said, I was hoping to put together an archive of facts, a museum of American reality.

The interview was broadcast on the first Saturday in October, exactly one year ago today. Since that time, I have received more than four thousand submissions. This number is many times greater than what I had anticipated, and for the past twelve months I have been awash in manuscripts, floating madly in an ever expanding sea of paper. Some of the stories are written by hand; others are typed; still others are printed out from e-mails. Every month, I have scrambled to choose five or six of the best ones and turn them into a twenty-minute segment to be aired on *Weekend All Things Considered.* It has been singularly rewarding work, one of the most inspiring tasks I have ever undertaken. But it has had its difficult moments as well. On several occasions, when I have been particularly swamped with material, I have read sixty or seventy stories at a single sitting, and each time I have done that, I have stood up from the chair feeling pulverized, absolutely drained of energy. So many emotions to contend with, so many strangers camped out in the living room, so many voices coming at me from so many different directions. On those evenings, for the space of two or three hours, I have felt that the entire population of America has walked into my house. I didn't hear America singing. I heard it telling stories.

Yes, a number of rants and diatribes have been sent in by deranged people, but far fewer than I would have predicted. I have been exposed to groundbreaking revelations about the Kennedy assassination, subjected to several complex exegeses that link current events to verses from Scripture, and made privy to information pertaining to lawsuits against half a dozen corporations and government agencies. Some people have gone out of their way to provoke me and turn my stomach. Just last week, I received a submission from a man who signed his story "Cerberus" and gave his return address as "The Underworld 66666." In the story, he told about his days in Vietnam as a marine, ending with an account of how he and the other men in his company had roasted a stolen Vietnamese baby and eaten it around a campfire. He made it sound as though he were proud of what he had done. For all I know, the story could be true. But that doesn't mean I have any interest in presenting it on the radio.

On the other hand, some of the pieces from disturbed people have contained startling and arresting passages. Last fall, when the project was just getting under way, one came in from another Vietnam vet, a man serving a life sentence for murder in a penitentiary somewhere in the Midwest. He enclosed a handwritten affidavit that recounted the muddled story of how he came to commit his crime, and the last sentence of the document read,

"I have never been perfect, but I am real." In some sense, that statement could stand as the credo of the *National Story Project*, the very principle behind this book. We have never been perfect, but we are real.

Of the four thousand stories I have read, most have been compelling enough to hold me until the last word. Most have been written with simple, straightforward conviction, and most have done honor to the people who sent them in. We all have inner lives. We all feel that we are part of the world and yet exiled from it. We all burn with the fires of our own existence. Words are needed to express what is in us, and again and again contributors have thanked me for giving them the chance to tell their stories, for "allowing the people to be heard." What the people have said is often astonishing. More than ever, I have come to appreciate how deeply and passionately most of us live within ourselves. Our attachments are ferocious. Our loves overwhelm us, define us, obliterate the boundaries between ourselves and others. Fully a third of the stories I have read are about families: parents and children, children and parents, husbands and wives, brothers and sisters, grandparents. For most of us, those are the people who fill up our world, and in story after story, both the dark ones and the humorous ones, I have been impressed by how clearly and forcefully these connections have been articulated.

A few high-school students sent in stories about hitting home runs and winning medals at track

19

meets, but it was the rare adult who took advantage of the occasion to brag about his accomplishments. Hilarious blunders, wrenching coincidences, brushes with death, miraculous encounters, improbable ironies, premonitions, sorrows, pains, dreams — these were the subjects the contributors chose to write about. I learned that I am not alone in my belief that the more we understand of the world, the more elusive and confounding the world becomes. As one early contributor so eloquently put it, "I am left without an adequate definition of reality." If you aren't certain about things, if your mind is still open enough to question what you are seeing, you tend to look at the world with great care, and out of that watchfulness comes the possibility of seeing something that no one else has seen before. You have to be willing to admit that you don't have all the answers. If you think you do, you will never have anything important to say.

Incredible plots, unlikely turns, events that refuse to obey the laws of common sense. More often than not, our lives resemble the stuff of eighteenth-century novels. Just today, another batch of e-mails from NPR arrived at my door, and among the new submissions was this story from a woman who lives in San Diego, California. I quote from it not because it is unusual, but simply because it is the freshest piece of evidence at hand:

I was adopted from an orphanage at the age of eight months. Less than a year later, my adoptive father died suddenly. I was raised by my widowed mother with three older adopted brothers. When you are adopted, there is a natural curiosity to know your birth family. By the time I was married and in my late twenties, I decided to start looking.

I had been raised in Iowa, and sure enough, after a two-year search, I located my birth mother in Des Moines. We met and went to dinner. I asked her who my birth father was, and she gave me his name. I asked where he lived, and she said "San Diego," which was where I had been living for the last five years. I had moved to San Diego not knowing a soul — just knowing I wanted to be there.

It ended up that I worked in the building next door to where my father worked. We often ate lunch at the same restaurant. We never told his wife of my existence, as I didn't really want to disrupt his life. He had always been a bit of a gadabout, however, and he always had a girlfriend on the side. He and his last girlfriend were "together" for fifteen-plus years, and she remained the source of my information about him.

Five years ago, my birth mother was dying of cancer in Iowa. Simultaneously, I received a call from my father's paramour that he had died of heart complications. I called my biological mother in the hospital in Iowa and told her of his death. She died that night. I received word that both of their funerals were held on the following Saturday at exactly the same hour — his at 11 A.M. in California and hers at 1 P.M. in Iowa.

After three or four months, I sensed that a book was going to be necessary to do justice to the project. Too many good stories were coming in, and it wasn't possible for me to present more than a fraction of the worthy submissions on the radio. Many of them were too long for the format we had established, and the ephemeral nature of the broadcasts (a lone, disembodied voice floating across the American airwaves for eighteen or twenty minutes every month) made me want to collect the most memorable ones and preserve them in written form. Radio is a powerful tool, and NPR reaches into almost every corner of the country, but you can't hold the words in your hands. A book is tangible, and once you put it down, you can return to the place where you left it and pick it up again.

This anthology contains 179 pieces — what I consider to be the best of the approximately four thousand works that have come in during the past year. But it is also a representative selection, a miniaturized version of the *National Story Project* as a whole. For every story about a dream or an animal or a missing object to be found in these pages, there were dozens of others that were submitted, dozens of others that could have been chosen. The book begins with a six-sentence tale about a chicken (the first story I read on the air last November) and ends with a wistful meditation on the role that radio plays in our lives. The author of that last piece, Ameni Rozsa, was moved to write her story while listening to one of the *National Story Project* broadcasts. I had been hoping to capture bits and fragments of American reality, but it had never occurred to me that the project itself could become a part of that reality, too.

This book has been written by people of all ages and from all walks of life. Among them are a postman, a merchant seaman, a trolley-bus driver, a gas-and-electric-meter reader, a restorer of player pianos, a crime-scene cleaner, a musician, a businessman, two priests, an inmate at a state correctional facility, several doctors, and assorted housewives, farmers, and ex-servicemen. The youngest contributor is barely twenty; the oldest is pushing ninety. Half of the writers are women; half are men. They live in cities, suburbs, and in rural areas, and they come from forty-two different states. In making my choices, I never once gave a thought to demographic balance. I selected the stories solely on the basis of merit: for their humanity, for their truth, for their charm. The numbers just fell out that way, and the results were determined by blind chance.

In an attempt to make some order out of this chaos of voices and contrasting styles, I have broken the stories into ten different categories. The section titles speak for themselves, but except for the fourth section, "Slapstick," which is made up entirely of comic stories, there is a wide range of material within each of the categories. Their contents run the gamut from farce to tragic drama, and for every act of cruelty and violence that one encounters in them, there is a countervailing act of kindness or generosity or love. The stories go back and forth, up and down, in and out, and after a while your head starts to spin. Turn the page from one contributor to the next and you are confronted by an entirely different person, an entirely different set of circumstances, an entirely different worldview. But difference is what this book is all about. There is some elegant and sophisticated writing in it, but there is also much that is crude and awkward. Only a small portion of it resembles anything that could qualify as "literature." It is something else, something raw and close to the bone, and whatever skills these authors might lack, most of their stories are unforgettable. It is difficult for me to imagine that anyone could read through this book from beginning to end without once shedding a tear, without once laughing out loud.

If I had to define what these stories were, I would call them dispatches, reports from the front lines of personal experience. They are about the private worlds of individual Americans, yet again and again one sees the inescapable marks of history on them, the intricate ways in which individual destinies are shaped by society at large. Some of the older contributors, looking back on events from their childhood and youth, are necessarily writing about the Depression and World War II. Other contributors, born in the middle of the century, continue to be haunted by the effects of the war in Vietnam. That conflict ended twenty-five years ago, and yet it lives on in us as a recurrent nightmare, a great wound in the national soul. Still other contributors, from several different generations, have written stories about the disease of American racism. This scourge has been with us for more than 350 years, and no matter how hard we struggle to eradicate it from our midst, a cure has yet to be found.

Other stories touch on AIDS, alcoholism, drug abuse, pornography, and guns. Social forces are forever impinging on the lives of these people, but not one of their stories sets out to document society per se. We know that Janet Zupan's father died in a prison camp in Vietnam in 1967, but that is not what her story is about. With a remarkable eye for visual detail, she tracks a single afternoon in the Mojave Desert as her father chases after his stubborn and recalcitrant horse, and knowing what we do about what will happen to her father just two years later, we read her account as a kind of memorial to him. Not a word about the war, and yet by indirection and an almost painterly focus on the moment before her, we sense that an entire era of American history is passing in front of our eyes.

Stan Benkoski's father's laugh. The slap to Carol Sherman-Jones's face. Little Mary Grace Dembeck dragging a Christmas tree through the streets of Brooklyn. John Keith's mother's missing wedding ring. John Flannelly's fingers stuck in the holes of a stainless-steel heating grate. Mel Singer wrestled to the floor by his own coat. Anna Thorson at the barn dance. Edith Riemer's bicycle. Marie Johnson watching a movie shot in the house where she lived as a girl. Ludlow Perry's encounter with the legless man. Catherine Austin Alexander looking out her window on West Seventy-fourth Street. Juliana C. Nash's walk through the snow. Dede Ryan's philosophical martini. Carolyn Brasher's regrets. Mary McCallum's father's dream. Earl Roberts's collar button. One by one, these stories leave a lasting

25

impression on the mind. Even after you have read through all fifteen dozen of them, they continue to stay with you, and you find yourself remembering them in the same way that you remember a trenchant parable or a good joke. The images are clear, dense, and yet somehow weightless. And each one is small enough to fit inside your pocket. Like the snapshots we carry around of our own families.

PAUL AUSTER
*October 3, 2000*

# ANIMALS

# THE CHICKEN

As I was walking down Stanton Street early one Sunday morning, I saw a chicken a few yards ahead of me. I was walking faster than the chicken, so I gradually caught up. By the time we approached Eighteenth Avenue, I was close behind. The chicken turned south on Eighteenth. At the fourth house along, it turned in at the walk, hopped up the front steps, and rapped sharply on the metal storm door with its beak. After a moment, the door opened and the chicken went in.

LINDA ELEGANT
*Portland, Oregon*

# RASCAL

The resurgence of the Ku Klux Klan in 1920s was a phenomenon nobody has fully explained. Suddenly Midwestern towns found themselves in the grip of this secret order, which aimed to eliminate Negroes and Jews from society. For towns like Broken Bow, Nebraska, which only had two Negro families and one Jew, the targets were the Catholics. Klansmen whispered that the pope was preparing a takeover of America, the church basements were arsenals, and priests and nuns had orgies after mass. Now that World War I was over and the Huns had been defeated, there was a new focus for men who needed somebody to hate. The astonishing thing was the number of such people.

In Broken Bow and Custer County, scores were lured by the mystique of the secret, masculine society that appealed to the "Us vs. Them" urge that seems universal among men. Two of the people who held out against them were the local bankers: John Richardson and my father, Y. B. Huffman. When a Klan phone call warned them to boycott the Catholics, they defied it. Inasmuch as both banks resisted, that Klan effort was frustrated, but my mother, Martha, paid for it when the school board election came around. She was decisively defeated by slanderous gossip that she was carrying on an affair with the leading druggist.

Came the time for the annual parade of the Ku

30

Klux Klan around the town square. They always chose a summer Saturday when the town was crowded with ranchers and farmers. Clad in white robes and conical caps and masks with eyeholes, they strode forth to remind the citizenry of their dignity and their power, led by the powerful but anonymous figure of the grand kleagle. The curb was lined with people speculating about the marchers and whispering about their mysterious powers.

Then there came bounding out of an alley a small white dog with black spots. Now, just as the folks in Broken Bow knew everybody in town, they also knew the dogs, at least the prominent ones. Our German shepherd, Hidda, and Art Melville's retriever were famous personages.

The spotted dog ran joyously up to the grand kleagle and jumped up on him, clamoring for a pat on the head from that beloved hand. "Rascal," the word started around. "That's Doc Jensen's dog, Rascal." Meanwhile, the majestic grand kleagle was thrashing his long legs through the robe trying to kick away what was obviously his own dog. *"Home,* Rascal, *home!"*

Now the word was running along the curb ahead of the procession. People weren't whispering, they were talking out loud to show how knowledgeable they were. Elbows nudged fellow watchers, snickers moved along the lines like rustling leaves before an errant gust of wind. Then Doc Jensen's boy appeared and called off the dog. "Here Rascal! Here Rascal!"

That broke the tension. Somebody took up the cry, "Here Rascal!" That was when the snickers turned into guffaws, and a great gale of laughter swept around the town square. Doc Jensen stopped kicking his dog and resumed his stately march, but the spectators were having none of that. "Here Rascal! Here Rascal!"

So that was the last of the Ku Klux Klan in Broken Bow. Doc Jensen was a fair-to-middling large-animal vet and kept a good practice among the ranchers and the farmers. Maybe they enjoyed calling him for the conversational value with their neighbors, but few teased him. Once in a while some smart-ass kid would see Doc Jensen driving by and holler, "Here Rascal!"

And the small white dog with black spots was kept close to home after that.

YALE HUFFMAN
*Denver, Colorado*

# THE YELLOW BUTTERFLY

In the Philippines, the tradition was to begin the rites of Holy Communion in the second grade. Every Saturday, we had to go to school to rehearse how to walk, how to carry the candle, where to sit, how to kneel, and how to stick out your tongue to accept the Body of Christ.

One Saturday my mother and uncle picked me up from practice in a yellow Volkswagen Beetle. As I slid into the backseat, my uncle attempted to start the car. It gave several dry coughs, and then the engine stopped turning over. My uncle sat in silent frustration, and my mother turned around and asked me what we should do. I was eight years old, and without hesitation I told her that we had to wait for a yellow butterfly to touch the car before it would work again. I don't know whether my mother believed me or not. She only smiled, and then she turned back to my uncle to discuss what to do next. He got out of the car and told her that he was going to the nearest gas station for help. I fell in and out of sleep, but I was awake when my uncle returned from the gas station. I remember him carrying a container of gas, filling up the car, the car not starting, and him tinkering some more, and still the car wouldn't start. My mother then got out of the car and hailed a cab. A yellow cab stopped. Instead of taking us home, the driver looked at our predicament and suggested that my uncle squirt some gas on the engine. This seemed to do the trick, and after thanking this Good Samaritan, my uncle turned the ignition and the car started right away.

I began falling back to sleep. Half a block later, my mother woke me up. She was all excited, and her voice was full of wonder. When I opened my eyes, I turned to where she was pointing. Fluttering around the rearview mirror was a tiny yellow butterfly.

SIMONETTE JACKSON
*Canoga Park, California*

# PYTHON

Vic bought the python after a very bad week at the halfway house. His clients were flipping. Mellow Marty brought in some street drugs, which was a definite no-no. Then the Midget went ballistic, grabbed one of the wussy college volunteers, and held her captive for two hours. When the Midget nearly choked the college girl, Vic tackled him and got him to the hospital. The buck stopped with Vic, Manager, Big Nurse — mess after mess piled up on his shoulders.

To make things worse, the media were waging a war against privately run mental-health facilities. On the six o'clock news, Vic defended the corporation's McLoony approach to group homes. He believed that private houses were a big improvement over gray-brick institutions, that patients were better off living in the community than being warehoused behind barred windows. Why shouldn't the folks who did all this good work make a profit? After shooting his mouth off, Vic felt a powerful need for a relaxing distraction.

His wife, Carrie, had insisted that snakes were her limit, but with her day job teaching and her nighttime gigs playing saxophone, she was out a lot. Besides, she and the girls had really dug it when he'd brought the iguanas home. Zoloft, the silvery one, posed all day in her floor-to-ceiling glass cage in the middle of the dining room. At

35

dinner, Vic felt calmed by her blinking yellow eye. Prozac, the pink one, had his own plywood box in the kids' room. When Sherry, their four-year-old, got down on her hands to push kale and lettuce leaves into Prozac's lair, Vic kept a close eye on her. Iguanas had sharp claws, and he'd been scratched pretty badly himself.

Vic read all about pet therapy and the calming effect dogs and cats could have on old people. Though the snake was his own particular therapy, he could claim it as a job-related expense. Maybe that would convince Carrie. He took the girls along to shop for snakes; then he enlisted them in his campaign.

"Mom, it's so cool," Ella, the older one, begged.

"He can keep Prozac company," Sherry said.

"What does it eat?" Carrie wondered. Vic could see her softening.

"No problem," Vic said. "He eats rats and rabbits, but I can get them at the reptile supply store. You won't have to look at them."

"Please, Mom," the girls said in unison.

Carrie agreed — she was cool. Vic never complained about her music gigs. Why should his hobby bother her? Just wait until she saw how beautiful the python was — that thick, leathery skin with its gorgeous diamond pattern. She'd have to agree it would be the best piece of art they'd ever owned.

Vic named the python Jung. He considered calling him Freud, but that was a bit over the top. The first time he took Jung out of the cage and draped the fat serpent around his neck, Carrie and the

36

girls were dazzled. He let them touch the hard, scaly skin. They loved watching the little tongue — it flickered and shimmered, a thin flame, moving so fast it almost seemed like a mirage. Vic felt the snake's power, its danger, yet he could control him. Compared to a houseful of schizophrenics, the python was a breeze.

He knew it would be a hassle getting Jung out of the cage and into a carrying case, but he needed something different at work. At the home, Vic carefully balanced Jung on his shoulders. Silence descended on the noisy common room as the eight schizophrenics sat transfixed. Slowly, Vic circled, letting anyone who was brave enough touch the python's skin. Mellow Marty's grin seemed to stretch all the way to the Midget's pudgy face. Better than drugs, better than group; their attention didn't waver. Vic felt the powerful beast wrap itself more tightly around him. He held out his arms, letting Jung uncoil. Scales glittering, the python seemed to enjoy his performance. Slithering from Vic's shoulders, he wound himself around his owner's broad chest. As the crazies watched in awed silence, Jung coiled his way down Vic's torso, trapping him in an astonishing embrace.

JUDITH BETH COHEN
*North Weymouth, Massachusetts*

# POOH

In my hippie days thirty years ago, I took on the ownership of a dim white German shepherd, the former pet of a married couple moving to a no-pets condo in Aspen, Colorado. I was living in Leadville, a rough mining town ten thousand feet up in the mountains.

I was two people, as many wage-earning hippies were. One of me lived for free as the caretaker of a house in downtown Leadville and worked as a reliable medical transcriptionist at the hospital. The other me lived in the endless pine woods, sharing a two-story converted garage with Pooh and Jak, an energetic six-foot-three Dutch-Korean speed-freak gunsmith with long black hair tied in a pony-tail. The wage-earning Jak was a reliable machinist who possessed a presidential commendation letter for machining components used in a moon lander.

Like most of the pets that lived outside of town, Pooh roamed freely in the woods and checked in at home base more and more infrequently as winter turned into spring. We saw that she was pregnant, but then she was off and away. Next, we received a complaint from some neighbors that Pooh had given birth under their trailer. Thirteen puppies! We brought the dogs back home. Dim little Pooh became a pretty good mom.

One morning, just as I was starting work at the

hospital, the sheriff called. Pooh had moved her pups back to the neighbors'; they'd called out animal control, and could I please come to the sheriff's office and do the paperwork to get my dogs out of the pound? My motherly boss, a stout Oklahoman named Lahoma, allowed as how usually I was not a troublesome girl and gave me an early coffee break. I tore downtown. To my horror, there was a release fee of ten dollars per dog. One hundred and forty dollars! It might as well have been a thousand. I raised a huge stink, to no avail, and stomped out.

Up the revolution! I was a wolf in sheep's clothing! I rushed to my "town house," grabbed implements of destruction and a big clothes basket, and headed out to the dog pound. Astonishingly, at ten in the morning the runs were unlocked and unguarded. I heaped the pups into the basket, threw Pooh in after them, and drove hell-for-leather up the mountain pass. A mile out of town, I decanted everybody by the river and drove back to work.

About an hour later, the phone rang. It was Jak. The puppies and Pooh were missing! The sheriff's office was mortified! An all-county alert had been issued for the dognappers!

At lunchtime I joined the law and Jak at the pound. Jak went satisfactorily berserk, so much so that I took him aside and filled him in before he could organize a lynch mob. He wasn't much of an actor, so we decided that I would live in town for a while, leaving him in the dark about developments to preserve his innocent relationship as a good drinking buddy of the sheriff and his depu-

39

ties. Not that he wasn't extremely proud of me. But I was a criminal now, and on my own.

After work I drove to a neighboring town to buy a big bag of Purina. In the cold night, under a big moon, I took food to Pooh by the river. And every night I visited the dog family. Here would come proud Pooh, looking like a white wolf. And after her, flowing toward me in the moonlight, stumbling a bit over the willow roots, came her thirteen beautiful, sturdy puppies, eager to be cuddled. It was one of the most magical times of my life.

Then, one night, nobody came to meet me. The dogs were gone. I had no way to investigate, and the only thing I could do was wait at the town grapevine.

When Pooh's puppies were given out for adoption from the sheriff's office, wasn't it strange that nobody phoned to let us know that they had been found?

A few weeks later, Jak got into a bar fight when one of the deputies got to boasting about how he shot himself some white bitch that was guarding her pups so ferociously he couldn't get near them.

PATRICIA L. LAMBERT
*Eugene, Oregon*

# NEW YORK STRAY

In one of my moments of despair following my husband's death, I decided to go to a play, hoping that a night at the theater would lift my spirits. I lived in the East Village, and the theater was on Thirty-fourth Street. I decided to walk. Within five minutes, a mongrel dog started to follow me. It did all the things that a dog normally does with its owner — exploring some distance away and then running back to check on its companion. I became intrigued by the animal and stooped to pet it, but it scampered away. Some passersby also seemed taken with the dog and tried to coax it to come to them, but it ignored them. I bought an ice-cream cone and offered some to the dog, but it still wouldn't come near me. As I approached the theater, I wondered what would become of the dog. Just before I entered, it finally approached me and looked me full in the face — and I saw the compassionate eyes of my husband.

EDITH S. MARKS
*New York, New York*

41

# PORK CHOP

Early in my career as a crime-scene cleaner, I was sent to the house of a woman living in Crown Point, Indiana, about two hours from where I lived.

When I arrived, Mrs. Everson opened the door, and I could immediately smell the scent of blood and other tissues emanating from the house. This told me that there was a real mess inside. A rather large German shepherd followed Mrs. Everson everywhere she went.

Mrs. Everson told me how she had come home to find the house silent, even though her aging and quite sick father-in-law was living there. Her German shepherd sniffed me with the curiosity usually shown by a large carnivore.

The basement light had been on, so she knew he must be down there. She found him sitting slumped in a chair. He had stuck a twelve-gauge shotgun in his mouth and pulled the trigger, removing most of his head and splattering brains, bone, and blood all over the finished basement.

I went down there for just a quick look and knew I would have to put on a Tyvek suit. More to keep blood off of my clothes than for protection against anything in the blood.

"Wow, what a mess," I thought to myself. In spite of my best efforts, I was soon covered from head to toe with blood. No matter how long I do this work, I still find it to be gross and disgusting. I guess that's a good sign.

I made several trips to my truck with contaminated items from the basement: ceiling panels, odd pieces of clothing, parts of the chair the old guy had been sitting in. I noticed that the curious dog was beginning to follow me around with increased interest.

I have learned that it's often better to say nothing than to say something really awkward during someone's time of grief. But this lady was sitting at the kitchen table with her head down, sobbing as though she had never cried before in her life. I felt that I had to say something to ease the tension. Her dog was still following me around the house while I worked, so I thought I would use that to break the ice. I said, "Ya know, Mrs. Everson? This must be the friendliest dog I've ever seen."

Suddenly, as if a cold glass of water had been dumped on her head, Mrs. Everson sat straight up, looked at me as if I were stupid, and said, "Well hell! . . . Ya smell just like a pork chop!"

ERIC WYNN
*Warsaw, Indiana*

43

# B

As a girl of fifteen, I was introduced to a dog whose breed was quite rare in this country. There was a remarkable chemistry between us. He had a strong personality and a strong name to go with it, a single syllable beginning with the letter B. I visited B every day after school. When I went off to college and left the dog behind, I missed him terribly. Ten years later, I contacted a breeder and inquired about a puppy like B. I was told that a single-parent household in New York City was no place for such a noble puppy. They refused to sell me one.

I registered with the SPCA and left the next day on a business trip to another country. There a friend took me to spend a weekend at his mother's country house. She had wanted to meet me. A place was always set for her at mealtime, but the woman never showed up. On Sunday, driving down a wooded lane on our way back to the city, we came upon a very tall, austere woman flanked by two of the biggest, quietest retrievers I had ever seen. My friend introduced me to his mother. I didn't get out of the car, and she only said a word or two to me. As I watched her speaking, giving no excuse for her conspicuous absence, I was struck by a feeling I had not felt since my school days with B. There seemed to be the same inexplicable kinship between the woman and the two dogs standing beside her. We said a brief good-bye and drove on.

Back in New York one morning about two weeks later, I got a call from the SPCA. There was a large-breed puppy for adoption. They had given up on me because I had not answered any of their previous calls during the time I was out of the country. This call was a database glitch. But the puppy did exist; I called in sick at work, got a taxi, and went straight to the SPCA on Ninety-second Street by the East River. I was taken to a small cage in a small room in a vast maze of kennels three levels high. Lying there listlessly on ground level was a black puppy. Except for the fact that he was emaciated, he looked exactly like B. I opened the door, crouched low, and tried everything I could to get the puppy to come to me. The stern, emotionless orderly assured me I did not want this puppy. He was obviously too willful. I stood up and turned to leave. But then for some reason the word "Ben" came to mind. I said the name aloud and stopped in my tracks. When I turned around, the puppy bounded out of the cage, jumped up, put his paws around my neck, licked my face, and peed all down my front. Against the protestations of the orderly, I adopted the retriever puppy called Ben.

Both of us were exhausted when we arrived at my apartment late that night. When I opened the door, a blue air-mail envelope, apparently mis-delivered, was lying on the threshold. The puppy froze, fixed on the envelope, and would not enter my apartment until I had picked it up. He sat and looked at me as I read the letter. It was from my friend's mother, the one who lived abroad. She apologized for writing, since we hardly knew each other. She had gotten my address from her son. For some reason, she wrote, she felt that it was important to tell me that her dog, Ben, the one I had met on the wooded lane, had died suddenly. She just wanted me to know. She asked, in closing, if I had found the puppy I had been looking for.

SUZANNE STROH
*Middleburg, Virginia*

# TWO LOVES

In October 1977 I was twelve years old and nuts for both baseball and Colby (our swaggering, sophisticated black cat). One afternoon, those two loves collided eerily.

Having tired of pitching tennis balls against the wall behind our driveway, I hoisted my Wiffle bat and began driving my four or five Spaldings back and forth across the yard. One by one, the balls became snared in the limbs of an old pear tree. Soon I was down to one surviving tennis ball — which finally surrendered to the same fate. At this point, I was very dismayed. I knew I couldn't quite climb that tree. I began heaving my Jim O'Toole-model glove at the balls. The glove got stuck. I resorted to chucking my flimsy bat at the balls. The bat got stuck. Before I had a chance to lose my sneakers, Colby swayed upon the scene. He sat briefly, head cocked, studying my helplessness. My hero then resolutely scaled the tree, expertly negotiating its far reaches to locate and deftly swat at each hostage sporting good. Moments later, the last one successfully tumbled into my disbelieving grasp.

WILL COFFEY
*North Riverside, Illinois*

# RABBIT STORY

A couple of years ago, I went to visit a friend, carrying a new CD I thought we'd enjoy listening to together. I perched myself on a wooden chair in her living room, scrupulously avoiding contact with the cat lounging on the far-comfier couch.

After the music had been playing awhile, I spotted out of the corner of my eye a second cat creeping down the stairs. I made a mildly disapproving remark, the kind you might expect from someone with an allergy.

"But that's not a cat," my friend corrected me. "It's my daughter's rabbit."

I remembered something I had once heard. I asked her, "Aren't rabbits inclined, if you let them roam around the house unsupervised, to bite into electrical cords — and then . . . ?"

"Yes," she said. "You have to keep an eye out."

That's when I made my little joke. I told her that if she ever found herself with a zapped rabbit, she should call me right away. I'd come over and take it home and cook it for supper. We had a good laugh about that.

The rabbit wandered away. Shortly afterward my friend left the room in search of a pencil. Moments later, she reappeared with a spooky look on her face. I asked what was wrong, and she told me that the rabbit had just bitten into a lamp cord and electrocuted itself — exactly as I had described it.

She had reached the scene just in time to see it kick its legs and die.

I ran to the next room to view the evidence for myself. There lay the inert animal, its two front teeth still sunk in the brown cord. Every few seconds the teeth were bridged by a tiny arc of electricity.

My friend and I looked at each other, a little giddy and disoriented. We weren't sure whether to be entertained by the situation or unnerved. When something finally had to be done, I grabbed a broom and knocked the slowly cooking rabbit clear of the cord.

For another little while we simply stood there and gawked at the corpse. Then my friend spoke up. Something had occurred to her.

"Do you realize," she said, "that you could have wished for *anything?*"

"What do you mean?" I asked.

"Back when you mentioned taking the rabbit home and cooking it for supper," she said, "back when you suggested that possibility. You could just as easily have wished for a million dollars, or anything else you wanted. And that's just what you would have gotten. It was that kind of moment, a moment in which any wish would have been granted."

There has never been any doubt in my mind that she was absolutely right.

BARRY FOY
*Seattle, Washington*

# CAROLINA

When I was working in rural Honduras as a Peace Corps volunteer, the government sent a crew of surveyors to my village to map out the best path for laying down an electrical line. One of the men, Pablo, became obsessively infatuated with me. The feelings were far from mutual, not least because he was pathetically drunk whenever I saw him. He followed me everywhere, banged on my door, and asked the neighbors where the gringa was when he couldn't find me. Pablo then decided to carry positive thinking to the extreme. He announced that we were getting married on Sunday and invited everyone to our wedding, laying out the best food anyone in the area had ever seen. Unfortunately, nobody came to the big bash, not even the bride.

He then noticed that I confided in my mule, Carolina, who came trotting over to see me whenever I went out to her pasture. She nuzzled up to me as I poured out my troubles into her huge, sympathetic ears. Pablo decided to capture my heart by using the mule as an intermediary.

The problem with his strategy was that Carolina absolutely detested drunks. She stomped her feet and snorted whenever she smelled alcohol. Pablo was too drunk to get the hint. He approached her, and she tried to walk away from him. When he cornered her, she kicked him and knocked him to the ground. He pulled himself up, staggered back to the mule, and was promptly back on the ground again. He didn't give up until he was bruised from head to toe.

The next day, Pablo deluded himself into thinking that Carolina was dead, even as he stood outside the pasture where she was contentedly eating grass. He tried to recruit everyone who walked by to bring their shovels to help bury the mule because I was too distraught over her death to do it alone. He scolded everyone who refused to help, saying they were lazy and lacked compassion for me, especially since I was working so hard to help the children of the area.

Several friends then came to my house to let me know that the rumors of Carolina's death were greatly exaggerated. She looked healthy and peaceful in spite of what Pablo was saying. I decided to move her to another pasture so he couldn't hurt the mule or be hurt himself any more than he already had been. When I got there, he was passed out on the ground and never saw me take her.

A few days later, I was riding Carolina down a mountain path and met Pablo, who looked relatively sober but very perplexed. I exclaimed, "Mire! Se resucito!" (Look, she came back from the dead!)

Pablo turned white as a ghost and muttered "Dios mio!" (My God!) He turned and ran away as fast as he could, never to return.

KELLY O'NEILL
*Lock Haven, Pennsylvania*

51

# ANDY AND THE SNAKE

Andy was fascinated by animals. Every day he told us about snakes, dogs, and cats. He spoke with the passion of an animal-rights activist and, frankly, with the twisted love of a stalker.

He read me a story from his journal. He said it was a true story from his own past. He had been living in a new neighborhood in what had recently been country and near wilderness in Texas. He was about fourteen and had no friends, except for his little brother, who wasn't a friend so much as a punching bag. From living with Andy and listening to his stories, I'm sure his brother ran whenever Andy came near. It was a little before he became a drug addict, and his brother wasn't around to receive his attentions and divert his boredom. Andy went for a walk out past the new neighborhood and into what natural land was left.

This was an area where the dirt on the ground was thin. You could kick the topsoil off with the toe of your boot. Underneath, you'd find rock. The dirt couldn't support much growth, but the weeds didn't care. They grew tall and deep. There was a stream running through the area, which was diverted into a large underground pipe close to the neighborhood. The banks of the stream were deep, and when it rained the stream became a forceful and dangerous river. Andy and all the kids in the neighborhood were told every day to stay away from the area. Since he was bored, Andy went right to it. On his way, he saw a huge snake that must have been at least six feet long. It slithered along the bank of the stream, in and out of the weeds. It glowed and shined when the sun struck it. Its scales were like armor that held all colors and released them at the speed of light, but one at a time. Andy couldn't bring himself to stop looking at it. He thought the snake had been given to him as a special present from God. He followed it until it went down the bank of the stream. The bank was shale, crumbly and dangerous. It was dotted with potholes and caves. Clumps of weeds grew from the sides. Andy stood there and watched the snake. It had stopped. Even still, though, it glittered, glowed, and shined.

Andy was in a trance, a state he wouldn't reach again until he started shooting cocaine into his bloodstream, mixing it with just the right amount of LSD. He didn't hear the cars come up behind him. He didn't move until a rock hit him.

"Hey!" he said. "What the fuck are you doing?" He turned and saw a group of about five guys and three girls, none of whom looked to be over twenty. He thought he recognized some of them from school.

"Who's saying 'fuck'?" said one guy, who was also looking bored. Andy could smell the need for blood excitement on that guy, too, but he was cautious. "I did," said Andy. Then he immediately said, "There's a snake over there so big I bet you'd never touch it." Everyone immediately looked to where the snake was. The guy said, "What the fuck you talkin' about? I don't need to touch it to

53

kill it." Then he went to a car and brought out a little pistol. He took aim and shot at the snake. He missed, but shale splinters went everywhere. The snake slithered down the sides of the bank and into a cave.

The guy said, "What snake?" and then turned to look at Andy, with the pistol still in his hand. "You got another snake I can shoot?" he asked. Andy said, "No. But I can get you that snake." All the guys started to laugh and call him names. No one could get down the bank — except a snake. Andy said, "If I get down there and get the snake, you gotta give me your gun." The guy said, "No way, man." Andy said, "You scared I can do it?" In front of his group, the guy said, "Okay. Go for it. You get that snake and bring it up here and you can have my gun."

Andy had no fear. Or, if he did have it, he never let it stand in his way with stuff like this. He walked to the edge of the bank and slid down to the cave where he had seen the snake go. The angle was so steep, the guys and girls on the bank could hardly see him. They kept yelling at him, "Stupid," "Dumb fuck," "Chicken." Andy said nothing. Knowing him now, I'm sure he had this intense, death-grip smile on his face.

He slowed down as he got to the cave. He went around it carefully. Then he leaned into the bank and slowly crawled up to the entrance. The cave was huge. If the sun hadn't been rising, no one would have seen the cave, let alone have seen inside it. But Andy saw inside it. He saw the snake, just beyond the entrance. He saw it shimmering and glittering in the sun against the background of the unseen cave walls. He saw the snake move its mouth as though it were yawning. He saw its green eyes stare at nothing. He saw it and then he grabbed it and then he killed it by smashing its head on the rock floor of the cave.

He had stopped hearing the cries of the kids up on the road, but now he heard them again. One insistent cry of "Hey man!" kept coming through. He yelled back, "I'm on my way up." New questions were yelled at him: "Did you get it?" which were answered by others: "No way, man. No way could he get that snake." The gun guy said, "He's chicken and stupid anyway." Andy said nothing as he crawled up the bank. He needed both hands, so he wrapped the dead snake around his neck as he inched up the shale on all fours, cutting the palms of his hands and the tops of his knees. He started sweating and wiped the sweat from his forehead with one bloody hand and then the other. He got to the overhang of the bank and stopped. No one could see him. He got his breath and then slung one leg over the overhang and pushed himself up with the other.

The guys and girls were startled. No one said anything, but Andy grinned. The gun guy was still holding his gun, but he dropped his jaw. The girls all looked at him as if he were more than just an attractive nuisance. The gun guy said, "Well, that's cool, man, but you ain't getting my gun." Andy said, "You promised." "Promises to nuts don't count." Andy walked up to the guy and said, "Don't make promises you can't keep." The guy backed up a step or two and started to raise his gun. "Get away from me, man." Andy said nothing, but he kept walking toward him. As he did, he unwrapped the dead snake, now colored only gray but still huge, and tossed it at the gun guy. The gun guy threw up his hands to keep it away and fell backward with the snake on him. Andy leaned over, picked up the gun, and said, "You can keep the snake, man. It's no good now anyway." The other guys and girls laughed. The gun guy stood up and said, "Hey, give me my gun back." Andy said, "My gun. You got a snake. Shoot it." The gun guy was ready to start a fight, but Andy got that look again that made his own brother run from him. Another guy, a big guy, said, "Cool it. You promised him your gun for the snake and he delivered." He then looked at Andy and said, "See you around, man." They all got in their cars and left. One girl looked back through the rear window. She smiled and waved. Andy walked home with the gun in his hand, the grin still on his face.

RON FABIAN
*Parma, Michigan*

# BLUE SKIES

In 1956 Phoenix, Arizona, was a city with boundless blue skies. One day as I walked around the house with my sister Kathy's new parakeet on my finger, I had the notion to show Perky what the sky looked like. Maybe he could make a little bird friend out there. I took him into the backyard, and then, to my horror, Perky flew off. The enormous, relentless sky swallowed up my sister's blue treasure, and suddenly he was gone, clipped wings and all.

Kathy managed to forgive me. With fake optimism, she even tried to reassure me that Perky would find a new home. But I was far too canny to believe that such a thing was possible. I was inconsolable. Time passed. Eventually, my great remorse took a modest place among the larger things of life, and we all grew up.

Decades later, I watched my own children growing. We shared their activities, spending soccer Saturdays in folding chairs with the parents of the kids' friends, the Kissells. The two families went camping around Arizona together. We piled into the van to go on outings to the theater. We became the best of friends. One evening, the game was to tell Great Pet stories. One person claimed to have the oldest living goldfish. Someone else had a psychic dog. Then Barry, the father of the other family, took the floor and announced that the Greatest Pet of All Time was his blue parakeet, Sweetie Pie.

"The best thing about Sweetie Pie," he said, "was the way we got him. One day, when I was about eight, out of the clear, blue sky, a little blue parakeet just floated down and landed on my finger."

When I was finally able to speak, we examined the amazing evidence. The dates and the locations and the pictures of the bird all matched up. It seems our two families had been connected long before we ever met. Forty years later, I ran to my sister and said, "You were right! Perky lived!"

CORKI STEWART
*Tempe, Arizona*

# EXPOSURE

My sister and I slowly walked the dirt road home from school. The air was warm like summer and I think we both wanted it to be summer, but it was fall. The aspens had lost their leaves. The deer and elk hunters had come and gone. The mountain valley was quiet once again.

I was thinking about what our teacher said we should do if there was going to be a bomb. She said we should go outside and crawl into the culvert and be safe under the road. I had looked into the culvert many times and it did look safe, but I never wanted to crawl into it. Our teacher said dirt would stop the radiation.

On the way home I asked my sister if she thought there would be a bomb. She said, "Not here, but over in Korea probably."

I thought of our teacher telling us every morning where the battle lines were while pointing to a map of Korea on the wall. I think she listened to the Durango radio station and then came to school and told us what she had heard.

When we got home, our dad was getting ready to butcher the steer we had been feeding grain to all summer. He asked if we wanted to help. My sister said no, but I said sure. I think my sister was friends with the steer.

My dad took his rifle from the pegs on the wall, got a handful of shells from the kitchen drawer, and we walked to the corral where the steer was standing alone. We opened the gate and went into the corral with the steer and then closed the gate so the steer wouldn't get away. While he loaded the rifle, my dad told me, as he had the last time we butchered, about drawing two imaginary lines from the steer's ears to his eyes and then shooting the steer where the lines crossed. He said, "That's where the most critical part of the brain is, and they're killed instantly without knowing what hit them."

The steer was looking at us, and I was glad he didn't know what was about to happen.

My dad aimed carefully and then fired the gun. To my surprise, the steer only flinched. I think my dad was even more surprised than I was. He said, "I couldn't have missed," and then he quickly shot again before the steer moved. But the steer just shook his head. My dad said "damn" and then fired the gun. Again, the steer shook his head, but then I saw that he had thick blood coming from his nose, and he dropped his head very low to the ground. My dad saw it too. He looked really angry, and he took out the handful of shells from his pocket and inspected them and yelled, "Where did these come from?" I looked into his palm, and he told me that the shells were filled with bird shot and were used for scaring away stray dogs, and then he threw the shells into the dirt, handed me the rifle, and left me standing in the middle of the corral, alone with the steer, while he went to get the right shells.

While my dad was away, the steer looked at me for a while with blood and snot oozing from his nostrils. Then he shook his head once more and began to trot along the corral fence. I kept my eyes on him and soon felt dizzy because I was turning as he ran. Finally my dad returned, and he took the rifle from me and put one shell in, raised the rifle to his shoulder, aimed, turning as the steer trotted, and then yelled loudly, "Hey!" The steer stopped running and we stood there waiting. Then the steer slowly turned his head toward us. His nose was inches from the dirt. His white face was splashed all over with blood and he looked like he knew what was about to happen.

MICHAEL OPPENHEIMER
*Lummi Island, Washington*

# VERTIGO

When I was ten, my family moved to Apple Valley, a small community in the California High Desert. My father was a test pilot who had been stationed at George Air Force Base since the summer of 1964. We settled in a mustard-colored house situated in a vast neighborhood that included a couple of other homes, a thousand creosote bushes, Joshua trees, and pear cacti on a three-mile stretch in every direction but one: the Mojave River blinked at us a mile down desert.

My father was six-three and had incredible, bushy eyebrows. He had a laugh so deep I could feel its peals vibrate in my own stomach. He could imitate a horse's whinny like no one I've ever met. He spoke a Taiwanese dialect and enough German to seem fluent. He used to give one-man air shows in the communities where we lived, and his picture hung in a gas station in his hometown, where he was considered a local hero. He died in a prison camp in North Vietnam in 1967, when he was forty-one.

I realize that I cherished my father for his strengths. He had a spirited investment in taking chances and a bottomless reservoir of optimism. When we lived in Taiwan, he rode the bus every week into Taipei, where he and a local carpenter built a Lightning sailboat. We hauled it back to the United States and came in last in every boat race we entered in Chesapeake Bay. My father was always eager to try new things, to bring fun changes to our lives. Sometimes one or the other of us was reluctant or afraid, but he had a way of encouraging us to take a chance.

Now that I look back on my father, under the focus of forty-four-year-old eyes, I know that what I loved most about him was his fragility, and because I sensed this, I developed a desire to protect him. I think everyone in my family felt the same. We were in awe of his exuberance but cradled fear for him, too. Maybe he carried so much sense of promise that we realized how hard it would be on all of us to see him disappointed, disillusioned, or hurt.

Soon after moving to Apple Valley, we adopted a horse we named Vertigo. Vertigo was a big, smart, stubborn palomino, an ex-parade horse whose years of showing off had left him savvy and embittered. I can't speak for my siblings, but I was afraid of Vertigo. He had a way of knowing my fear, too, and seemed to relish my uneasiness and hesitations, lifting a threatening hoof or slapping me with his tail whenever I came near. My father, on the other hand, was ready to ride, and spent hours learning the tack and the ways of horse care.

One Saturday afternoon in July 1965, my father saddled up Vertigo and set out for the Mojave River. We all came down to the corral to watch. Even my mother stayed close by, weeding the ice plant that crawled around the shade of the house. First my father curried Vertigo's mane and tail; as he worked, the horse reached around and casually lipped the hoof pick from the corral post; it dropped in the dry dirt. Undaunted, my father checked Vertigo's hooves. Vertigo sighed and snorted and then proceeded to untie the halter rope from the rail. Seconds later, he pranced away. "Rrrrrmmmph," my father whinnied softly to Vertigo as he reached for the swinging halter rope. He retied the horse to the post and set to work hitching the bridle, lifting the saddle on, and securing the buckles and cinch. Vertigo snorted and shook. He nodded his head and slapped my father's face with his mane. "Rrrrrmmmph," was all my father had to say. Finally they were ready. The day was hot and dry. It must have been about three in the afternoon.

I remember the vision of them heading out — my father shirtless and in jeans and tennis shoes, the horse plodding along with his head to the ground, starting to nibble at greaseweeds and snorting at ants. My father pulled steadily at the reins and Vertigo jerked his head and swung his white mane in the air. I don't know what held all of us to the corral rails, or my mother to the hoe and ice plant, but none of us moved. We watched them all the way down to the river, Vertigo's plodding and stalling, my father's hitch of the reins, the petulant sweep of the mane.

Finally they were out of sight, over the edge of the desert and into a more forgiving place, the cool world of the Mojave River. We kids must have all wandered off then, to our cooler house, to our own concerns. I can't remember where I went or what I did. I only remember that my mother called us back outside a couple of hours later. We stood in a line of six, our hands shading our eyes, searching the desert terrain between our house and the river. I saw Vertigo prancing at an angle toward us, his head and tail held parade-proud, a breeze combing his mane. He seemed in no hurry to return; he just stopped and grazed on weeds. He hadn't come far, and the river glinted just on the other side of him. My stomach ached as I wondered if my father was hurt — bucked off and lying alone, full of pear cactus or, worse, red ants and scorpions. But then I saw him, running awkwardly in the soft sand toward Vertigo. The horse shook his head but continued to graze on the useless weeds. His saddle hung precariously to the side.

My father approached, and I saw him reach out for the reins. Vertigo swung his head away and pranced, not in a beeline for home, but angled, his head held erect, as if he knew we were watching. Just as suddenly he again stopped and yanked at weeds. My father, still standing where the horse had left him, dropped his arms and was frozen for a moment. Then, he strode again toward the animal. Again, Vertigo waited until my father was within arm's reach of the reins. This time, the horse jumped sideways, as if startled, and pranced off once again. We watched in silence. My mother leaned on her hoe and sighed.

Vertigo teased my father again and again, in a zigzag all the way up the home stretch. By the fourth time my father reached for and missed the swinging reins, I was sure he was frustrated and angry. He slapped at Vertigo's rump as the horse trotted off; I heard a thread of his weary voice chastising the horse across the short distance between them, slowly coming closer to us.

65

My mother must have slipped inside at that point; none of us noticed as we worried my father up the slope of the desert. Finally, Vertigo pranced to the corral and stood waiting at the gate. He held his head high. His nostrils were wide and his eyes were glinting. I felt my mother standing again beside me, along with my brother and sisters, all of us silently watching my father walk the last stretch toward us.

The closer he came, the worse I felt. He looked hot and sweaty. His shoulders stooped forward and his head was down. "What happened, Daddy?" my brother asked. Without answering, my father walked over and swung open the corral gate and stood back. Vertigo walked slowly inside and calmly munched on hay. My father closed the gate and latched it. He came and stood near us. There were beads of sweat caught in his eyebrows. "That's a pretty smart horse. You have to be one step ahead of old Vertigo."

My mother held out a bottle of icy beer. No one spoke as he took a long sip. We all stood, looking down toward the river, the Santa Ana wind whistling; no one looked over at Vertigo. But when we all turned to walk back toward the house, we heard his contented snort. Next Saturday, my father was back out in the corral, currying and saddling our new horse for another ride.

JANET SCHMIDT ZUPAN
*Missoula, Montana*

# OBJECTS

# STAR AND CHAIN

In 1961, during a visit to Provincetown, Massachusetts, I bought a handcrafted one-of-a-kind Star of David on a chain. I wore it all the time. In 1981 the chain broke while I was swimming in the ocean off Atlantic City, and I lost it in the surf. In 1991, during Christmas vacation, my fifteen-year-old son and I were poking around in an antique shop in Lake Placid, New York, when a piece of jewelry caught his eye. He called me over to take a look. It was the Star of David that had been swallowed up by the ocean ten years before.

STEVE LACHEEN
*Philadelphia, Pennsylvania*

# RADIO GYPSY

This happened during my life as a radio gypsy. In March 1974, I'd taken a job as a news guy on WOW in Omaha and was in my VW Bug pulling away from my parents' house in a Denver suburb when I had to jam on the brakes. A tire had come rolling down a hill and crossed right in front of me. Poetic omen, I thought, and hit the road.

Two months later, the job I really wanted at KGW in Portland opened up, and while I was thinking about whether to quit the one in Omaha so soon, I looked out the window of my apartment and saw a tire rolling along in the parking lot. The tire has spoken, I thought, and I went for the Portland job.

A year passes and Portland's going well — so well that a promotion to the flagship station, KING in Seattle, is offered. But not before I'm driving my bug at Thirteenth and West Burnside late at night, and a tire appears out of the fog and rolls down the street.

But it doesn't end there. Another year — it's now 1976 — and the company wants to send me back to Portland, to KGW, as news director and morning news anchor. And this time, the rolling wheel — actually only a tire rim — appeared heading south on the Alaskan Way Viaduct. It was in the left lane.

Late '77. I'm on the road again, to KYA in San

70

Francisco. My old VW is packed with my stereo and my cat and all my stuff, and I'm about to get on the freeway. I haven't seen any rolling tires, but then I hear a grinding noise from the back of the car, and I feel like I'm skidding and the car doesn't steer. Scary. I put on the brakes — in time to see my own back right wheel, which had come loose, shooting down the road and coming to rest in a ditch. A mechanic had forgotten to put in a cotter pin. The rolling tire was my own damned wheel!

And there ended the chain of rolling tires. Or so I thought — until 1984. I was back in Seattle, a big radio executive now but still a gypsy of the business, and I accepted a job for lots of money in Houston, Texas. Every instinct spoke against it: the city, the vibes, the fact that I had two little kids now and really wanted to raise them in the Pacific Northwest. But the contract and the money clouded my judgment. I flew down there to begin the job, and my wife followed by car. She was driving on Interstate 5, coming through North Portland, when *crunch:* the hood of her Volvo took the impact of something that had come down from a road that ran above the freeway. It bounced off her car, hit two other cars, and was stopped by the median. Shaken but not hurt, she looked and saw what it was: a big, huge truck tire.

We did Houston, but it was terrible. It lasted only a year, and then we gratefully came back to Portland to raise our family. No more itchy feet, no more radio gypsy, and no more damned rolling tires.

BILL CALM
*Lake Oswego, Oregon*

71

# A Bicycle Story

During the 1930s in Germany, every child's greatest hope was to own a bicycle. I saved up for years, putting aside the money I was given for birthdays and Chanukah, along with the occasional reward for exceptionally good grades. I was still shy of my goal by about twenty marks. On the morning I turned thirteen, I opened the door of the living room and was shocked to see the bicycle I had admired for so long in Mr. Schmitt's shop window. It had a wide black seat and a gleaming chrome frame. But best of all, it had wide red balloon tires — the newest of inventions, which, contrary to the conventional narrow black tires, gave you more traction and made the ride smoother. I could barely wait for the school day to end so I could ride it all over town, glorying in the admiration of passersby.

The bicycle became my trusted companion. Then, one frosty January morning in 1939, I had to flee Germany and the Hitler regime. I was part of a hastily organized children's transport to England. We were only allowed one small suitcase, but my parents assured me they would somehow find a way to send my bike. Meanwhile, it would be stored safely in the cellar.

By a stroke of luck, newfound friends were active in the Methodist Church of Ashford, Middlesex. They convinced their congregation to raise funds to rent a flat for my parents, which, after official approval, would offer them a haven in Great Britain. With these preliminary papers, the German government let my parents ship a large wooden crate to my friends. Each item had to be approved: no valuables were allowed, but they did not object to my bike. Meanwhile, my parents' papers were ready at the British Home Office. Everything was in order except for one last signature. Then war broke out, and my parents' fate was sealed. They both lost their lives in camps in 1942.

In September 1939, all this was still in the future. One continued to hope for an early end to the war and to be reunited with one's family. A month later, I was accepted at a school where I would be trained as a children's nurse. St. Christopher's had moved from London — and the potential threat of bombs — to a small hamlet in the south of England. After six months I received permission to take a week's holiday. I had to follow protocol and label all the belongings I was not taking with me. I dutifully tagged my bike and left it in its accustomed spot in the bike rack.

A few days later I received a letter from the matron that a new law had been passed. I was now an "Enemy Alien" and could not be allowed within fifteen miles of the coast. Not only had my training come to a sudden halt, but I was also told that I had not complied with instructions and that none of my clothes could be found. As for my bicycle, they doubted that it even existed. I was furious, angry, and helpless in the face of such outrageous lies, but most of all I missed my bike, which had been such a good friend.

Over the next few years, I moved around a great deal, always complying with the law that required refugees to register with the local police whenever they were gone from their residence for more than twenty-four hours. In late 1945, when I was living in London, I received a postcard with an official police seal on it. It threw me into a panic. The card instructed me to report to the station as soon as possible. I trembled uncontrollably. What had I done wrong? Unable to cope with the fear and suspense, I immediately headed up the hill to the station and showed the card to the sergeant on duty.

"Hey, Mac. Here's the girl you've been waiting for!"

Another officer appeared. "Did you ever own a bicycle?"

"Yes."

"What happened to it?"

I told him the story. After a while, nearly everyone in the station was listening to me. I found that puzzling.

"What did it look like?"

I described it. When I mentioned the unusual red balloon tires, they all laughed with relief. One of the officers wheeled out a bike.

"Is this the one?"

It was rusted, the tires were flat, and the seat had a tear in it, but it was definitely my bicycle.

"Well, what are you waiting for? Take it home with you."

"Oh, thank you, thank you so much," I said. "But how did you ever find it?"

"It was abandoned, and someone found it. He hauled it in because it still had a name tag on it."

74

I wheeled it back to my apartment house full of happiness. When my landlady spotted me, however, she was horrified.

"You aren't going to ride that thing in London, are you?"

"Why not? It only needs a bit of repair and it'll be as good as new."

"It isn't that. Those wide tires are a dead giveaway that it's a German bike. The war is over, but we still hate those bastards and anything that reminds us of them."

I did have the frame painted, the seat and tires repaired, but a single ride in my neighborhood was enough to convince me that my landlady was right. Instead of admiring stares, I got shouts and jeers. Two years later, I sold it for a few shillings to a collector of wartime memorabilia.

EDITH RIEMER
*South Valley, New York*

# GRANDMOTHER'S CHINA

In 1949 my parents made the big move from Rockford, Illinois, to Southern California, along with three very tiny children and all their household possessions. My mother had carefully wrapped and packed many precious family heirlooms, including four cartons of her mother's hand-painted dinner china. Grandmother had painted this lovely set herself, choosing a forget-me-not pattern.

Unfortunately, something happened during the move. One box of the china didn't make it. It never arrived at our new house. So my mother had only three-quarters of the set — she had plates of different sizes and some serving pieces, but missing were the cups and saucers and the bowls. Often at family gatherings or when we would all sit down for a Thanksgiving or Christmas dinner, my mother would say something about the missing china and how she wished it had survived the trip.

When my mother died in 1983, I inherited Grandmother's china. I, too, used the set on many special occasions, and I, too, wondered what had happened to the missing box.

I love to prowl antique shops and flea markets, hunting for treasures. It's great fun to walk up and down the aisles early in the morning, watching as the vendors spread their wares on the ground.

I hadn't been to a flea market in over a year

when, one Sunday in 1993, I got the itch to go. So I crawled out of bed at 5 A.M. and drove an hour in the predawn darkness to the giant Rose Bowl Flea Market in Pasadena. I walked up and down the outdoor aisles, and after a couple of hours I was thinking about leaving. I rounded the last corner and took a few steps down the row when I noticed some china strewn on the macadam. I saw that it was hand-painted china . . . with forget-me-nots! I raced over to look at it more closely and gingerly picked up a cup and saucer . . . forget-me-nots! Exactly like Grandmother's china, with the same delicate strokes and the same thin gold bands around the rims. I looked at the rest of the items — there were the cups! The saucers! The bowls! It was Grandmother's china!

The dealer had noticed my excitement, and when she came over I told her the story of the missing box. She said the china had come from an estate sale in Pasadena — the next town over from Arcadia, where we had lived when I was a child. When she was going through the contents of the estate, she had found an old unopened carton stored in the garden shed, and the china was in it. She questioned the heirs about the china and they said that they knew nothing about it, that the box had been in the shed "forever."

I left the Rose Bowl Flea Market that day laden with my amazing treasure. Even now, six years later, I am filled with wonder that "all the pieces in the universe" tumbled together to let me find the missing china. What would have happened if I had slept in? What gave me the itch to go to the Rose Bowl on that particular day? What if I hadn't turned that last corner, choosing instead to leave and rest my aching feet?

Last week I had a dinner party for fifteen friends. We used Grandmother's china. And at the end of the meal, I proudly served coffee in those beautiful cups and saucers that had been missing for so long.

KRISTINE LUNDQUIST
*Camarillo, California*

# THE BASS

I was playing the second or third steady gig of my career, six nights a week in a hotel lounge in Toledo, Ohio. I was young and proud of the fact that I was playing music and getting paid pretty well for it. My old Epiphone hollow-body bass, a student model, was clearly not going to cut it for a professional like me.

I was very taken with a Fender Precision that was hanging on the wall at Ron's Music Store. It was a natural blond, its ash body finished to a perfect gloss, with a cream-colored pick guard and a natural maple neck. But the real standout feature of this magnificent instrument was that it was fretless. It even lacked a fingerboard; there was no thin slab of ebony or rosewood applied to the front of the neck, which on a normal bass would be home to the frets. There weren't even any position markers — the typical inlaid mother-of-pearl dots or bars or stars. Just a marvelously grained expanse of clear maple, interrupted only by the four strings that ran down its face. I thought it was beautiful, and I knew I would be able to play it. When I tried it out through an amplifier in the store, I knew I had to have this bass.

The resonance of the strings on a fretless electric bass is a wonderful thing. It's a heady blend of the sound of a modern electric instrument with that of a traditional, woody acoustical stringed instrument. The notes round off with a satisfying buzz as the string vibrates and ever so slightly touches the neck, string against wood. Varying degrees of expressiveness not possible on a fretted bass can be produced with nuances in the touch of the fingers.

The price of this bass, obscenely low by today's standards, was nevertheless a stretch for me in 1974, but I made the stretch, borrowed money, and bought this instrument of my dreams.

My father was in the hospital following open-heart surgery, and I went to visit him. I brought my new bass into the hospital, carried it in the bulky hard-shell case past the curious and wary eyes of the nurses to show it to him. I was that proud of it.

We were playing at the Hospitality Motor Inn in Toledo. Six nights a week of lounge music — pop, rock, swing, and funk. Everything from Sinatra to Stevie Wonder. After the gig each night the guitar player and I would stash our instruments (we were hip, we called them "axes") in the open coatroom and go sit in the coffee shop and eat bacon and eggs and drink coffee until three or four in the morning. I should have known better than to leave the bass in the coatroom. I had been touched by crime before, when my car was broken into. But I was young, stupid, trusting of people in general, and naive.

One night, my friend and I came out of the coffee shop to find our axes gone. We looked all over the building, twice, unable to believe that we had been violated in this way. A man's tools of his trade, his livelihood . . . how could anyone be so evil as to knowingly take these away? My glorious new bass was gone.

Two years later, a drummer whom I knew only as a casual acquaintance pulled me aside in a club and said that he had seen my bass at a jam session and that someone he knew was playing it. The bass was still probably the only one like it in Toledo, and every musician in town had been aware of my loss. It hadn't been difficult for the drummer to spot it. He gave me the address of the guy who had my bass.

The only possibilities were that the fellow who now possessed my Fender Precision had bought it "hot," knowing it was stolen property, or that he had stolen it himself. Either way, I decided I had the right to recover it.

I had a friend named Marek, a tall, muscular former boxer and trumpet player who was now a talent agent. I told him what I had in mind and asked him to come with me for moral, vocal, and possibly physical support.

We pulled up in front of a small ranch house with an unkempt yard, got out, and rang the bell. I was nervous, and I started to think that doing this might be a big mistake. A young woman answered the door. We introduced ourselves and explained why we were there. Marek asked her if we could come inside. She looked tentative and confused. She told us that her husband wasn't home. Then she let us in.

Sitting on a guitar stand, right there in the living room, was my fretless bass. I was stunned. Two years — and there it was right in front of me!

Marek very calmly explained to the young

woman that my bass was very distinctive and therefore easily recognizable. He told her that we were aware that the only ways her husband could have come by this bass were illegal ones. We didn't want to call the police or to press charges, he said, all we wanted was the bass.

She was looking more unsettled by the minute, and it was clear that she was not at all sure what to do. She told us again that her husband was not at home, and she didn't feel comfortable making any decisions about his bass without asking him.

It was then that I was glad that I am a pack rat and a saver of documents. And that Fender puts serial numbers on every instrument they make. I pulled out my wallet and extracted the original sales receipt from Ron's Music Store, complete with the serial number of the bass. I unfolded it and showed it to her, and then said, "May I?" I picked up the bass — marveling that just holding it brought back a rush of emotions, knowing that this instrument was my outlet, the extension of my body through which I could make something good happen. I slowly turned it over and looked at the serial number engraved in the neck bolt cover, where the slender neck joined the natural-blond ash body. The numbers matched.

I held the bass for her to see the number. She looked down at the receipt I had handed her, saw that the numbers matched, and looked back up at me. A very distressed look.

Marek said to her, "We're taking the bass." I picked it up, and we went out the door, leaving her standing there without the foggiest notion of what she should do. I felt sorry for her at that moment, but at the same time, I knew I was in the right.

I had my bass back. In spite of the huge odds against ever seeing it again, I had it back. I played that bass for many more years, in many more hotel lounges, nightclubs, and on concert stages. Meanwhile, I acquired other basses and built three of them myself.

Several years ago, I sold the Fender Precision fretless for considerably more than I had paid for it. I needed the money, but to this day I regret selling it. It played a large part in my development as a player, and it served me well for many years.

MARK SNYDER
*Milton, Massachusetts*

# MOTHER'S WATCH

It was a seventeen-jewel Elgin in a locket-style case, and my mother bought it before she was married in September 1916. It was a typical watch of the era, functional yet decorative — a prized piece of jewelry for a woman of that time. When you pressed on the winding stem, the locket would spring open, exposing the face of the timepiece. The watch was given to me around the time I was thirteen or fourteen, and I had it converted into a wristwatch. For me, it was just another one of the things I owned. When I left for the service in April 1941, I took the watch with me.

My unit was sent to the Philippine Islands. On board ship, crossing the Pacific, I almost lost the watch after carelessly leaving it tied to a water line while taking a shower. Thankfully, an honest GI found it and returned it. The watch still did not seem that special to me. It was just one of my practical possessions.

After the bombing of Pearl Harbor, we retreated to the Bataan Peninsula. Now I started to become a little concerned about my watch. With the enemy so close by, I felt foolish for bringing something that had been given to me by my mother. When we were told to surrender to the Japanese, I knew that my watch could become a Japanese souvenir. I couldn't bring myself to throw it into the jungle, but I didn't want to lose it to the enemy, either. I did what I could to out-smart my captors. I fastened the watch onto my left ankle and pulled my sock over it. For more protection, I put on a pair of leggings. Little did I know that I was about to embark on thirty-four months of playing a "hide the watch" game.

My unit surrendered, and then we were forced into the now infamous Bataan Death March. I wrapped the band around the watch and squeezed it into the small watch pocket of my pants. One day, while out on a work detail in northern Luzon, I was standing in the dump box of a truck, guarded by one of the ever present Japanese sol-diers. His eyes were at just the right level to notice the lump in my small pocket. He reached out with a gloved hand and touched the spot. I froze and held my breath, fearing that I was about to lose my now prized possession. Surprisingly, the guard was not curious enough to ask about what I had in my pocket, and again the watch was safe for a while. Later, I managed to find a new chamois, and I swaddled the watch in it, concealing it in my shirt pocket. No matter how wet I became, the watch remained safe and dry.

The work detail lasted about seventy days. After that, it was back to another death march and on to Cabanatuan Prison Camp, where I remained for two and a half years. There I removed the band from the watch and wrapped the face in medical gauze and tape. It made a small, easy-to-hide package. At last, when my camp was liberated, the watch and I made the trip home. When I walked through the door, I learned that my mother had died. Now her watch, which had become a reminder of my own survival, was also a reminder of her life.

I had the watch restored to its original case and added a chain identical to the original. Once again, my mother's watch was a delicate ladies' locket-style watch. I gave it to my wife. Later, I found that my brother still had the original watch chain. When he heard that I had restored the watch, he gave me the chain. Now, eighty-four years after my mother bought it, my daughter wears the watch. It is still in working condition.

RAYMOND BARRY
*Saginaw, Michigan*

# CASE CLOSED

As a teenager in the 1950s, I went to visit my cousins in Bloomington, Illinois. While walking together one day, we were arguing about the wording of a popular song. I said that they were saying, "an Indian named Standing Bear." My cousin said it was "Standing There." As we continued along, I noticed a piece of paper on the sidewalk. I picked it up, and it was the sheet music for that very song. There was no further argument. I was right, of course.

JERRY HOKE
*Torrance, California*

87

# THE PHOTO

One night I was working late in my office at home. Out of the corner of my eye I saw a photo flutter to the floor. I looked to see where it had fallen from, and then I laughed at myself because I knew full well that only the ceiling was above me and it couldn't have fallen from there.

After I had finished what I was working on, I picked up the photo, which had fallen facedown, and turned it over and looked at it. I had never seen the picture before, and I didn't recognize the people in it — a man, a little girl, and a younger boy, all wearing Mouseketeer ears. I puzzled over it, looked around again for the place where the picture might have come from, and then decided that I was too tired to figure it out. I went to bed and forgot about it.

The next day, the young woman who lived across the street got married in her backyard. The wedding was lovely, and I met lots of people for the first time. The maid of honor told me that she had grown up in my house, but she had moved out when she was eighteen — which would have been about ten years before, I guessed. Her maternal aunt was at the wedding, and so were some of the maid of honor's cousins. She said that some time she would love to come back and visit the house and show her relatives where she had grown up. I invited them all over right then, and we walked across the street and into the house.

I teased the maid of honor about my having known her name, Jane, before I knew her, because she had carved it onto a countertop in the kitchen. She went right to the spot and showed it to her relatives. In the midst of laughing about how she and her brother had slid down the back stairs and crashed into the wall at the landing, she suddenly became very sad. She said that she had lots of sad memories about living here, too, because her mother, Nancy, had died in this house.

We went upstairs, and I was showing the aunt the beautiful tile in the bathroom when suddenly Jane called out from my office, "Oh my God! Where did you get this picture? It's my father, my brother, and me!" I told her that it had fallen onto the floor last night, but I couldn't really explain where it had come from because I had never seen it before. More tears . . .

I told Jane to take the picture. She was meant to have it, I said.

Now, sometimes, when I leave the house, I call out, "Bye, Nancy. Look after the house for me until I get back, okay?"

BEVERLY PETERSON
*Uniontown, Pennsylvania*

# MS. FOUND IN AN ATTIC

In the mid-1970s I took a job at the Des Moines *Register*. When I told my father that I was moving to Des Moines, he told me about the only time he'd been there. It was in the 1930s, he said, when he was the business manager of the *Southwest Review*, the literary magazine of Southern Methodist University in Dallas. His friend Lon Tinkle, who later became a well-known Texas writer, was the review's editor. Lon also taught English at SMU, and there was a student in his class who had a severely deformed back. It was the Depression, and the young woman came from a family that was so poor she couldn't afford the operation that would correct the problem.

Her mother, who ran a boardinghouse in Galveston, was cleaning out the attic one day when she came across an old dusty manuscript. Scribbled across the top were the words, "By O. Henry." It was a nice story, and she sent it along to her daughter at SMU, who showed it to Lon. Lon had never seen the story before, but it *sounded* like O. Henry, it had an O. Henry story line, and he knew that William Sydney Porter, aka O. Henry, had lived in Houston at one time. So it was entirely possible that the famous author had gone to the beach and stayed in the Galveston boardinghouse, had written the story while he was there, and had inadvertently left the manuscript behind. Lon showed the manuscript to my father, who contacted an O. Henry expert at Columbia University in New York. The expert said he'd like to see it, so my father got on a train and took it to him.

The expert authenticated the story as O. Henry's, and my father set out to sell it. Eventually, he found himself in Des Moines, meeting with Gardner Cowles, a top editor at the Des Moines *Register*. Cowles loved the story and bought it on the spot. My father took the proceeds to the young woman in Lon Tinkle's class. It was just enough for her to have the operation she so desperately needed — and, as far as we know, to live happily ever after.

My father never told me what the O. Henry story was about. But I doubt that it could have been better than his own story: a story about O. Henry that was an O. Henry story itself.

MARCUS ROSENBAUM
*Washington, D.C.*

# TEMPO PRIMO

I needed a few moments alone with the car. To my surprise, saying good-bye to "Old Unreliable" was sad.

That car was my first major purchase, a symbol of postdivorce independence. It wasn't the privileged new Honda Accord, externalization of our privileged marital accord, but it was a Tempo — a chance for the beat to go on, to get in step. Maybe a better idea from Ford would give me a better idea for the road ahead. Maybe our mechanic's burst of sales generosity ("the divorce price") portended good luck. I had no idea I was so mechanically superstitious, but I opened the door to the Tempo as if it were a large tin fortune cookie.

At first the Tempo was great. It took the kids to school, took me to work, and took us all to Jones Beach. It sprouted pails, shovels, melted crayon bits. It was slept in, cried in, kissed and hugged in, eaten in, thrown up in. Those vinyl seats came in handy. It developed that "lived in" look, and actually having to live in it no longer seemed a real probability . . . no breakdowns, no collisions. Our tempo, and the Tempo, were steady.

However, into the second year, the fortune-cookie theory began to crumble. As a matter of fact, I would have been better off driving a rickshaw. Triple A told me that my limit of tows had been reached — and that's not counting the time the DOT truck pushed me off the Triborough Bridge (a recounting of which caused the boy to ask, "How did you live, mommy?"). I was spending more time and money with my mechanic than with my kids. The Tempo had to go. We definitely had reached the coda.

I couldn't sell this car in good faith, except for parts. I couldn't find anyone to buy it for parts, although there were certainly plenty of brand-new ones. Where are those damn chop shops when you need them? Do car thieves just sell the whole thing for fifty dollars and then take a cab home? I donated the car to charity.

Yet when the flatbed pulled up to carry Old Unreliable to its final resting place, instead of a steely relief at not having to pay the insurance or play the alternate-side shuffle, I felt sad. After all, we'd had some good times in that car. Good-bye is good-bye, even to an inanimate object, especially when that inanimate object has transported you through both mile and milestone. I told the car that I was sorry to have to let it go, that it would be helping people who need it. Then I walked home, Club lock in hand, with tears streaming down my face. Hey, people have written songs about railroads, odes to flowerpots, plays about trees, movies about baseball fields. I'm in good company, crying about my car.

LAUREN SHAPIRO
*Bronx, New York*

# A LESSON NOT LEARNED

I lost everything. That is, I'd either lose it or destroy it. Jewelry. Dolls. Games. Whatever made its way into my hands I chewed on, mangled beyond recognition, or sent to a premature death. I ate paper, and once consumed an entire book. Poor Curious George didn't stay curious for long around me. He was eaten. Mom and Dad called me "instant disaster" for inanimate objects. And because I was so messy, they always sat me at the dinner table next to the guests they weren't planning to invite back.

One day in the second grade, I walked home from school, and my surprised mother looked at me as I walked through the front door. "Carol," she asked calmly but with a confused look on her face, "where's your jumper?" I looked down and saw my patent leather buckle shoes; white leotards that were ripped at the knees; and white (but dirty) cotton turtleneck. Until my mother pointed out that I wasn't fully dressed, I hadn't noticed. I was just as surprised as she was, for we both remembered that I had been wearing the jumper that morning. My mother and I walked across the street to the school, looked on the sidewalks and all over the playground and in the halls, but no plaid jumper was to be found.

The following winter, my mother and father bought me a faux-fur brown coat with a matching hat. I loved my new coat and hat and felt like a big girl wearing the coat because it didn't have clip-on matching mittens. They had planned to buy me a coat with a hood because they knew how I was, but I begged and promised that I would be careful and not lose the hat. I especially loved the big fur pom-poms on the end of the hat's strings.

One day my father came home from work and called me downstairs from my room. He bent down to my size and hugged me, and he asked me if I would try on my new coat and hat and model them for him. Upstairs I galloped, two steps at a time, excited to put on a fashion show for my father. I threw on the coat, but I couldn't find the hat. I nervously looked under my bed and in the closet, but it was nowhere. Maybe he wouldn't notice that I wasn't wearing it.

I flew downstairs and twirled around as if on a runway, posing and smiling, modeling my new coat for my father who was paying attention to me and telling me how pretty I looked. Then he said he wanted me to model the hat, too. "No, Daddy, I just want to show you the coat. Just look at the coat on me!" I said, still sashaying around the hallway and trying to avoid the subject of the missing hat. I knew the hat was history. He was giggling, and I thought I was adorable and loved because he was laughing and playing with me. We went around a couple times about the hat, and in the middle of his laugh, he slapped me. He slapped me hard on the face, and I didn't understand why. At the sharp sound of his hand on my face, my mother yelled, "Mike! What are you doing! What are you doing!" She was breathless and stunned. His rage gored both my mother and me. I just stood there holding my hand to my burning cheek, crying. And then he took my new hat out of his coat pocket. He had found it lying in the street, and as he looked at me over the top of his glasses, he said, "Maybe now you'll learn not to be careless and lose things."

I'm a grown woman now, and I still lose things. I'm still careless. But what my father taught me that day was not a lesson of responsibility. I learned not to trust his laughter. Because even his laughter hurt.

CAROL SHERMAN-JONES
*Covington, Kentucky*

# A FAMILY CHRISTMAS

*My father told me this story. It occurred in the early 1920s in Seattle, before I was born. He was the oldest of six brothers and a sister, some of whom had moved away from home.*

The family finances had taken a real beating. My father's business had collapsed, jobs were almost nonexistent, and the country was in a near depression. We had a tree for Christmas that year but no presents. We simply couldn't afford them. On Christmas Eve, we all went to bed in pretty low spirits.

Unbelievably, when we woke up on Christmas morning, there was a mound of presents under the tree. We tried to control ourselves at breakfast, but we rushed through the meal in record time.

Then the fun began. My mother went first. We surrounded her in anticipation, and when she opened her package, we saw that she had been given an old shawl that she had "misplaced" several months earlier. My father got an old axe with a broken handle. My sister got her old slippers. One of the boys got a pair of patched and wrinkled trousers. I got a hat, the same hat I thought I had left in a restaurant back in November.

Each old castoff came as a total surprise. Before long, we were laughing so hard that we could barely pull the strings on the next package. But where had this largesse come from? It was my brother Morris. For several months, he had been secreting away old things that he knew we wouldn't miss. Then, on Christmas Eve, after the rest of us had gone to bed, he had quietly wrapped up the presents and placed them under the tree.

I remember this as one of the finest Christmases we ever had.

DON GRAVES
*Anchorage, Alaska*

# MY ROCKING CHAIR

In the summer of 1944, I was eight years old. I was an active kid and enjoyed exploring the woodlands that surrounded our house in northern New Jersey. During one of these adventures, I happened upon an old homesite. The house was collapsed and decayed, but there was evidence of former occupancy scattered on the ground. I gathered up some of these bits and pieces and discovered that I had most of the parts of a small rocking chair, made of sturdy maple and fruitwood. It looked as though it had survived many winters in the forest.

I took these pieces home to my mother (my father was overseas with the navy in the Pacific). My mother loved antiques and was especially fond of American colonial furniture. She took the pieces to a restorer she knew down near Trenton. He rebuilt the chair, replacing a few missing spindles.

The chair turned out to be a lovely example of a child's rocker from the colonial era. I kept it in my room all through my childhood. At one point, I got some small bird decals from a breakfast-cereal box and put them on the backrest. The restored chair was the first piece of furniture that was truly my own. It eventually came to the West Coast after I graduated from college. It survived numerous moves, from apartments to rented houses to houses I eventually built for my family. In 1977 the chair was lost during a move from a rental to my current residence on an island in Puget Sound. Apparently, the chair had fallen off a truck that was moving furniture from another part of the island. The loss left me with a heavy heart. Periodically, I would remember the chair and chastise myself for not being more careful during the move.

Ten years later I was driving down the main highway on the island (the island is nearly twenty miles long) and I saw a similar child's rocking chair on the porch of the local antique shop. It wasn't my chair, but it reminded me of the one I had lost. I stopped and asked the owner, who was a friend of mine, how much she wanted for the chair on the porch. In the course of the conversation, I told her the story of my lost chair, describing it in detail. She began looking at me very strangely and then said, "That sounds like a chair I recently sold to a California dealer. In fact, it's upstairs in my storage room. It's to be shipped to the dealer tomorrow." I told her my chair had a decal of a duck on the backrest. The store owner then went upstairs to inspect the chair. The decal was just where I said it would be, and that was all the proof she needed. Needless to say, I got the chair back. It now sits in a special room filled with other objects from my childhood. It's my "Rosebud."

DICK BAIN
*Vashon Island, Washington*

# THE UNICYCLE

In 1978, after working hard to develop a reputation as a player-piano restorer, I found myself overwhelmed with work and losing the affection of my beautiful, long-devoted girlfriend. Besides a considerable backlog of work for customers, I was distracted by a huge pile of unrestored instruments that I had bought and was not giving her the attention she deserved. In a last-ditch attempt to show my fiancée that she meant more to me than the pianos, I put them up for sale by taking out an ad in a newsletter for collectors. I sold them all to the first person who called — a man who lived on the opposite coast.

It didn't work. My companion defected, and at the buyer's suggestion I moved to Tacoma to help him restore the pianos.

I didn't like the West Coast. It differed too much from the East, and I was without a loved one for the first time. I quit working with the buyer. Then my truck developed problems, and I ran out of money. Desperate to leave, I barely got the truck running, drove to the airport, abandoned it, and went to the ticket counter. My brother was living near Chicago. I asked how much it would cost to fly there, and then I reached into my pocket and pulled out all of my remaining cash. It was, to the penny, the exact price of the ticket.

101

After failed attempts to reconcile with my fiancée and a couple of years exploring the country by rail and thumb, staying in monasteries and so on, I again found myself on the West Coast. And once again I was broke.

Then Mount Saint Helens exploded. I was in the University of Washington library at the time, and we all ran to the front steps to watch the eruption on the horizon. It was very ominous and made many people quite nervous.

The next day, one exceptionally nervous man was driving near the Pike Street Market and plowed through a crowded crosswalk, killing four people. I saw the whole thing happen, with the four bloodied and motionless bodies spread out across the pavement. I sat right down on the sidewalk and vowed to leave town.

That evening, while standing alone at that same intersection, I cried to the heavens with outstretched arms: *God, I hate the West Coast! If I had a unicycle, I'd ride all the way to Connecticut on it!*

I walked away then and crawled into my sleeping bag down by the harbor.

The next morning, at that same intersection — but across the street and lying on the sidewalk — there was a unicycle.

I don't usually steal, but under the circumstances I felt I had better show some gratitude. So I got on it, pointed it down the hill, said "Thanks," and took off.

After about three hundred feet, my ankles became so bloodied from banging on the cranks that I had to stop. I was also starting to get worried about taking it, so I put the unicycle back where I found it. It lay there for three days, at one of the busiest intersections in town, before it finally vanished.

I hopped a train out instead.

GORDON LEE STELTER
*Bogart, Georgia*

# MOCCASINS

"I think I want to be a priest," I said. It was 1953, and I was in the eighth grade. My parents didn't say anything, and the subject wasn't brought up again. One day during the summer, I came home and threw my first-baseman's glove on the dining-room table. My mother was ironing. I said to her, "I really think I want to go to the seminary."

Only then did I learn that my parents had already talked to Fr. McCollow, the pastor. He had told them that there were three high-school seminaries in our area. A short time later he took me to visit Queen of Apostles in Madison, Wisconsin. I registered for the next school year.

My father was happy with my decision. One day he mentioned it to a salesman who came regularly to the shoe store where he worked. The salesman told him that there was a seminary in his territory near Fond du Lac, Wisconsin. The following Saturday, I traveled with my parents and three brothers to Saint Lawrence Seminary in Mount Calvary.

The school sat at the top of a hill. We drove up to it in our wooden-body station wagon. There was no one in sight, but the Milwaukee Braves baseball game was being broadcast over the public-address system. A door opened, and a shaft of light streamed across the deserted corridor. Into the light walked a man in what looked like a brown bathrobe and open-toed shoes. He was the first Capuchin-Franciscan I had ever seen. He looked strange to me. That Capuchin introduced us to Fr. Gerald, the rector, who toured us around the grounds and buildings. Back in his office, Fr. Gerald gave us an application form. As we got back into the station wagon, my father asked, "Well, what do you think?"

"That's the place," I said.

I attended high school and one year of college at Saint Lawrence Seminary. During my freshman year of college, I realized that I was seriously drawn to the idea of joining the Capuchins. In September 1958 I received my very own brown bathrobe and open-toed shoes. I was invested in the Capuchin habit. In 1965 I was ordained a Capuchin priest. Any time I had to preach on divine providence, I said, "Next to God, the person most responsible for my being a Capuchin is a shoe salesman whom I have never met, and whose name I don't even know."

In 1975 I was stationed in Huntington, Indiana. Joe, a college student who frequently visited with me, asked if I would be going to Wisconsin on my vacation that summer. I told him that I was. He reached down and took a soft-soled moccasin off his right foot. It was worn through at the toe. "Find me a pair of these," he said. "They only sell them in Wisconsin." He didn't know what size he wore, so I slipped my foot into the moccasin. It was a little too large for me.

I stopped at several stores during my vacation, looking for a pair of "those moccasins." I also visited the college dorm at Saint Lawrence Seminary and was given a tour of the rooms, which students had decorated with imaginative posters and banners. There, next to one student's bed, was a pair of "those moccasins." "Whose bed is that?" I asked my tour guide. "Tom Roportal's," he said, and he told me the boy was in class in the main building. When I found Tom, I asked him, "Where did you get those moccasins?"

"Jahn's Shoe Store on Main Street in Fond du Lac," he said.

I drove the twelve miles to Fond du Lac, and there in the store window were "those moccasins." I entered the store and told the gentleman that I would like a pair. "What size do you wear?" he asked. "They're not for me," I said, "but I'll try them on, and if they're a little too big, I'll know they're the right size."

The clerk rolled his eyes heavenward, and I said, "I know that's not the way to do it. I was raised in a shoe store."

"Where?" he asked.

"In Monroe, Wisconsin," I said.

"Which shoe store?" he asked.

"The Monroe Shoe Store," I said.

"Are you Vern Peterson's son?" he asked.

"No, I'm Don Clark's son," I answered.

"Oh yes," the clerk said. "Don had a boy who went to the seminary, didn't he?"

"Yes," I said. "I'm that boy. Are you the salesman?"

He was.

FR. KEITH CLARK, CAPUCHIN
*Mount Calvary, Wisconsin*

# THE STRIPED PEN

It was a year after World War II ended, and I was part of the Occupation Army in Okinawa. For the past few months, there had been several robberies in our base's yard area. Window screens had been cut, items in my shack had disappeared — but strangely, the thief had taken nothing more than candy and little doodads, nothing of real value. On one occasion, I had seen dried-mud prints of bare feet on the floor and wooden table. They were tiny and seemed to belong to a child. It was known that small bands of orphaned kids roamed the island in packs, living off whatever they could find, taking anything that was not bolted down.

But then my prized Waterman fountain pen disappeared. And that was going too far.

One morning, we picked up a man from the prisoner compound. He was assigned to work duty. I had seen him several times before. He was quiet, he was handsome, he stood erect, he listened attentively. Looking at him, I imagined that whatever his rank in the Japanese army had been (possibly an officer), he had performed his duties well. And now, suddenly, there was my Waterman pen, clipped to the pocket of this dignified Japanese man.

I couldn't believe that he would steal. I was usually a good judge of character, and this man had impressed me as reliable. But I must have been wrong this time. After all, he had my pen, and he had been working in our area for several days. I decided to act on my suspicions and ignore the compassion I felt for him. I pointed to the pen and held out my hand.

He drew back, surprised.

I touched it, and again asked him, by gesture, to hand it over. He shook his head. He seemed slightly afraid — and totally sincere as well. But I wasn't going to let myself be scammed. I put on an angry face and insisted.

Finally, he gave it to me, but with great sadness and disappointment. After all, what can a prisoner do if a representative of the conquering army gives him an order? Punishments had been meted out for refusing to obey, and he must have had his fill of that kind of thing.

He didn't come back the next morning, and I never saw him again.

Three weeks later, I found my pen in my room. I was horrified by the atrocity I had committed. I knew the hurt of being victimized — of being unjustly outranked, of watching a trust killed in cold blood. I wondered how I could have made such a mistake. Both pens were green with gold stripes, but on one the stripes were horizontal; on the other, they were vertical. To make matters worse, I knew how much more difficult it must have been for this man to come by one of these prized American artifacts than it had been for me.

Now, fifty years later, I don't have either one of those pens. But I wish I could find the man, so that I could apologize to him.

ROBERT M. ROCK
*Santa Rosa, California*

# THE DOLL

For seven years I lived in L.A., where I worked at a job I didn't like very much. After a while, it made me not like myself very much. It got to the point where I only went to the office for the air-conditioning and the free coffee. But after I gave up coffee, it seemed pretty pointless to go in at all. For about a year, I kept figuring out my net worth; every morning I did a countdown of days until I'd have enough money to quit and move to North Carolina and live in the woods.

Last spring I developed a cough. I started coughing in May and then kept coughing all through July. By August my coworkers had rec-ommended all sorts of doctors and drugs, but I knew what was wrong. The job was like a noose around my neck; I was being strangled by the wrong life. After four months of coughing so hard I thought I might crack my ribs or spit up my guts, I finally resigned. On Labor Day I drove cross-country to do what I said I would do. Every-body thought I was crazy to go live in the woods. Truth is, much as I believed it was the right thing, sometimes I wondered myself.

One night during my first month after leaving L.A., I went a little stir crazy. I made dinner but somehow couldn't eat. I couldn't sit still. I was feeling some of that old work depression and anxi-ety, and I felt trapped. I wanted to get outside to watch the sunset. I got so antsy that I just left my food on the stove and drove off, with no idea where I was going.

After a while I found myself driving along the French Broad River listening to a story on NPR about an incident that had taken place in L.A. Something about computers and Y2K. My mind wandered to my friend and former coworker, Marcus, who works with computers. I realized that I hadn't talked to him since I'd moved, but now I was suddenly worried: Marcus was in pain, and I swore I'd contact him the second I could.

In the meantime, something kept pulling me along. There's this park where I sometimes sit and watch the river rush past, but I didn't stop there. Instead, I went to an old post office right by the river. It's a spot so beautiful that I've often considered taking the postmaster's exam. Even though there's a post office closer to where I live, I drive out of my way just to stand at the rail and watch the water go by. I mean, usually I just stand there watching. But that day watching wasn't enough; I had to get close.

There had been three months of drought, so the river was the lowest I'd ever seen it. I walked out on the rocks, still thinking about my friend. I remembered that Marcus couldn't swim and that he'd never do anything like this — walk across a river on rocks. I tried to forget about Marcus because I was feeling so uneasy. I tried to imagine a beautiful mermaid who would come to my cabin on cold nights for warmth and to share a bottle of wine; but her image kept fading and Marcus kept appearing. I couldn't get him out of my mind.

Marcus is a stocky black man. Highly intelligent, and so logical that he's often illogical. He can be sensitive and generous, and yet he often brusquely pushes people away. Once, when I asked if he'd visit me when I moved, Marcus played "Strange Fruit," sung by Billie Holiday. He said it was a song about whites lynching blacks in the South. I told Marcus they didn't do that where I lived. He grinned the grin of a man who doesn't believe.

I was missing Marcus out there on the rocks. But mostly I was worried. He sometimes drank too much and drove too fast. He's the kind of person who hates his job so much that he becomes a workaholic to mask his sorrow. He's come to identify so closely with computers that in some ways he's become one. Sometimes it's as though Marcus is carrying the burdens of the world around his neck on FireWire. And yet, despite all this, one image of Marcus's face kept coming back as I walked over those rocks: the way he'd held back tears the day I left the parking lot and drove away from L.A.

For half an hour I crouched in the middle of the river wondering what I was going to do with my life. Money was already tight. I was lonely in the mountains and wondered (as Marcus had prophesied) if I'd made a mistake, if I'd go nuts in the quiet. I didn't know why I was here. I felt lost. I didn't even know why I'd come to this spot on the river. All I really knew was that I missed my friend and was worried that he wasn't okay. Finally I started home, thinking that there was nothing I could do to help him because he was so far away.

And that's when it happened. . . .

Close to the riverbank, I saw something wedged between two rocks under the water. I went closer, and when I reached down, I found a doll stuck in the mud. I picked it up and saw that the doll was a small black man — stocky and wearing a hat. His arms were stretched wide, as if in a posture of surrender. At first I smiled because the resemblance to Marcus was so uncanny. I might have even laughed because they looked so much alike.

But when I had the doll in my hands, I froze. Suddenly, I was engulfed by a terror that temporarily made me insane. Someone had put a noose around the doll's neck; they'd rigged him to be hung, then tossed him into the river to drown. Now I knew why I'd been pulled there, why I'd been thinking of Marcus all day. I was sure he was in pain. And it was my job to help. So I took off the tiny rope, cleaned the doll in the river, and then carried him home.

I knew I'd helped my friend from three thousand miles away, but I never called Marcus to tell him what had happened. He's an MIT computer genius who's far too logical (cynical?) to take stock in voodoo, synchronicity, or the mystic wonders of the world.

But on the very day I rescued that doll from the river, I received a terse e-mail from Marcus. From the computer clock, I could see that he wrote it at exactly the same time that I was down at the river. He was at work, in the middle of chaotic preparations for Y2K. It was a wild stream-of-consciousness diatribe about women and work in which he talked openly about doing something he really wanted to do with his life. He said he might sell his house to go live in France or maybe sail around the world. He ended with: "But something strange and wonderful is happening to me today. I feel lighter. I've somehow gained sudden clarity, and I know that they don't own me anymore. I'm still here, but they don't own me anymore. For the first time ever, I feel free."

I never told Marcus this story. The doll from the river now lives in my house, in a room where there are no computers or electronic devices of any kind. He sits on a shelf in open view of the window, the trees, and the light. The doll seems pretty happy to be living like this.

ROBERT MCGEE
*Asheville, North Carolina*

# THE VIDEOTAPE

I work at a library, where my job is to buy video-
tapes for the film collection. Over the years I've
seen thousands of tapes. It gets to be pretty routine
after a while. Then, last week, I put in a tape and
started to watch the movie. A mother and her children are riding in a car. The children ask where
they're going. The mother replies, "We're going to
Santa Rosa." I give a mental thumbs-up. After all,
Santa Rosa is my hometown. I watch awhile, checking for sound and picture quality. I eject the tape
and put in part II. It's night. A young girl is running
down the street. She approaches a house, runs up
the steps, crosses the porch, and climbs in through
a bedroom window. I move forward in my seat. It
can't be. That's my porch, and the window leads
into my bedroom. Two girls are talking, but I don't
hear what they're saying. I'm busy looking at the
room. Window to the right, no closets — the house
is too old for that. The fourteen-foot ceilings, so
hard to find curtains for. I stop the tape; my mind is
spinning. This is the bedroom in the house I grew
up in. I slept in that room with my grandmother, in
a small iron bed across the room from her. I eject
the tape and put in the first tape again. Mother and
children driving along the street. Now they are entering a neighborhood made up of different ethnic
groups. Hispanic children playing in the street, a
Vietnamese woman reading the paper, black men

114

wearing gang colors talking in an alley. The car turns the corner. I lean forward in my chair. I've been on this street. I've ridden down it on my blue Sears bicycle with the sheepskin seat, the summer wind blowing in my face. The car pulls up to a house. The mother gets out and climbs the porch steps. A woman comes to the door. Through the screen I can see the gingerbread along the arch that leads to the dining room. They are in the kitchen talking. Everything is exactly the same. The kitchen table under the window, the big white enamel stove, the single cabinet by the sink. A man steps from another room, my bedroom. He has a towel around his shoulders. He is coming from the only bathroom in the house. My bedroom door has a small oval-shaped knob that is high up on the door. I can remember reaching for it. I strain forward as though I can see more this way. I can make out the side door to the porch where I made mud cookies for my dog. I know just beyond this are the steps that lead to the backyard where I buried the dead bird I found, the apple tree with the swing, and my grandfather's garden. I stop the tape. Suddenly thirty-five years and thousands of miles are gone. In some subtle way I am changed. I can feel the sun on my skin, see my dog's face, and hear the birds singing. In a world where life is sometimes mundane, repetitive, and often cruel, I am filled with wonder.

MARIE JOHNSON
*Fairbanks, Alaska*

115

# THE PURSE

In the early '70s I worked as a meter reader for PG&E in San Mateo. I was one of only three women in the department. Once a month I would go to a neighborhood in Redwood City. The people who lived there were mostly elderly Italian couples, widows, and widowers, and when they died their children would fix up the houses and rent them out. You could usually tell by the front yards. The flowers and tomato plants would be replaced by easy-to-care-for lawns.

That was where Joe lived: in a small bungalow on the last block of my route. He had a large front yard and a beautiful, well-tended garden in back.

Every month I would read the gas meter in front and then knock so that Joe could let me walk through the house and go to the electric meter out back. He was a plump little man with once-black hair that was almost all gray now, and smiling dark eyes, and from the beginning he had insisted that I call him Joe. He was probably in his seventies and was always at home and apparently lived by himself. He would open the door and say with an Italian accent, "Good morning! Good morning!" no matter what time of day "Come in! Come in! Come! Come! Come!" Joe would always remain in the house until I had finished reading the meter. Afterward we would walk through the garden, and he would give me fruit or vegetables to take

116

home with me, whatever was in season.

The electric meter was on the house above an old picnic table that had been pushed up against the wall under the shade of a large grapevine. On the table — near the edge — was an old purse. It was the type of purse an old lady would own: it had a hard, curved shell covered with dark brown leather that was scuffed and worn. The clasp was the type that pinched shut and was tarnished and discolored from years of use. At first I wondered where she was . . . the owner of the purse. . . . Was she ill? Or maybe this was to test me, to see if I was honest. Eventually, I stopped questioning its presence. I would stand next to the bench in front of the purse and read the meter, but I was always aware of it — solid and unmovable. Once I almost touched it.

One August day about two years after I started coming to his house, the weather was unusually warm. By the time I knocked on Joe's door, I was dehydrated and suffering from the heat. We walked through to the patio and he insisted that I sit down on the bench by the picnic table. As I sat there looking at the purse, I heard him say in a soft, trembling voice, "We were going shopping. . . . She put the purse down. . . . She needed to sit for a minute. . . . I couldn't touch it after. . . . I can't move it." When I looked up at him, he turned away and walked quickly into the house. When he came back outside, his eyes were smiling and he proudly handed me a large bag of tomatoes and zucchinis and a Fanta orange soda.

I thought about the purse a lot over the next month and was anxious to see Joe again. When I finally arrived at his house in September, I noticed immediately that something wasn't quite right. His garden was yellowed and there were rotting vegetables on the ground. Thinking that he might be ill, I ran to the door and knocked loudly. A slim man with Joe's eyes — but they weren't smiling — opened the door. I said, "Where's Joe!"

He stared speechlessly at the girl with long blond hair dressed in a man's uniform. Unsure what to say next, I told him that I was there to read the meters. He turned to another man and asked him to open the side gate for me, a route I had never taken before. I walked quickly through the gate to the back of the house and around the giant grapevine up to the picnic table. The man stood near me and waited. I stared at the meter and wrote some number down in my book. When I was finished, I walked past the man without saying a word. I left the yard and closed the gate behind me.

The purse was gone.

BARBARA HUDIN
*Bend, Oregon*

# A GIFT OF GOLD

It was the winter of 1937, just after Christmas. The Depression was still going on, but I was in good spirits. At the end of January, I was going to graduate from elementary school. I was just twelve — younger than all the other boys in my class and much smaller. My mother still dressed me in shorts, and when the cold weather came, I wore woolen knickers and knee-high socks. Most of my classmates had given up wearing shorts, but even though they were older and taller than I was, they still wore knickers. Only a couple of the taller fourteen-year-old fellows had moved on to long pants.

However, for the graduation ceremony, all the boys were expected to dress the same way. They were supposed to wear white shirts, navy-blue knitted ties, and dark-blue wool serge pants. When I asked one or two knickered kids what they were going to do, they said that they were going to show up on graduation day wearing long pants.

I waited until a week before graduation before I told my mother. I figured I'd better break the news to her as gently as I could.

I remember that it was a cold Monday afternoon. I had come home from school after crunching my way over the treacherous streets and crosswalk. There were deep ruts and tracks cut into the thick layers of melted and refrozen snow. Inside the house it felt warm and comforting. I put

119

my heavy coat away in the hall closet, all the while inhaling the tantalizing smell of fish being fried in butter. I went into the kitchen for a glass of milk, one of the few luxuries of life in our house.

"Boy, Mom," I said, "that smells good. I love fish."

"Don't start bothering me for some now," she said, "the way you always do. Remember, if you have some now, you won't get your share at dinner."

This was a little game we played, always with the same result. I would pester her until she swore that I was driving her to distraction. Then she'd give in and let me have a generous sample. I'd invariably get my full share at dinner.

This time, I didn't put the game in motion.

"Mom," I said, "about graduation . . ."

"Yes?" she answered, shuffling the skillet on the burner.

"They're going to give me the first-prize medal," I said.

Still working over the stove, she looked over her shoulder at me and smiled broadly. "That's wonderful, Babe. Dad and I will both be there, and we'll be the proudest parents in the place."

She must have seen by the look on my face that something was wrong. She turned her back to the stove and said, "So?"

"So, I have to get long pants," I said.

It didn't take long to get the answer I expected.

"Babe, we don't have the money for new pants right now," she said very quietly. "You know that."

"Okay," I burst out. "Then I won't go to graduation. Plus, I'm running away from home!"

120

I waited. My mother shook the pan several times and then turned over the pieces of fish one by one. It was very quiet except for the sound of melted butter sizzling in the pan.

She turned to me. Her outstretched hand held the spatula on which she had balanced a golden piece of sautéed fish.

"Here," she said. "Cut one of the rolls on the table and make yourself a nice fish sandwich. And if I were you, I wouldn't pack my bags just yet. We'll solve the pants problem somehow."

My mother watched me make the sandwich. She continued to watch me eat it, obviously amused by the way each bite was accompanied by moans of delight. "That ought to hold you," she said.

The following Saturday, when my mother said, "Let's go shopping," I knew that she had solved the problem.

Midmorning we bundled up against the bitter cold that had settled over the city and took the trolley that ran along Westchester Avenue. We got off at Southern Boulevard, the best shopping street in the East Bronx. Our clothing store was just a couple of blocks away. We had been getting my pants there from Mr. Zenger ever since I could remember. I liked Mr. Zenger, and I enjoyed hearing him say, as he always did, "Trust me, sonny, I'll give you the best, and with those pants, you'll look like a million dollars."

But first we walked a short way down the boulevard and stopped at a place I had never noticed before.

My mother said, "Wait here."

121

She opened the door and entered a storefront that looked a little like a bank. I read the sign over the door: Home Thrift and Loan.

She came out about ten minutes later, and we went to the pants store. There Mr. Zenger fitted me with what was surely the greatest pair of 100 percent pure-wool navy-blue serge trousers ever to be had in the whole world.

Mr. Zenger measured me for the inner seam length and then sewed the cuffs while we waited. The cost was three dollars and fifty cents, including the alterations.

The new trousers were wrapped up in brown paper and tied with string. I was holding the package tightly under my arm when my mother went to pay Mr. Zenger. I saw her take a tiny brown envelope from her purse, tear back the sealed flap, and remove the contents. There were four brand-new one-dollar bills inside. She carefully unfolded them and handed them to Mr. Zenger. He rang up the sale and gave my mother the fifty cents change.

Sitting next to my mother on the trolley, I had the window seat and looked out for most of the ride. About halfway home, there wasn't much to look at rattling over the Bronx River Bridge, and as I shifted around in my seat to face forward, I glanced down at my mother's hands folded across her purse, which was resting on her lap. It was then that I saw that the plain gold wedding band that had always circled the ring finger on her left hand was no longer there.

JOHN KEITH
*San Jose, California*

# FAMILIES

# RAINOUT

The last time I went to Tiger Stadium (then known as Briggs Stadium) I was eight years old. My father came home from work and announced that he was taking me to the ball game. He was a fan, and we had gone to several day games before, but this would be my first night game.

We got there early enough to park on Michigan Avenue for free. In the second inning, it started to rain, and then the rain turned into a downpour. Within twenty minutes, they announced over the loudspeaker that the game had been canceled.

We walked under the stands for about an hour waiting for the rain to let up. When they stopped selling beer, my father said that we should make a run for the car.

We had a black 1948 sedan, and the door on the driver's side was broken and could only be opened from the inside. We got to the door on the passenger's side panting and soaking wet. As my father fumbled for the keys, they dropped out of his hand and fell into the gutter. When he bent down to retrieve them from the rushing water, the door handle knocked the brown fedora off his head. I caught up with the hat about halfway down the block and then raced back to the car.

My father was already sitting behind the wheel. I jumped in, collapsed onto the passenger's seat, and dutifully handed him the hat — which now looked like a wet rag. He studied it for a second and then put it on his head. Water poured out of the hat, splashing onto his shoulders and lap and then onto the steering wheel and dashboard. He let out a loud roar. I was frightened because I thought he was howling with anger. When I realized he was laughing, I joined in, and for the next little while we just sat there in the car, laughing hysterically together. I had never heard him laugh like that before — and I never did again. It was a raw explosion that came from somewhere deep within him, a force that he had always kept dammed up.

Years later, when I spoke to him about that night and how I remembered his laughter, he insisted that it had never happened.

STAN BENKOSKI
*Sunnyvale, California*

# ISOLATION

A week after my mother's body was cremated, my father borrowed an Econoline van from someone and piled us into it. We sat in cheap beach chairs in the back drinking beer, which spilled off when he took the corners too fast. He drove us out to a place called West Meadow Beach on Long Island's North Fork. The bungalow had been lent to us out of pity. My mother had just been murdered, and my father had been left alone with six teenage children.

We were used to a rough and windy ocean beach. Our summer house was on the Atlantic, in Neponsit, a small town in Queens, and we loved it there. But that place was now contaminated by death. My mother had been strangled in her bedroom there one night late in June. We couldn't have stayed in that house even if we had wanted to. People kept driving by and pointing, and the police had messed it up with their coffee cups and fingerprint stuff.

The stranger's bungalow was on Long Island Sound. There were no waves or pebbles in the sand, and tame, civilized things kept floating by, rocking silently in the water. I was eighteen. Sarah, the youngest, was twelve. Gaby, the oldest, was twenty. Blaise was sixteen, Mark was fourteen, and Heather was thirteen. My father was fifty-one. He had no comfort to offer us, so he

127

gave us isolation instead.

Before West Meadow Beach, we had been a fairly happy, drug-riddled bunch of sniping American kids. We shared our pot but not our favorite clothes; we hated each other's music but loved each other's friends. That all changed when we found ourselves in that house, bound together by cynicism, depression, and alcohol.

Everything inside the bungalow was cold and clammy. There was an unfamiliar cheerfulness to it, with toys and floral cushions lit by bright, un-shielded bulbs and hurricane lamps. We all shared a sensitivity to light, having been brought up in a dark house and the dark houses of our grand-mothers. We sat with the lights out, in the glow of our cigarettes. My father had brought along plenty of booze, every kind of liquor in the book, as well as several cartons of cigarettes, but hardly any food. That was how we inaugurated our tradi-tion of drunken familial empathy.

The drinking didn't make a difference, but it was something to do, something that felt like progress. Nobody had much to say. So we sat on the stranger's wicker furniture and drank very strong drinks: gin and tonic, vodka and grape soda, rum and anything. Somewhere outside, the neighbors were happy. It was around the Fourth of July and they were having parties.

The next day, we parked ourselves at the back of the beach, sprawled out in lounge chairs behind the dunes and grass with our long hair and long legs and burning Marlboros in the sun. To anyone else, we would have looked bored, but we were ac-tually deep in thought. Deep in thought. The

Sound was like a big, dull swimming pool. We started drinking first thing, which seemed like a good idea. Nobody went swimming.

We had a canoe, which had fallen off the van in the middle of a road on the way out, nearly killing the guy behind us. That had been one of the high points of the trip. After a few drinks, Heather and Sarah and Dad took the canoe out to the sandbar, and Dad pulled them along, leaning into the breeze like a giant, gray-haired Goliath. The water made his gray chest hair all bedraggled, and his loose shorts clung to his skinny butt. He pulled the canoe with pain all over his face, as though it were a penance. The girls sat in the canoe, silently holding their highballs and staring at my father's back.

We continued like that through the hot, sunny days and long, strange nights. On the fourth day, my cousin came to check on us and spend a few days in the sun. She was loud and talkative and moved through us like a walking television that's been left on and that you don't want to watch. She said she thought that maybe my father shouldn't let the little girls drink. We laughed at that, and then we were very quiet and some of us started to cry. She left the next day.

That was in 1980, twenty years ago. I find that hard to believe, because I know that all of us are still there, floating and rocking back and forth, letting the time pass as we wait for things to get better.

LUCY HAYDEN
*Ancram, New York*

# CONNECTIONS

My father had two sisters, Layna, a pediatrician, and Rose, a photographer. They lived in Berlin, where they shared an apartment. Being Jewish, they fled Germany soon after Hitler took power in 1933 and eventually made their way to the United States. They settled in New York, where they again shared an apartment.

In 1980, after the second sister had died, I received a phone call from the lawyer of her estate. The lawyer told me that he was eager to wrap up his work and that her apartment had to be cleared out. Among the remaining odds and ends were some one hundred German books. He said that most of the refugees from Hitler's Germany had settled in New York and had brought their German books with them. The market was flooded, the books were worthless, and they couldn't be sold or even given away. His recommendation was to throw them out. That suggestion offended my sensibilities, raising memories of Nazi book burnings. I begged him to give me a few days to find a different solution.

I live in Bloomington, Indiana, the seat of Indiana University. My thought was to offer the books to the German Department as a gift. Here, I found, German books were not considered worthless, and the chairman was happy to accept my gift for the departmental library.

The books arrived, and while they were still in boxes, one of the German professors, rummaging through the collection, suddenly let out a gasp of astonishment. He had found the owner's name, Layna Grebsaile, inscribed on the title page of several volumes. He told the chairman that he had known someone by that name during his boyhood in Berlin, and he wanted to know how these books had wound up in Bloomington. The chairman gave him my name. When we met, we confirmed that I was indeed the niece of the Layna he had known. Then he told me a bit of family lore that I had never heard before.

The professor had grown up in Berlin. His mother died when he was quite young, and his widowed father, resolving to remarry, began courting Layna, the older of the two sisters. Nothing came of the courtship, but the future professor, then in his teens, formed his own friendship with Layna, and they remained friends even after his father and Layna parted ways.

The young man was also Jewish, and he, too, fled Germany. His odyssey took him to Bloomington, where he was first a student and later joined the faculty of Indiana University. He settled down, married, and raised a family, but throughout those years he and Layna kept up their friendship, exchanging occasional letters until her death in 1957.

After Rose's death in 1980, a trunk full of family letters, documents, and memorabilia made its way into my basement. On dreary evenings, when I feel nostalgic, I open the trunk and riffle through its treasures. One evening, I came across a greeting card from the professor to Layna. I gave it to him as a gift.

MIRIAM ROSENZWEIG
*Bloomington, Indiana*

# THE WEDNESDAY BEFORE CHRISTMAS

This happened the Wednesday before Christmas a couple of years ago. We had just finished choir rehearsal at the church. The decorations were already up — wreaths on the columns, which filled the church with a smell of pine. In the sanctuary, there was a big artificial Christmas tree. That was the drop-off spot for the Toys For Tots program, and there was a small pile of presents under it.

It was almost midnight, and I was standing in the parking lot with a friend. The other members of the choir had already gone home. We'd shut off the lights in the church and locked the front doors, but the side door by the chapel was always left unlocked.

As my friend and I were talking, a red Jeep 4x4 drove slowly into the parking lot. When the driver saw us, he turned around and left. This was strange, and it worried me. Churches get vandalized. The door is always open in God's house, and occasionally some drunk will stumble into the chapel to sleep it off — or maybe to drink the wine and steal the gold altar service. But the odd, appraising drive-by of an expensive SUV — that gave me pause.

My friend and I said nothing about it. After we finished our conversation, we got into our cars, but I didn't go home. I circled the block and returned to the church. When I came back, the Jeep was parked by the chapel door and the lights in the church were on. I sat in my car for a little while, feeling pretty nervous. Then I got up and went into the church.

Expecting to take a bullet in the head at any moment, I went through the lower church, flipping on light switches, making a whole lot of noise so they'd know I was coming. I didn't want jumpy, startled intruders on my hands. Halfway up the stairs I found myself singing "King of the Road" at a decent volume (don't ask me why).

I rounded the bend in the stairs and came out into the sacristy, and there, by the altar, I saw a man and a woman whom I knew by sight as members of our parish. From my spot in the choir, I see everybody. The woman always sat in the center aisle, seven pews back on the right. She had a strong, pure soprano voice. I'd spoken to her once and asked her if she'd considered joining the choir, but she was too shy. She usually came to church alone, but I'd seen the man a few times and knew he was her husband.

They were each holding huge white plastic shopping bags, and both of them were filled with new toys. There had to have been at least five hundred dollars' worth of stuff in those bags. They were piling the toys under the artificial Christmas tree for the Toys For Tots program.

The woman gave me an embarrassed half-smile and raised a finger to her lips. "Please," she said, "not a word to anyone."

I nodded dumbly and left.

134

This woman and her husband were in their late forties. I knew a little about them. They had no children. They'd never had children. Never could. Infertile.

There's no punch line here: this is just something that happened. But when I got in my car and drove home, I was shaken by sobs that did not stop for a long time.

JACK FEAR
*somewhere in Massachusetts*

# HOW MY FATHER LOST HIS JOB

At the age of sixty, just a few years from retirement, my father lost his job. For most of his working life he had managed a small printing department in a Connecticut rubber factory. Long owned by B. F. Goodrich, the operation had recently been sold to an eccentric Midwestern businessman known for quoting scripture one moment and cursing the next. To no one's surprise, the business rapidly began losing money. Fortunately, my father was able to escape the frequent layoffs, and because management would always need forms and printed stationery, he assumed his luck would continue a little longer.

But on the night of March 1, 1975, three armed men wearing ski masks appeared at the plant, abducted the night watchman and a custodian, and abandoned them, blindfolded and bound, in a lumberyard some miles away. The intruders had planted explosives, and by midnight the factory was leveled, the blast shaking the sidewalks and shattering windows on both sides of the Housatonic River. No one was killed, but the next morning nearly one thousand workers found themselves without jobs. Despite the gunmen's claims that they were part of a radical leftist organization, an FBI investigation revealed that the company's owner, with the help of his equally strange adviser, a self-styled psychic, was responsible. The pair

136

had hoped to reverse their financial slide by collecting insurance on the ruined buildings. Though the investigation was quick, the subsequent trial was not, and my father's pension would be frozen for several years.

I was away at graduate school when he called to tell me the startling news. The community was stunned; the area already had one of the highest unemployment rates in the state. Most of the people had lived in the Housatonic Valley all their lives. Where would they find work? My father hated the idea of collecting unemployment; it contradicted his beliefs about how an honest person earns his way through life. If he had managed to find a job digging ditches as a teenager during the Great Depression, then by God he could find a job now.

My father had taken good care of himself and still looked like a man in his early forties. His jet-black hair, thick and wavy like Fred MacMurray's in *Double Indemnity*, showed barely a trace of gray, and a daily regimen of sit-ups had kept his stomach flat. Surely no one could hold his chronological age against him. He scoured the want ads with a vengeance, considering everything from night watchman — my mother quashed that possibility — to shipping clerk. There wasn't much demand for printers.

Finally, after months of rejections and poor prospects, he heard about an opening for a print-shop manager at a local college. The position was a perfect match for his skills. It didn't pay as much as his old job, but it offered him a chance to use the technical knowledge he'd acquired over the years. He rushed to apply.

He got on well with the young personnel officer, who reviewed his application with obvious interest and enthusiasm. My father liked the guy and loved the thought of being in an academic environment. He had always regretted not finishing high school, and working on a college campus would be the next best thing to heaven.

After some friendly conversation, the personnel officer leaned back, slapped his hands down on his desk, and said, "Well, I think we've found our printer." He asked my father how soon he could start. Though policy required one more bureaucratic stage of approval, he told my father that he was by far the most qualified applicant and that he could expect to be officially notified of his hiring within days.

They shook hands, but as my father walked to the door, the young man called him back. "One little thing," he said, smiling, "you forgot to fill in your age on the application." This was no mistake. Having been brusquely disqualified so often because of his age, my father had learned to forestall the inevitable by leaving the line blank. But this time was different. He was the best person for the job. He was practically hired. Why not be honest?

"I'm sixty," my father said, with a touch of pride. The young man's smile faded. "Sixty?" he repeated. He lowered his head; his forehead furrowed. It was as if someone had turned off a light. "I see," he said, his voice suddenly flat and impersonal, "well, we do have several more applicants to interview, so I can't make any promises. We'll let you know. Have a nice day."

There was no call, no letter. My father lost his spirit, any hope that his last working years would be of real value. Feeling desperate, even with six months of unemployment benefits left, he took a job as a laborer at a dye works. There was no union. The work was physically grueling, breaks were minimal, and he was forced to eat lunch on the job, grabbing bites as he could from a sandwich he kept in a back pocket. Surrounded by recent immigrants from Eastern Europe and Central America, people so hungry for a good life in the United States that they would accept any working conditions without complaint, my father was nearly the only person in the plant who spoke English. He was also the oldest.

I visited my parents that Thanksgiving, less than two months after my father had started his new job. When he rushed forward to hug me, as he always did whenever I came home, I saw that his hands were stained with indelible dye, and that his hair had turned completely gray.

FRED MURATORI
*Dryden, New York*

# DANNY KOWALSKI

In 1952 my father quit his job at Ford to move us to Idaho and start his own company. Instead, he got polio and spent six months in an iron lung. After three more years of therapy, we moved to New York City, where my father finally got a sales job, this time with the English car company Jaguar.

One of the perks of the new job was a car that he was given to drive. It was a two-tone gray Jaguar Mark IX, the last of the elegant, rounded models. It looked like something that belonged in a movie star's garage.

I was enrolled at St. John the Evangelist, a parochial school on the East Side with an asphalt playground separated from the street by a high wire fence.

Every morning my father would drop me off at school in his Jaguar before heading off to work. Being the son of a blacksmith from Parsons, Kansas, he was proud of his car and thought I should be proud to be driven to school in it. He loved its genuine leather upholstery and the small burled walnut tables that were attached to the backs of the front seats, on which I could finish my homework.

But I was embarrassed by the car. After years of illness and debt, we probably didn't have any more money than the rest of the mostly working-class Irish, Italian, and Polish kids in the school.

But we had a Jaguar, and so we might as well have been Rockefellers.

The car separated me from the other kids, but especially from Danny Kowalski. Danny was what they called a juvenile delinquent in those days. He was slight and had a mound of blond hair sculpted with grease and spray into a tsunami-like pompadour. He wore the shiny, pointed boots we called "Puerto Rican fence climbers," his collar was always up, and there was a permanent, practiced snarl on his upper lip. It was rumored that he had a switchblade, maybe even a zip gun.

Every morning Danny Kowalski would wait in the same spot at the school fence and watch me as I climbed out of my two-tone gray Jaguar and entered the school yard. He never said a word; he just stared at me with hard, angry eyes. I knew he hated that car and that he hated me, and that someday he was going to beat me up for it.

My father died two months later. We lost the car, of course, and soon I'd have to go live with my grandmother in New Jersey. Mrs. Ritchfield, an elderly neighbor, offered to walk me to school the day after the funeral.

When we approached the school yard that morning, I could see Danny hanging on the fence, same place as always, his jacket collar turned up, his hair perfectly coifed, his boots recently sharpened. But this time, as I passed him in the company of this feeble, elderly woman and with no elitist English car in sight, I felt as if a wall had been taken down between us. Now I was more like Danny, more like his friends. We were finally equals.

Relieved, I walked into the school yard. And that was the morning Danny Kowalski beat me up.

CHARLIE PETERS
*Santa Monica, California*

# REVENGE

My grandmother was an iron-willed woman, the feared matriarch of our New York family back in the 1950s.

When I was five years old, she invited some friends and relatives to her Bronx apartment for a party. Among the guests was a neighborhood big shot who was doing well in business. His wife was proud of their social status and let everyone at the party know it. They had a little girl about my age who was spoiled and very much used to getting her own way.

Grandmother spent a lot of time with the big shot and his family. She considered them the most important members of her social circle and worked hard at currying their favor.

At one point during the party, I made my way to the bathroom and closed the door behind me. A minute or two later, the little girl opened the bathroom door and grandly walked in. I was still sitting down.

"Don't you know that little girls aren't supposed to come into the bathroom when a little boy is using it!?" I hollered.

The surprise of my being there, along with the indignation I had heaped upon her, stunned the little girl. Then she started to cry. She quickly closed the door, ran to the kitchen, and tearfully complained to her parents and my grandmother.

Most of the partygoers had overheard my loud remark and were greatly amused by it. But not Grandmother.

She was waiting for me when I left the bathroom. I received the longest, sharpest tongue-lashing of my young life. Grandmother yelled that I was impolite and rude and that I had insulted that nice little girl. The guests watched and winced in absolute silence. So forceful was my grandmother's personality that no one dared stand up for me.

After her harangue was over and I had been dismissed, the party continued, but the atmosphere was much more subdued.

Twenty minutes later, all that changed. Grandmother walked by the bathroom and noticed a torrent of water streaming out from under the door.

She shrieked twice — first in astonishment, then in rage. She flung open the bathroom door and saw that the sink and tub were plugged up and that the faucets were going at full blast.

Everyone knew who the culprit was. The guests quickly formed a protective barricade around me, but Grandmother was so furious that she almost got to me anyway, flailing her arms as if trying to swim over the crowd.

Several strong men eventually moved her away and calmed her down, although she sputtered and fumed for quite a while.

My grandfather took me by the hand and sat me on his lap in a chair near the window. He was a kind and gentle man, full of wisdom and patience. Rarely did he raise his voice to anyone, and never did he argue with his wife or defy her wishes.

He looked at me with much curiosity, not at all angry or upset. "Tell me," he asked, "why did you do it?"

"Well, she yelled at me for nothing," I said earnestly. "Now she's got something to yell about."

Grandfather didn't speak right away. He just sat there, looking at me and smiling.

"Eric," he said at last, "you are my revenge."

ERIC BROTMAN<br>
Nevada City, California

# CHRIS

It was the year my mother stopped drinking, so it was two years after a careless driver killed my sister in a crosswalk, one year after my father died of a massive coronary on the front stairs, eight months before my brother Ronnie died of AIDS, and six months before he revealed his situation.

It was summer, that unbearably hot summer when Rachel, my daughter, and I went to Boston University for her freshman orientation and visited what was left of my family. We had traveled at enormous expense from New Mexico.

Before I left home, I discussed the trip with my friend Janie. Because of traveling this route for so many funerals, I had become apprehensive of flight. At one point in the conversation, I said, "I would really like to see my cousin Chris once more before he dies, but the chances of that are slim." He had been diagnosed with AIDS and had told the family several months earlier. "He isn't seeing anyone these days. He doesn't answer my letters. He's somewhere in Provincetown."

She said, "Just do it."

"What do you mean?"

"Just go to Boston. Just go to Provincetown. Don't think about it. Do it."

It was the best advice anyone has ever given me.

After the orientation, we went to the family home, and I called Chris to ask if he would see us.

146

I left a total of eight messages on his machine. This was one of those years when my mother was not speaking to her sister — Chris's mother — and even though I was an adult and knew that I had not, at least not very often, caused her drinking, I determined that I would do nothing so uncouth as to call my Aunt Lorraine.

And Janie's words came back to me. "Just do it."

I rented a car and told my mother that Rachel and I were going to see if we could find Chris. As an afterthought I said, "Would you like to join us?"

"Yes." Since quitting the bottle, she had become curt.

And thus our various destinies were set. Getting to P-town was a challenge. Chris had answered none of my phone calls, and we didn't know where he lived. After stops at Triple A and the ever necessary "coffee and," we set out with maps and TripTiks in the general direction of Cape Cod. Rachel dozed and my mother examined the windshield. We got there sometime after the lunch crunch.

I found a phone booth, conveniently located outside a fish restaurant, and left another message, telling him where we were.

Ma, Rachel, and I went into the darkened restaurant overlooking the ocean. My mother had a beer. I did not remark on this. I enjoyed my scallops. Rachel had lobster salad. As the beer began working its wonders, my mother shared confidences with Rachel. I enjoyed my scallops.

After lunch, I left another message for Chris, feeling more and more hopeless. I slumped against the cool glass of the booth and watched my mother play some game in the sand with her only grandchild.

I just didn't know what to do next.

"He's still not home," I announced, stepping out of the phone booth. They looked at me, waiting. "Well, I guess we can walk around a bit. Since we're here." They were amenable.

"Right or left?" I asked. This seemed to be an important yet illusive decision. We were about midway between each end of a street of taffy shops, hotels, restaurants, and souvenir shops, the bay behind us, hills ahead. I had no idea what lay in either direction.

Rachel shrugged her shoulders and my mother examined her fingernails.

"Okay," I said, "right it is." If my mother picked up the sarcasm, one of her specialties, she ignored it. Rachel smiled encouragement, and we ambled right.

What I remember is a blur of hot red-orange-blue color flapping and shimmering in the heat, kids darting in and out among men in shorts and women in sundresses.

We crossed the vehicleless street diagonally, drawn, I suppose, by the absence of color on the sparkling city hall building with its lush lawn rolling down to several inviting benches in the shade of two trees. As we approached, my mother stopped to read a sign on the side of the tourist tram — something about its route and costs.

"Look," she said, pointing. She turned to me and started to say something, but I was watching Rachel, who was watching something behind me.

148

"Rachel," I said.

"Patti?" a vaguely familiar voice said at my ear.

I turned and saw my cousin Chris. Time stopped. I am certain of that. The whole of Provincetown stopped until the bell on the trolley rang.

"Chris!" I shouted, and my voice rose high and screechy as it does when I'm scared or incredulous.

"Yes, it's me." He hugged me lightly, protecting a plastic bag of liquid attached to his shirt, its tube disappearing between two buttons. He was thin in the way I imagined British sailors with rickets to be. His hair was thin. Even his lips were thin. Only his voice was what it had always been. He wore tight, bleached-out shorts, a fitted plaid shirt, sunglasses, and the plastic package of life at his breast, like a yellow Jewish star announcing the Holocaust. He wasn't my boy-cousin in that moment, he was every man dying of AIDS. He was my brother, dying secretly of AIDS. He was my cousin dying of AIDS.

I was incredulous and it showed on my face. Chris said, "This is my bench," pointing, "I figured you'd pass by sooner or later. Or not."

"Auntie Mame!" Chris shouted his endearment and hugged my mother. "And this must be Rachel. . . ." Another careful hug.

We all sat on Chris's bench and talked pleasantly and banally, as if we did not share family secrets. Rachel said very little, but smiled. She's an observer. In a few months, she would, literally, watch her Uncle Ronnie die.

My mother smiled a lot, too. The beer luster had worn off, so she didn't say much. After a bit, we simply ran out of things to say. No one asked Chris about his treatments. I may have remarked that I thought he wasn't supposed to be out in the sun on that medication. He may have laughed derisively. We all came to "good-bye" naturally, hugged, and kissed. I know I whispered, "I love you, Chris." It seemed so inadequate. We three turned and walked slowly toward the Authentic Salt Water Taffy Shop ahead.

None of us looked back to see Chris one more time. We went into the store and bought taffy. By the time we came out, he was gone.

I felt empty. "Let's look for shells," I said, appealing to Rachel's childhood obsession, and we crossed the bay, shedding our shoes and wading in the cool sand.

Rachel found a shell shaped like a big toenail. Ma captured a silvery purple mussel shell, and I found a piece of beach glass, a shard of blue, honed, buffed, and rounded by eons of salt water, sand, and wind. As we walked along the beach, heading toward the car and ultimately Boston, I remembered, and I hope I told them, that it was Chris who had introduced me to beach glass so many years ago when I was a young woman in a bikini and he was a boy-cousin.

I keep Chris's piece of blue in an empty artichoke jar alongside Rachel's "toenail" and Ma's mussel shell.

The following summer, the city of Provincetown dedicated a bench in front of city hall to Chris Locke.

EDWINA PORTELLE ROMERO
*Las Vegas, New Mexico*

# PUT YOUR LITTLE FOOT

I hated it when Mama tied a bow in my hair. My blond hair was too fine, and we both knew that it would slip off long before the evening was over. I didn't like bows and dresses and only wore them when pressured.

Tonight was different. I was going to a barn dance. I started to sway to the imaginary music in my head. I decided that I would survive if I pretended that I was my cousin Emma.

"Stand still. I need to straighten the sash on your dress. I expect you to mind your manners tonight and don't forget that you and your brother are going to dance 'Put Your Little Foot.' I want everyone to see how well both of you are learning to dance."

"Oh Mama, I don't see why I have to dance with Raymond. He doesn't want to be seen dancing with his little sister. Besides, all of our cousins will be watching and will tease us."

For days Mama made us practice "Put Your Little Foot." I thought it was a simple dance that didn't require too many brains, much less a lot of practice. I didn't understand why Mama was making such a fuss. All you had to do was stand side by side and move from left to right according to the music. You crossed your right foot over your ankle and put it down — then you switched sides. Raymond and I caught on from the beginning, and the only reason we had trouble with the dance was that we tried to trip or kick each other.

I knew there would be snickers and giggles from our cousins, whose parents never made them show off. But Mama had made it clear. The price for us to stay up late, watch the adults, and have a late-night supper was "Put Your Little Foot." My brother and I shook hands and agreed that we wouldn't embarrass Mama. We also agreed to band together and beat up our cousins the next day if they made fun of us.

It was a big barn dance. People were coming from the surrounding ranches and towns. Every spare bedroom and the bunkhouse were filled. There had not been a barn dance for a long time. In 1942 gasoline was rationed, and many of the men were in the war. However, this year quite a few men were home on leave, and my aunt and uncle decided that everyone needed a party — the soldiers, the cowboys, the relatives, and even the kids. It was a big "eatin' and meetin'."

People were already arriving, and I could hear the greetings. "Howdy! Glad y'all could come. Sure a nice night for a barn dance." The fiddler was tuning his fiddle, and some of the ladies were giving the barn floor one last sweeping. I saw my cousin Emma going into the barn, and I took out after her.

"Emma, Emma, wait for me."

She turned and took me by the hand. "Don't run, Anna Bess. You'll get all sweaty and spoil your pretty dress." Then she leaned down and whispered to me, "Besides, your mother won't like it if that bow falls out of your hair."

I loved my cousin Emma. She could always make me laugh, and I thought she was the most beautiful, perfect person in all the world. She squeezed my hand as we went into the barn.

"Go and find your friends, Anna Bess. I'm going over to see Betty Sue." I looked wistfully at the young adults, but I knew that I was expected to sit with the children. However, I did pretend that I was Emma as I walked over to join the children in the corner.

The music started. The dancers jumped to their feet, and the dance was in full swing. My mother, a widow, was on the floor for every dance. I had never seen Mama dance, and she was wonderful. She always had a partner and never made a mistake in the square dances. The "Texas Star" was my favorite. I pretended I was dancing all the steps. I was tapping out time with my feet and could hardly sit still. I had completely forgotten about "Put Your Little Foot" until I heard the music. I hung my head down as far as I could, hoping that Mama wouldn't see me or that my brother couldn't find me. I heard steps approaching but I kept my head down. I didn't want to have to look up at my brother's smirking face.

A deep voice said, "Anna Bess, would you like to dance?" I slowly raised my head, hoping the ribbon was still in my hair, and there was Mr. Hillary Bedford, one of my grandfather's best friends. He had on his best clothes, and his gray hair shone in the light. He bowed, took my hand, and led me to the dance floor. Then he smiled, put his arm around my shoulder, and we started to dance.

The slow waltz tempo was perfect. He was elegant. I didn't know that dancing felt like this. It was like ice skating — smooth and easy. He gently led me and turned me until I felt that I was the most wonderful dancer in the world. Everyone stopped dancing and watched us. Mr. Bedford was one of the most important men in our community, and he was dancing with me.

Soon all the young girls were dancing with their fathers or uncles or grandfathers. Mr. Bedford and I swirled past my brother, who was dancing with one of our cousins. Mama was dancing with my grandfather. On and on the circle expanded until everyone was on the dance floor, with Mr. Bedford and me in the center. When the music stopped, everyone clapped and cheered. People hugged each other. For one special moment we were all part of the same family. I felt so happy to be in the center of so much love. I didn't feel like a kid. I felt like a grown-up who could dance.

ANNA THORSON
*Sarasota, Florida*

# AUNT MYRTLE

When I was growing up, my mother always told us true stories about our relatives and ancestors who lived in rural Point Cedar, Arkansas. The stories usually had a point or a moral to them.

Once, when my sister and I were teenagers in high school, we were fighting over the bathroom mirror, each of us trying to apply our makeup. My mother told us the story of her beautiful but very vain aunt. We had heard a little bit about Aunt Myrtle from our grandparents, uncles, and aunts, because she had died recently and left some property but no will. Her closest heirs were her brothers, one of them my grandfather. My sister and I had seen an old photograph of Aunt Myrtle and thought she was pretty.

According to our mother, Aunt Myrtle was a naturally beautiful woman who always kept herself very thin. She cut her hair fashionably short and dyed it coal black, a shocking thing for a woman to do in rural southern Arkansas in the early 1930s. She wore lots of lipstick, eyeliner, rouge, and nail polish, even if she was just staying home. She had the finest clothes, the latest fashions, and was probably the only woman in the community who spent her money this way. Aunt Myrtle had lots of boyfriends, most of them traveling salesmen, although some, according to rumors, were married men who lived in the area.

The boyfriends bought her furs and jewelry and took her on trips to hotels in the city.

Aunt Myrtle was the local elementary-school teacher when my mother started going to school, no doubt because she was one of the only people in that area who had been to college, for a year. My mother told us about an assignment Aunt Myrtle gave the class: to draw a house. My mother said that my uncle, who was in first grade, took his time and drew a detailed pink house, and Aunt Myrtle gave him an F because, she said, "houses aren't pink." When he was grown and married, my uncle bought some farmland and built his own house, and the bricks he chose were a soft pinkish color.

When she quit teaching a few years later at age thirty-eight, Aunt Myrtle was still unmarried. She shocked everyone when she had a baby. Nobody in the community, not even Great-Grandma nor the local doctor, had even suspected Aunt Myrtle was pregnant: she hadn't gained an ounce of weight, and she wore a corset to keep her tummy flat. Aunt Myrtle's father, my mother's grandfather — who was the local grocer — was utterly embarrassed. After the birth, he stood up in church one Sunday and told everyone that Aunt Myrtle had been secretly married to a traveling salesman but that the relationship had gone sour and the marriage was being annulled.

"Nobody knows for sure," Mother said, "but everyone thought that the reason cousin Marcia Lynn was born with a clubfoot was because of the tight corset Aunt Myrtle wore during her pregnancy. Aunt Myrtle was so vain that she couldn't stand to see her baby pooching out her belly, and she wanted to keep the baby a secret." Because of the baby's clubfoot, Aunt Myrtle kept the baby at home, away from family and the community. The doctor said that an operation and a brace would improve Marcia Lynn's leg and foot, but Aunt Myrtle didn't get this done.

Marcia Lynn stayed in her room and was not allowed to be seen by anyone. Aunt Myrtle kept the windows closed and the curtains open only a small crack for light. As a baby, Marcia Lynn lay in her crib without a lot of attention. Aunt Myrtle's mother wanted to see her granddaughter, but she wasn't allowed to. My mother's mother and father begged Myrtle, "Let us see Marcia Lynn! Let her be with other children!" Aunt Myrtle would say, "Stay out of my business!" As Marcia Lynn grew up, she wasn't taken to church, or picnics, or anywhere.

Aunt Myrtle's house was on the other side of the field from where my mother grew up, so Mother and her brother would cross the field and peek in Marcia Lynn's window. Marcia Lynn was always babbling to herself. The children would try to talk to Marcia Lynn: "Come on out and play, Marcia Lynn!" If Aunt Myrtle heard them, she'd come outside with a broom and say, "Get away from this house!" Marcia Lynn was alone in her bedroom, where she was brought only food and a bedpan. The children felt sorry for her because she was not allowed to go to school or to play with other kids.

My mother was about five years older than Marcia Lynn. When my mother was twelve, the doctor

157

was summoned to Marcia Lynn's bedside. She had a fever. My mother and her brother ran across the field and peeked in the window, where they saw the doctor bending over the lifeless body of Marcia Lynn.

My mother and uncle looked out at the field, and they both saw Marcia Lynn running through the grass! Marcia Lynn turned around and looked at them and smiled, and then she was gone. Though they knew they had seen a ghost, neither one of them was afraid. They knew that Marcia Lynn was at last free of her tyrannical mother and her terrible, lonely life.

LAURA BRAUGHTON WATERS
*Eureka Springs, Arkansas*

# American Odyssey

Things began falling apart for us in the summer of 1930. That's when my father refused to take a cut in pay and wound up losing his job. He spent a long time looking for something else, but he couldn't find work, not even for lower wages than what he had already turned down. Finally he settled into a chair with his *Argosy* magazine, and my mother began to nag and fuss. Eventually we lost our house.

I remember a dream I had about finding jewels for them, but when I put my hand in my pocket, all I found was a hole. I woke up crying. I was six years old.

An uncle wrote from Texas that he'd heard about a restaurant in Kansas that was supposed to be a real moneymaker. My parents sold whatever they had and bought an old touring car and some canvas canteens. We left California for the unknown plains of Kansas.

Kansas was as poor as California, only colder. Farmers couldn't sell what they grew, and they certainly couldn't eat out.

My folks saw that at least the farmers could put food on the table. They decided to become farmers, too. Land was cheaper in Arkansas, so that's where we headed. But what did my father know about farming? My mother, my two little brothers, and I settled into a small house on a bit of land, and my father went to work for a lady outside of town. We seldom saw him.

My mother later said she thought he worked the lady's bed more than her fields.

My mother traded her California dresses for a bucket of sorghum molasses and some flour. All that winter, we ate flour-and-water pancakes and sorghum molasses. My mother would stand by the window with tears in her eyes as her pretty dresses passed by on the seat of our neighbor's wagon.

When spring came around again, my mother packed a suitcase with a change of clothes for each of us. She took my baby brother on her hip and the suitcase in her other hand. Then she told my four-year-old brother and me to stay close, and we started to walk back to California. It would take a large book to tell all that happened on that journey. I remember so much.

Once, when I fainted in Oklahoma, my mother waded through poison ivy to get to a stream and dip a cloth in the water for me. By the time we were in Texas, her legs were so swollen that we had to stay in Dallas until she could walk again.

Once a bad man put us out in the desert because my mother turned down his plans for that night's sleeping arrangements. The sun set, and no cars drove by. We were miles from any town, from any house. He had chosen a good spot for his revenge. We were rescued by a telephone man who took us to an auto court and paid for the night's lodging.

Once we stayed for a while in a little house near a Mexican fieldworkers camp. Never have I known such kindness. They lived in makeshift shelters, built from whatever they had found. Always, from everyone, there were smiles, pats on

160

the head, fresh hot tortillas, and, on payday, a handful of mints.

Finally, Los Angeles. My mother's sister was going to meet us by the lake in Lincoln Park and show us where our grandmother now lived. We waited all day. Whenever one of us said we were hungry, my mother would point to the ducks on the lake or take us for a walk to show us an unusual flower.

As it turned dark, an old man who had been tossing crumbs to the ducks asked my mother when she was going to take us home.

She told him that she had brought her family many miles and that with the help of God and some very kind people "something would turn up."

He said he guessed it was his turn. He reached into his wallet and pulled out two of those large old dollar bills and handed them to her. That was enough. One dollar paid for a cabin at the Lincoln Auto Court. The other bought a can of pork-and-beans and a loaf of bread, and there would be enough left over for carfare if Aunt Grace ever showed up. I had learned all I would ever need to know about charity, faith, trust, and love.

It was 1931, and I was seven years old.

JANE ADAMS
*Prescott, Arizona*

# A PLATE OF PEAS

My grandfather died when I was a small boy, and my grandmother started staying with us for about six months every year. She lived in a room that doubled as my father's office, which we referred to as "the back room." She carried with her a powerful aroma. I don't know what kind of perfume she used, but it was the double-barrel, ninety-proof, knockdown, render-the-victim-unconscious, moose-killing variety. She kept it in a huge atomizer and applied it frequently and liberally. It was almost impossible to go into her room and remain breathing for any length of time. When she would leave the house to go spend six months with my Aunt Lillian, my mother and sisters would throw open all the windows, strip the bed, and take out the curtains and rugs. Then they would spend several days washing and airing things out, trying frantically to make the pungent odor go away.

This, then, was my grandmother at the time of the infamous pea incident.

It took place at the Biltmore Hotel, which, to my eight-year-old mind, was just about the fanciest place to eat in all of Providence. My grandmother, my mother, and I were having lunch after a morning spent shopping. I grandly ordered a Salisbury steak, confident in the knowledge that beneath that fancy name was a good old hamburger with gravy. When brought to the table, it was accompanied by a plate of peas.

I do not like peas now. I did not like peas then. I have always hated peas. It is a complete mystery to me why anyone would voluntarily eat peas. I did not eat them at home. I did not eat them at restaurants. And I certainly was not about to eat them now.

"Eat your peas," my grandmother said.

"Mother," said my mother in her warning voice. "He doesn't like peas. Leave him alone."

My grandmother did not reply, but there was a glint in her eye and a grim set to her jaw that signaled she was not going to be thwarted. She leaned in my direction, looked me in the eye, and uttered the fateful words that changed my life:

"I'll pay you five dollars if you eat those peas."

I had absolutely no idea of the impending doom that was heading my way like a giant wrecking ball. I only knew that five dollars was an *enormous*, nearly *unimaginable* amount of money, and as awful as peas were, only one plate of them stood between me and the possession of that five dollars. I began to force the wretched things down my throat.

My mother was livid. My grandmother had that self-satisfied look of someone who has thrown down an unbeatable trump card. "I can do what I want, Ellen, and you can't stop me." My mother glared at her mother. She glared at me. No one can glare like my mother. If there were a glaring Olympics, she would undoubtedly win the gold medal.

I, of course, kept shoving peas down my throat. The glares made me nervous, and every single pea made me want to throw up, but the magical image of that five dollars floated before me, and I finally gagged down every last one of them. My grandmother handed me the five dollars with a flourish. My mother continued to glare in silence. And the episode ended. Or so I thought.

My grandmother left for Aunt Lillian's a few weeks later. That night, at dinner, my mother served two of my all-time favorite foods, meatloaf and mashed potatoes. Along with them came a big, steaming bowl of peas. She offered me some peas, and I, in the very last moments of my innocent youth, declined. My mother fixed me with a cold eye as she heaped a huge pile of peas onto my plate. Then came the words that were to haunt me for years.

"You ate them for money," she said. "You can eat them for love."

Oh, despair! Oh, devastation! Now, too late, came the dawning realization that I had unwittingly damned myself to a hell from which there was no escape.

"You ate them for money. You can eat them for love."

What possible argument could I muster against that? There was none. Did I eat the peas? You bet I did. I ate them that day and every other time they were served thereafter. The five dollars were quickly spent. My grandmother passed away a few years later. But the legacy of the peas lived on, as it lives on to this day. If I so much as curl my lip when they are served (because, after all, I still hate the horrid little things), my mother repeats the dreaded words one more time:

"You ate them for money," she says. "You can eat them for love."

RICK BEYER
*Lexington, Massachusetts*

# WASH GUILT

When I was a teenager, my bedroom was under an eave on the second floor of our two-hundred-year-old house. I slept in a twin iron bed beside the window, and there was a small table for a lamp and books next to the bed. In the summer the wide pine floors in the rest of the house never stopped creaking with visiting relatives coming and going and someone always making something to eat. My mother, a single parent who worked long hours at the hospital, would often nap in my room to escape the confusion. It was not unusual for me to find her list pad on my bedside table.

The summer of my eighteenth year, for the first time in my life, I began staying out too late. I had been adrift in adolescent confusion for years by then but was finally giving my mother concrete trouble. I would go out after my summer job and stay out much too late with "inappropriate" friends. I knew my mother was upset by this, but I also knew her fear of direct confrontation. When our paths crossed, usually in the kitchen at about 6:30 P.M., her "angry parent scene" meant chilly glances and cupboard doors slammed shut.

One night, returning to the dark house, I slipped into my bedroom, turned on the light beside my bed, and saw my mother's list pad lying there. Printed neatly on the top page in my mother's large, round lettering were two words: "wash guilt."

166

I turned from the page quickly, hurriedly pulling on my pajamas. What was my mother trying to tell me? Wash guilt. Before my mother started working on Sundays, the closest we had come to religion was a few visits to the Unitarian Church of Baltimore. The tone of this message was too Baptist for my mother, but the cryptic abstraction, I decided, was just her style. Most mothers would wave a wooden spoon at a belligerent teenage daughter and say, "You be home by ten o'clock or you're grounded!" My mother would send a message through a burning bush before she would sit down at the kitchen table with me and lay down a curfew.

I left the pad exactly where it was and never said a word about it. I guess I thought that if I didn't move it, I wouldn't have to acknowledge it.

My mother left for work too early for me to see her the next morning, but the words stayed with me. Wash guilt. Riding my bike to my job, I kept repeating them: wash guilt, wash guilt. What was this about? What was my mother trying to tell me? Why couldn't she be normal and just yell at me? When I returned home that evening, the page and neat lettering were still lying there. Again I didn't touch it. When I met my mother in the kitchen, she stayed silent. Expecting to feel studied, I peered into the refrigerator, waiting to receive her prying looks. She should be fishing for a reaction, a sign of change in me. Her eyes never found my face, but they didn't seem to be avoiding me either. Did she regret the dagger she had put in my heart and hope to pretend that none of it had happened? If so, why didn't she just take away that list pad? Did she feel, as I did, that if she moved it she would have to acknowledge that it had been there, whereas if she let it be, we could both pretend that it had never been written? Ah-ha. Did I just see an inquisitive look? Did she try to catch a glimpse of my face? Was she inspecting my demeanor, looking for a sign of change? No. She just looked strangely interested in making dinner, strangely normal.

The next morning, I dressed looking at that page. Wash guilt. Still I didn't move it. Again I spent the day with those words. Again, in the kitchen that evening, my mother said nothing.

It continued like this for about a week. The list pad never moved. My mother never said anything about it. The words went with me everywhere. Each night I returned to them. Sometimes it felt as though I had a screeching parrot in the room, repeating harshly, "Waaaaash guilt!" Sometimes it felt as though there were a hooded monk standing silently beside my bed with that list pad in his hand.

For a week I wallowed in those words. They didn't necessarily change my behavior, although I did eventually lose the boyfriend, but I wore those words like a hair shirt. Then, one lovely, miraculous day, it must have been sunny and clear. I came home, went up to my room, looked at the list pad — and it read: "wash quilt."

HEATHER ATWOOD
*Rockport, Massachusetts*

168

# DOUBLE SADNESS

"I keep worrying about Martha," my mother said as we sat in the hospital corridor, waiting for my father to be examined by the doctor. "We left her playing in the yard and didn't tell her where we were going. I hope she's not sitting somewhere crying."

I wiped away tears that were streaming down my cheeks. "But I'm Martha. I'm right here with you," I tried to reassure her.

"No, not you," my mother answered. "My little Martha."

Fears of abandonment, past and present, enveloped us as we tried to adjust to my father's sudden incapacity.

The call had come the night before. My father had fallen and broken his hip; an operation to replace the hip joint was scheduled for the next morning. A friend was staying with my mother for the night. "I'll come as soon as I can — on the early morning plane," I promised.

My mother and father, married for fifty-eight years, had never had a serious emergency before, although my mother had become increasingly confused in the last several months. "And is your mother still alive?" she had asked me on my last visit, with a sociable interest in the young woman she had never seen before. Now, with the daily routine disrupted and the nearly constant companionship of my father removed, her disorientation was more severe.

"But I'm worried about Martha," my mother said again when we had returned home and sat down for lunch. "I'm going out to look for her."

"But I'm Martha," I tried again. "Little Martha grew up and turned into me."

"That's ridiculous," my mother said. She tugged open the front door, went out to the street, and stood tensely, looking up and down for the little girl she was sure she had seen just that morning. No one in sight. Then to the back of the house and through the back lot to the other street. "I'm going to ask those people over there if they've seen her." My mother, becoming increasingly frantic, was ready to plunge into traffic and cross the busy street.

"Let's go home and call the church office," I pleaded. "Maybe someone there can help."

On the way back to the house, my mother said, "It's not like Martha to go away like that without telling me. If only she had left a note."

A note! Seeing a way to relieve my mother's agitation, I scribbled a note as soon as we were in the house, and left it where it could be discovered a minute later. "Mama," it said, "I have gone to stay with Mary Ann for a few days. Please don't worry. I'm okay. Martha."

"Look," I said, "here's a note. What does it say?" My mother read it aloud slowly and immediately began to calm down.

"Thank goodness," she said. "She's all right. She's with Mary Ann." With the tension gone, we sat down to finish lunch and spend a peaceful afternoon at home.

That evening in the hospital, my mother told my father that Martha had gone to stay with Mary Ann for a few days but that she was still worried about her. My father said, "Don't go looking for another Martha. We already have one, and that's enough."

The next day, Martha's absence was still very much on my mother's mind. "What can she be doing?" she wondered. "She's never gone off like that without arranging it with me ahead of time. Besides, I want her to go to the hospital to see Daddy."

I assured my mother that her daughter would come home soon. "Besides," I said, "Martha is a clever little girl. She can take care of herself."

"She needs a clean dress for church on Sunday," my mother said.

"It's only Thursday," I replied. "Plenty of time."

"Where did you learn to take over a kitchen like this?" my mother asked as I fixed dinner that night. "It's nice of you to come and stay with me. Do you have a family?" Having been accepted as a companion, if not a daughter, I settled into an amicable routine with my mother.

Friday morning we went to the hairdresser, the chiropractor, and the grocery store. I overheard Lynne, the hairdresser, say to my mother, "It's nice that your daughter could come to stay with you."

"That's not my daughter," my mother confided, "she has the same name, but she's not my daughter." Lynne looked quickly at me to see if she had misunderstood one of us, and I gave her a rueful smile.

On the way home my mother said, "Lynne thought you were my daughter."

"You don't mind, do you?" I asked.

"No," she said.

It wasn't until my brother came on Saturday that I was recognized as part of the family. "Bob will take this bed, and you can sleep in your old room," my mother said that night. It felt good to be legitimate again.

"You see," my father said the next day, "Martha has been here all the time. There was no need to worry."

"But there was a note!" my mother wailed.

"I wrote the note," I explained. "I wrote it to calm you when you were so anxious," and comprehension flickered for a moment in my mother's gradually dimming eyes.

MARTHA RUSSELL HSU
*Ithaca, New York*

# A PICTURE OF LIFE

My marriage to my lawyer husband was going badly. He filed for divorce on my birthday, November 15, 1989, and had me served with the papers. One of his girlfriends, a woman who had been my friend, came to tell me that I would have to leave the house we had lived in, as he did not want to continue paying the rent. He stopped our joint bank account. I had not worked away from home since before becoming pregnant with the older of our two children, nearly ten years before. I found and rented a large old house in a derelict neighborhood in the Houston Heights and moved the children and my pottery kilns and all our possessions into it in January 1990. Within a month, I had begun making pots and teaching pottery classes in this new home. I taught three or four nights a week for four years, made pots to sell at my yearly Christmas sales, got small boys off to school in the morning, and helped with homework and read bedtime stories in the evening after my classes. I made three meals a day from scratch, for the wholesome food and to save money, except some nights when, for a treat, we'd buy a pizza. When it became apparent that I would financially survive the breakup of my marriage, my husband, a child-support lawyer working for the state, filed suit to have me declared incompetent and my children taken away, on the grounds that I was a stay-at-home mom and depressed over the state of my marriage. He often called me "a vegetable."

My mother and father said that I would have to hire an attorney and, after a lifetime of living on a tight budget, loaned me $15,000 of their retirement money. This sum did not pay for an attorney, it merely ensnared one: a very gentle and caring lawyer who would not drop the case when the deposit money ran out. She managed to have the children awarded to me "temporarily" throughout the six years the case stayed in the courts. That alone was worth the $15,000. For the next six years, my children and I lived in a goldfish bowl with a dark cloud over it. There was one court date after another. Court-ordered psychologist after court-ordered social worker combed our past, present, and future, looking to make a Solomon-like judgment about my fitness to raise my children. Our divorce was granted on June 6, 1992. For twenty-two years, June sixth had been our wedding anniversary.

The custody battle raged on. Years earlier, at the temporary-custody hearing, I had been ordered not to leave town with the children, on the grounds that being near their father was more important even than their safety. Burglars broke into my house and took what they pleased on six occasions, before a policeman advised me to get a dog. Nighttime gunshots began to be a regular feature in the park across the street from my house, and I began to fear for our lives. I often stayed up sitting near the children as they slept, afraid that something would happen to them in the night. After my Christmas sale in December 1993, I had the extra money I needed to move home to the small town where I had been raised, where my parents were still living, and where it was safe to raise my children, two hundred miles from Houston and their father. Throughout Christmas that year, I said nothing to anyone about my plans. On Christmas Day 1993 I handed over my two boys to their father at noon, as I had been doing for the past four years, and began the next day to look for temporary lodgings. On January 1 I drove to Houston to pick up the boys from their father, grateful to have them back, and drove them straight home to their grandparents. January 2 I rented the first of two moving vans and began moving out of Houston, with only my best friend and her husband to help, hurrying against the prospect of being served with a restraining order to stay in town. When I had made it home with the second van, I told the boys' father. Within days, he had filed a suit in Houston to make me move back.

It is a wonder to me now that I wasn't arrested. I was back in court on a weekly basis again. I had to send photos of our new home (the house my grandfather had built in 1930 and the yard in which I played as a child) to caseworkers in Houston for evaluation. The boys' new school, the one from which I had graduated in 1965, had to be investigated for wholesomeness and teaching strength. The children and I had to face the psychologists again. The children were depressed that they had left their old friends and their father. I was trying to get the pottery back on line and subbing in the schools. I was looking after my sister, who was ill, and her young children and helping my elderly parents, who had been finding it hard to handle everything by themselves. No one, not even my loyal and hardworking attorney, expected me to win. I was told to start looking around Houston for a place to return, in the certainty that the courts would not agree with me.

I had begun praying years before, or talking, really, to anyone who would listen. I prayed to God, I prayed to the Great Mother, I spoke to my dead grandparents. I told them what was happening to us. I asked that they give me what relief they could and the strength and courage to handle the rest. I asked them to make me a wiser, gentler, more useful, more effective person for having gone through this. I asked them to impart to my children the same ability to distill strength and wisdom from overwhelming danger and distress. I asked them to allow us joy and pleasure in the midst of calamity, for I feared we wouldn't make it through to the end without these. A jury trial was scheduled, and a jury impaneled. For four days in November 1995, I drove in the dark early mornings to the center of Houston to attend the trial and then drove home in the dark evenings to be with my children and my parents. Every evening, things looked worse. On the fourth day, my mother got up early and rode into Houston to testify on my behalf. My best friend testified that day, too. Then, as the last witness, I took the stand. I sat proud, full of unreasonable hope, certain that the courtroom was full of my gods and grandparents long gone, and told my story simply to the jury. I was asked to show the jury a portrait of my children and myself that had been taken at Christmas the year before. It showed me to be a happy, glowing woman sitting with my arms protectively around my two bright and glowing children, in a room with a large decorated Christmas tree and a snowy window seat piled high with cozy pillows in red and green. There was no hint of the pain, sorrow, and fear that had haunted us for the past six years. I remember seeing that photo for the first time, sure that there was magic loose in it. I handed the photo around the jury box and heard gasps of amazement and understanding from almost everyone in turn. The jury retired to deliberate and a few minutes later sent a note to the judge asking if they could give me a larger settlement than I was asking, since they thought it was too small. As they filed past, several of them said to me that they had believed my husband until I took the stand and showed them the picture.

I never got that picture back. It was large and framed in red and green wood. It is still being kept as an exhibit somewhere in the family-court building. I have other copies of it, though, and I am still sure there is magic in it. I make a point of looking at it every day.

JEANINE MANKINS
*Orange, Texas*

# MARGIE

In 1981, when my son, Matthew, was thirteen years old, we had an argument over an essay he'd been assigned to write. He simply did not want to do his homework — it was a beautiful Sunday afternoon — and I refused to allow him to leave his room until the assignment was completed. Later that day I returned to find Matthew gone and the essay left conspicuously on the dining-room table. Unfortunately, what he'd written was a parody of the assigned topic, and every third word or so was an obscenity. My son was obviously angry with me, not surprising for a thirteen-year-old, yet I found the writing deeply disturbing. My husband, Richard, Matthew's stepfather, assured me that I was making too much of the incident. "Come on," he urged, "let's go for a walk and I'll tell you what happened to me when I was thirteen."

At that time we lived on the beach in Venice, California, where a "walk" meant becoming part of a carnival-like free-for-all. A dense crowd of locals and tourists shuffled along the boardwalk. Musicians, mimes, break dancers, fortune-tellers, and singers further clotted the thoroughfare. Korean vendors hawked sunglasses, socks, silver jewelry, and hash pipes while adults on roller skates wove at alarming speeds through the crowd. I remember a constant background beat created by drummers on bongos, tin pans, and empty bottles. Richard linked his arm through mine. Then we stepped into the current and he began his story:

"This happened when my family first moved to New Jersey. I was in the eighth grade — a painfully skinny kid who had trouble fitting in. The first day there, I got a crush on a cute, redheaded girl named Margie, who also seemed to like me. But Margie and all the kids in that group were much more sexually experienced than I was, or at least that's how it seemed at the time. So I was nervous. So nervous that every time she wanted to kiss, I told her that I had a cold or made up some other dumb excuse. I was afraid she'd find out that I didn't really know how to kiss. Before long, Margie got tired of my stalling and moved on to some other guy. I was hurt, and I wrote an angry letter to her using every four-letter word I could think of. Thinking, in fact, that I was being pretty clever. Then I put the letter in my desk drawer, where my mother eventually found it. You know my parents: The Panic Family. They couldn't believe what I'd done. They wanted to call Margie's parents immediately to find out what was going on. I must have cried and begged for quite a while until I finally got them to agree to drop it. So nothing really came of the letter. At the end of the school year, Margie and her parents moved to New York and I never saw her again."

At the *moment* my husband said those words, I looked up to see a slender, redheaded woman in her early thirties standing directly in front of us. The herd of tourists continued to thrust themselves forward, all colors and ages and sizes of

179

people pushing both north and south along the boardwalk. Everyone seemed to be moving except Richard and me and the redheaded woman. I suppose that the drummers and tin-pan bangers and bottle clinkers never let up, but in memory there was a grand moment of silence as the three of us just stood there and looked at each other. "Margie?" Richard said, and the woman calmly replied, "Richard?" My husband lit up. "What a surprise! I was just telling my wife about you."

This is a true story. It had been seventeen years since Richard and Margie had last seen each other as young adolescents in New Jersey. But that isn't *my* ending to the story. Seventeen more years have passed since the events of that day, and I now know that Margie's near-miraculous appearance is not the only conclusion to this tale. It's merely the one my husband and I tell at dinner parties. I think, to be true, the story must include the fact that my instincts about my son were also correct that day. His essay was not only a show of adolescent anger, but a turning point in his life: a turn toward a darker, difficult future which has never, to this day, sorted itself out.

Over the years, remembering our encounter with Margie, my husband and I have often asked ourselves: What were the odds of that happening? Now, I'd only like to know: What are the odds of a happy ending?

CHRISTINE KRAVETZ
*Santa Barbara, California*

180

# ONE THOUSAND DOLLARS

I came to Los Angeles with the idea of making it in the entertainment business. I started as an actress and worked my way down. I truly believed that I would be the lucky one who returned home rich and famous and would at last become the apple of her father's eye. I failed miserably. One of my schemes led me to a job as a receptionist at a talent and literary agency. My motive was to become a talent agent and have my script sold through the literary agent I was working for. It was a job that barely paid my bills.

My first year with the company, I lived off my credit cards. I was banking on the fact that as soon as I sold my script, I wouldn't have to worry about money again. The second year with the agency was worse. My credit cards were maxed. I was struggling every month to pay the rent, the car payments, and the high auto insurance. I was getting further and further behind on my bills. The tactic of pay one month and skip the next was not balancing out as planned. To make matters worse, I was told I had to move within the month. The simple job of receptionist ended up being more than I had been told. I had to spend nights trying to finish the large amount of work that was heaped on me: pulling pictures and résumés, keeping files in order, writing letters, and learning nothing about being an agent. Weekends were planned around working with my writing partner. I had no personal life. Still, I had the script to put my hope into. The literary agent thought it was quirky and fun, and I believed that once it sold, all this struggling would have been worth it. I would be a success.

The lack of money had always been the center of our lives at home. Every day seemed to end in a fight about the cost of food, braces, school equipment, trips, camps, girl-scout uniforms. In my late teens, the arguments shifted to the old car breaking down, my college costs, the trips to Los Angeles I took with the car, and phone calls. Though my father stopped hitting me as I got older, the dirty looks continued. They were almost as stinging as the slaps used previously for discipline. My father had come to this country with no money and a disabled wife. My mother was a responsibility he promised the American government he would take care of all his life. He even signed a contract to guarantee it.

I became increasingly desperate for money. Obviously, I couldn't turn to my father for the cash. He had never approved of any of my choices in life. I had no other relatives to turn to. My Los Angeles friends had all left me, either for a return ticket home or because they were afraid of being near someone who was so hopeless. I thought of jumping off the building where I worked. I began to daydream of robbing banks and old people. In my mind, I had settled on the sum I thought I needed. Ten thousand dollars would be perfect, and one thousand would give me a chance to catch up. There are free newspapers that live off the darker side of the city's population. Advertisements for prostitutes and ads looking for models and actresses to work in porno. I called one ad that boasted a payment of one thousand dollars.

A man returned my call. He was offhanded yet businesslike. He began by asking me standard questions about my height and weight, then moved on to more detailed, personal questions, such as which sexual acts I would and wouldn't perform. It all seemed so bizarre. I was twenty-six then. I had dyed my brown hair blond and kept slim and somewhat composed by smoking cigarettes constantly. At that time I believed in God but did not believe in evil. I became nervous on the phone. This was something I did not want to do. The man must have heard the hesitation in my voice. An instant later, he started talking about how I could make up to ten thousand a week. With ten thousand dollars I could pay off all my bills, pay off the car, breathe again. I was to audition for the leading role in a porno movie that afternoon at a nearby motel.

I was told by the man that the star of the movie was handsome. The star turned out to be short and dark-skinned, with long curly black hair and an ordinary face, far from handsome. I took his hand and shook it before entering the motel room.

He told me to take off my clothes, and I did as he asked. He instructed me on what he wanted done and how I should moan loudly, and I followed his directions. I remember looking up and seeing a large mirror on the ceiling. I thought how beautiful I looked. I had never really looked at myself naked before. Somewhere between the mirror

183

and another sexual act, I had to vomit. I excused myself to go to the bathroom. When I returned, we completed the scene. He banged against the wall and said, "We're finished in here." Outside the door he told me that he would "let me know."

When I returned home, I took a hot bath and scrubbed the man off my body. I cried, but I needed to pull myself together quickly for another interview. With that one, I failed to go any further than talking. I couldn't do a porno movie. I couldn't stand what I had just done. I went out to dinner with my second interviewer, who turned out to be a very nice man, even though he was a porno director. He told me I had been scammed. I went to bed with him later that evening. After all, who was I to say no?

Somehow, I managed to get through the month without the one thousand dollars. I moved into a house with a female roommate. I stopped dating. Every night, I would eat and vomit up the chocolates my new roommate laid out on the coffee table. I cut my hair short and dyed it dark brown. Otherwise, I went on with my life as usual. I never thought of the incident. It happened. It was over. It could have been worse.

The following month, I went to my parents' for a birthday celebration. My mother, who had lost her husband's love, had always enjoyed putting up barriers between me and my father. She told me that they had received some unexpected money about a month ago. The amount came to a thousand dollars. My mother had asked my father to give it to me, but he had said no. I broke down. I ran out into the backyard, sat on the grass, and

184

sobbed. Crying without any thoughts or restraint. My parents stood by the kitchen screen door. They kept calling me to come inside, but I couldn't move and they wouldn't come to me. Eventually I got up without saying good-bye and drove home.

I.Z.
*Los Angeles, California*

# TAKING LEAVE

For the last fifteen years I've been confined to a nine-by-seven cage of solid steel bars, squeezed between walls I can touch with my fingertips if I stretch my arms. On my right is my bed. Its mattress is as flat as a pancake, and next to it is a ceramic toilet, which is covered with a wooden board to keep the stench out.

I was in bed, on the verge of falling asleep, when my cell gate cracked. Any time it opened was a welcome relief. I jumped up, stepped out on the gallery, and called to the officer at the control booth a hundred feet away.

"The chaplain wants to see you. Get dressed," he said. I laced my boots, snatched my jacket, and hurried outside. A call from the cleric's office usually meant bad news. As I whizzed past my neighbor's crib I heard him say, "Is everything all right, Joe?"

"I hope so," I said. "I think I'm going to make an emergency phone call."

As I hurried across the snow-covered yard, groups of prisoners huddled together against the freezing wind. Blacks, whites, and Latinos bundled in multicolored hoods, hats, gloves, and mittens. Some were familiar, but most were just faces in a vast sea of lonely insignificance. A few walked endless laps around the yard, others stared at one of four TVs. Most were lost in self-imposed distractions, doing the best they could to kill time the only way they knew how.

At the wire gate leading to the guidance unit, I shoved my pass into the tiny slot of the guard's wooden shack. The officer scrutinized it like a suspicious cashier looking at a counterfeit fifty-dollar bill. Then, dismissing me like a foreigner at a border crossing, he said, "Go ahead." Relieved, I sprinted toward the building. At last I was going to speak with my grandmother, a tough eighty-year-old lady who could curse you out in a minute if you got her angry.

We had not spoken in several weeks, because my father, who had just completed a ten-year federal sentence, had disconnected the three-way service at Nan's house as a condition of his parole. When I spoke to my father, he said, "Your grandmother's in the hospital, but she should be back in three days."

Although her health was deteriorating, I never expected such a sudden decline. I remembered our last conversation, when she had cried and complained about her swollen legs.

"Nan, you got to try and walk around, stretch your legs and get some exercise," I pleaded.

"I do. You don't understand. My legs are no good anymore. Last week I went to the bank and fell down on the sidewalk."

I tried to ease her pain by talking about the good old days, when we lived on Ninety-eighth Street and when Grandpa was alive. I pictured myself in the kitchen, watching her open the oven to peek at the golden-brown loaves of Sicilian bread she baked for me and my grandfather. Back then one

187

of my favorite treats was a hot round loaf of home-made bread stuffed with chicken roll and washed down with a tall glass of milk. Those were great times, and now, here I was, clinging to them the same way my grandmother was.

But even as we spoke about the happy times, she had still cried bitterly. Her greatest fear was that she'd be forced to live in an old-age home.

"I want to die in my own house. I don't want to live with strangers."

"Nan, I promise no one's going to stick you in a home. Don't worry, when I get out I'll take care of you."

"Did you talk to the lawyer?"

"Yes, they're still working very hard."

"I hope to God you come home before I go."

"I will, Nan, you just take care of yourself." Although I was able to reassure her, my feelings of guilt lingered in my mind like the taste of spoiled milk.

Now, as I arrived at the chaplain's office, an officer said, "The imam wants to see you." The imam? I said to myself. Randazzo, my counselor, must have made arrangements with him to call my grandmother. Inside the small room, four Muslims were busy filling tiny bottles with scented oils. The room smelled like jasmine, musk, and coconut incense, penetrating and pungent, like the fragrance of head shops in the '60s. Imam Khaliffa was talking on the telephone. He removed the receiver from his ear and cupped the mouthpiece. In a soft voice he told the men to leave the room.

As they filed past me, he continued talking on

the phone while I impatiently scanned the room. Although his desk was cluttered with bottles and papers, my eyes were drawn to one particular document that seemed out of place. On it I noticed my name written in bold letters above my grandmother's. It was a business letter from the Francisco Funeral Home.

The imam hung up the phone, and I asked, "What's going on?"

"Your brother Buddy called. He needs to speak with you."

Two days later, at 6:00 A.M., I was awakened by a young officer named Rizzo. He was thin, had short-cropped black hair, and a voice that spoke with the soothing calm of a priest in a confessional booth. Perhaps he also knew what it felt like to experience the loss of a loved one. I was grateful.

When we crossed the yard, it was windy, dark, and pouring with rain. Inside the administration building, a burly Irishman with blond hair and rosy cheeks approached me and said, "I'm sorry to hear about your grandmother." I put on the garments given to me by the prison for the trip: blue jeans, a white shirt, and a tan jacket. I wore my own sneakers. I glanced at myself in the mirror and was disgusted by my reflection.

At last we climbed into a specially equipped van with a thick Plexiglas partition separating me from the officers, who carried .38-caliber pistols strapped to their hips in black leather holsters. My legs were shackled by a twelve-inch dog chain, secured tightly at each ankle. I was also handcuffed with a belly chain. This was fastened to my cuffs with a master lock. To eat I had to bend forward and strain my neck to peck at a sandwich clasped in my fingers.

I had not been outside the stone walls of the prison for fifteen years. We drove past mountains, trees, and farms with black-and-white cows grazing leisurely on the grass. I felt like I was part of a surreal three-dimensional photograph. Soon we entered a valley that was covered in thick fog. It consumed us like the smoke in woods after a smoldering forest fire. Suddenly a deer darted from the mist. It leapt onto the highway and into the front end of the pickup truck that was ahead of us. The driver didn't have a chance to swerve. I whipped my neck around and slid to the edge of my seat.

"Did you see that?" Officer Warren asked.

I peered out the side window, through beads of raindrops scurrying across the glass, and saw the deer sprawled on the perimeter of the roadway. As I strained forward in my seat, my shackles and restraints dug deep into my flesh. The deer's tongue dangled from her soft furry jaw, and her mouth was slightly open as she exhaled nervous, panting puffs of steam.

*"It's still alive!"* I exclaimed.

"Yeah, but she don't look good," Officer Warren said. I wanted to see her sprint back into the woods. Instead she lay motionless, as still as the fog hanging over the valley, as stiff as the trees.

By midafternoon trees were replaced by apartment houses and commercial brick buildings with an assortment of bubble-shaped, multi-colored, bright bold letters. Some of the structures were boarded up. Finally we exited Lexington Avenue, passed the piers of Manhattan, crossed the Brooklyn Bridge, and emerged on Atlantic Avenue. The city was vaguely familiar, dreamlike.

I imagined myself in the old days, leaning on the armrest of my black 1983 Ninety-Eight Oldsmobile. I'd be listening to music with a thick joint burning in the ashtray. Inhaling the smoke of the sweet sticky weed, its pungent aroma drifting through a crack in the moonroof in swirling plumes. Once I had had it all.

On Atlantic Avenue there were rows of stores and bodegas and people buzzing everywhere. Beautiful women wearing tight pants, platform shoes, and leather jackets strolled by, swinging shopping bags. They swayed their hips in sync with the seductive rhythm and style that spelled attitude with a capital *A* in the barrio. There were furniture shops with sofas outside, a black homeless man begging, and an amputee in a wheelchair hurrying across the street.

When we pulled up in front of the funeral home, Officer Warren said, "Hold on. I have to check it out."

Two minutes later he appeared and nodded to his partner. Then, with Rizzo's assistance, I carefully climbed out of the van. "Wait," Rizzo said, stopping me in midstride. "Let's take the belly chain and cuffs off first."

He inserted a key into the master lock and with a quick, practiced twist snapped it open. He reached around my back, unwrapped the chain, and then removed the handcuffs. I stretched and rubbed my wrists. They were swollen and red and had deep creases in them. Followed by Rizzo, I limped inside the lobby, taking slow, even steps to

191

avoid tripping on the tether still attached to my ankles.

My brother Buddy appeared. He was tall and broad and impeccably dressed in a fine black suit. I could tell he was shocked and glad to see me. We shook hands and kissed. Then my uncle, whom I hadn't seen in fifteen years, sauntered in. He looked much older, seemed shorter, and was as round as a wine barrel. He paused for a second, studying me the same way I pondered him. Fifteen years was a long time.

"Joey," he said in his distinctive Sicilian brogue.

I wrapped my arms around him. "It's great to see you, Uncle Charlie."

"I'm a grandfather now," he said, proudly slipping a photo from his wallet. "Your cousin Joey and his wife had a boy. His name is Cologero."

I took the picture and glanced at it and wondered where all the years had gone. I remembered my cousin Joey when he was a teenager wearing a football jersey rushing out of his house in College Point to play two-hand touch. Now he was a father. I handed the photo back to my uncle and said, "Congratulations."

I stepped into the viewing room and encountered my sisters, Gracie and Maria. Both were drowned in black clothes. We hugged and kissed and each cried on my shoulder. I was quickly surrounded by other family members, including my father, whom I had not seen in ten years. His hair was pure white and as fine as rabbit's fur.

"You made it," he said.

We embraced. "Yeah, Dad, security cleared me."

Because of restrictions, I had not spoken to my father while he was away. I stood there and scrutinized him, searching for the man I had last seen on a visit ten years ago. I knew I'd never find him again.

The room was still and quiet. Chairs lined one wall and a sofa the other. There were tables with lamps on them, and others that held crystal bowls filled with mints. At the rear of the room my grandmother lay lifeless, surrounded by an assortment of colorful floral arrangements. As I approached I could smell the familiar fragrance of freshly picked roses. I placed my hand on the edge of her bronze casket and gazed at her face. She was thinner than the last time I had seen her, five years ago. Her skin was pale and colored with a thick coat of makeup that made her look unnatural. She wore a smile that seemed more like a contrived grin. On her wrist was the same gold bracelet that she always wore on special occasions. It was heavy and adorned with several medals that jingled like bells when she walked. Now the charms — large solid-gold hearts and diamond-studded medallions inscribed with dates and heartfelt expressions — hung stiffly from her frozen wrist. She was dressed in a beautiful silk and lace pink gown that stretched to her ankles. On her feet she wore tiny pink shoes the color of seashells.

All these years I had expected this day. I just never thought it would happen so damn suddenly. Now all I had left were memories. Fragmented remnants of our lives scattered on the lid of her coffin. One was a picture of my grandmother taken in 1984, the year I went away, standing by the dock of our home in Howard Beach. Boats adorned with flags, some with fly bridges as tall as our house, floated on the surface of calm waters, waiting to cast off. She's wearing a pair of shorts and sneakers and has a huge grin on her face. And there beside her are the rosebushes she raised, exploding in brilliant full bloom.

At our house my grandmother usually kept large bowls of warm food in the oven. Pans of chicken cutlets and pasta, or meat and white potatoes, were always available for visitors who wanted to sit down and eat. On Sundays Nan always cooked a huge meal, large pastel-colored bowls filled with pasta, marinara sauce, garlic, and freshly picked basil. Then we passed around trays of meatballs, sausages, and meats stacked a foot high. I would wipe the sauce from my lips between mouthfuls of food and gulps of red wine mixed with 7Up. My grandfather wore a napkin tucked into his shirt and a pen in his pocket; he would busily grate a chunk of fresh ricotta cheese onto his macaroni. His arm moved in round, sweeping, circular motions. When he was finished, I took the cheese from him and did the same.

When I used to come home after junior high school to a house filled with the aroma of sauce simmering on the stove, I'd snatch a loaf of semolina bread, tear off a hunk, and soak it in the sweet red gravy. Before long, I'd hear my grandmother say, "Get outa here, will you?" She didn't say it in a mean way, she said it proudly, delighted by the thought of how much I loved her cooking.

The time to leave arrived with a nod from Officer Warren. Everyone surged forward to kiss me good-bye. My uncle and I grasped each other one last time, and he said, "You were your grand-mother's world, she loved you more than anything." Then my father held me and exploded into a violent, shuddering convulsion of sobs. We stood there clinging to each other like passengers on a plane about to crash, hurtling toward the ground. At that moment, with my dad's tears falling on my shoulder, I felt like I was his father and he was my son, and in the solace of my arms he discovered the safety I had once sought in his.

I walked to the van and extended my hands to Officer Rizzo to have the cuffs clamped on my wrists again. Instead, he said, "We'll put them on later, after we eat." This surprised me. I hopped into the van, slid close to the window, and peered out one last time hoping to freeze this moment that would have to last as a picture in my mind for-ever. I watched my uncle reach into his jacket pocket, pull out a cigar, and light it up, taking short, quick puffs. As we rolled away, I waved to him and wondered if my expression betrayed my sadness.

JOE MICELI
*Auburn, New York*

# ACT OF MEMORY

I was a young girl of eleven then, living in Brooklyn. My father had died unexpectedly that summer, and times were suddenly very hard for my mother, my two brothers, and me. My eighteen-year-old brother had been in the army for a year now. My other brother, who was thirteen, worked as a delivery boy after school to earn some sorely needed extra money. Mama had worked for a while too after Papa died, but had to stop when her health started to deteriorate.

Papa had always made a big deal out of Christmas. For as long as I could remember, the tree had always been at the center of our celebrations, along with the crèche and Santa Claus. There was a special little Kewpie-doll ornament with a red velvet circle around it that Papa always kept in its own little box. Every Christmas, when we were about to decorate the tree, he would make a little ceremony out of taking this doll out of its box, holding it up in front of me, and saying, "Maria, this doll is as old as you are." Then he would hang the little Kewpie on the tree.

Papa had bought that little doll the year I was born, and, without planning to, it had become a small tradition in our house for him to put my Kewpie ornament on the tree first, before any other decorations.

But this Christmas we were to have no tree.

My mother was a very practical woman, and she decided that the tree was a luxury we could well do without. I thought then, with quiet but keen resentment, that it had never meant as much to her as it had to Papa anyway. And if my brother minded, he didn't show it.

We had been to church that evening for a visit and were walking back home in silence. It was a beautiful, clear winter night, but all I could see were the tree-lit windows we passed. Their cheerful glow made my bitterness even more intense because I pictured whole, happy families in those houses, sharing laughter, exchanging presents, sitting at well-laden tables, talking, joking. Christmas had no deeper meaning for me that night than all of this. And I knew that when we finally got to our own house, we would be greeted by darkened windows, and that once inside our door, we would be together, yet eventually alone, each immersed in the almost tangible emptiness that had come to settle on us.

As we passed my girlfriend's house, which was a few doors down from ours, I noticed that the lights were still on in her living room. I asked my mother to please let me drop in for a while, just for a visit, before I came home. She said I could.

Only I never did go into my friend's house that night.

Instead I waited until my mother and brother disappeared inside our front door and then I impulsively turned and headed for my father's shop, about five long avenue blocks away. It was a small grocery store on the corner of Forty-fifth Street and Eleventh Avenue. For some reason I wanted to be there in front of that shop that had meant so much to him, even though it was now empty and for rent. It was as if somehow I would be closer to him.

There weren't many people about. It was very dark, but I noticed for the first time how beautiful the night was, so cold and crisp, with such a sky full of stars. The trees in the windows, still lit and glowing, didn't seem to be having the same effect on me as earlier that evening. Maybe it was the daring of being out and alone at night for the first time, or the sense that I was going to be closer to Papa somehow, that worked some strange effect on me. Whatever it was, it seemed to quiet my sense of resentment and grief.

When I finally got close to the shop, I noticed these great, odd-shaped masses on the sidewalk nearby. I stopped dead in my tracks. My imagination started to take hold, and I nearly turned and headed back home. But something made me keep on going. As I got closer, I realized that those masses were not monsters at all, but leftover Christmas trees from the store next to my father's shop. They were the trees that hadn't been sold and were left to be picked up by the garbageman or whoever it was that carted off such things.

I remember suddenly running to the pile of trees and trying, in the dark, to pick out the best one I could find. I seem to recall that the one I chose was huge, maybe ten or twelve feet high, but it couldn't have been that big. Anyway, I grasped my tree, grateful that I had worn my thick woolen mittens, and began half-carrying, half-dragging my treasure home.

My soul was full of Christmas. I knew that Papa was mixed up in all of this somehow. I don't know if I ever felt closer to him than I did that night. It was as if he was in the stars above me, in every lighted window, in the very tree I was carrying. I don't recall if I met anyone along the way. I guess I must have, and if I did, I must have seemed an odd sight: a young child, singing carols softly to herself, lugging a tree that was more than twice her size. But I know I wouldn't have cared what anyone thought.

When I got home, I rang the doorbell and was prepared to argue my tree into the house if need be. My brother answered the door and his startled look accompanied his amazed "Where did you get *that?*" We got the tree inside and he managed to find the stand for it, and we started to put it up. My mother came in and saw us but said nothing. She took no part, but neither did she do anything to stop us. And though she knew I had not gone to my girlfriend's house after all, she never said a word in reproof.

When my brother and I were done, we stood back and looked at the tree. To us it was perfect, without a single flaw. I was so excited I could have stayed up all night decorating it, but my mother insisted that it was late, nearly midnight, and that we should all get to bed.

Christmas was almost over. I was sure that she didn't approve of what I had done, and I even started to feel guilty, suddenly realizing what grief that tree might have brought to her, and the edge of my joy started to wear off.

I got ready for bed, my mind a confusion of ex-

199

citement and sadness. I went in to look at my tree one last time before Christmas was gone.

My mother was standing in front of it, holding a familiar small box. I don't know if she saw me in the doorway. Had she been crying?

Her hands seemed to tremble as she opened the box. She held the ornament up in front of her, not looking at me, but at the tree.

"Maria," she said, almost in a whisper, her voice somehow different, funny, ". . . this doll is as old as you are."

And she hung the Kewpie on the tree.

MARY GRACE DEMBECK
*Westport, Connecticut*

# SLAPSTICK

# BICOASTAL

In the mid-'80s, I worked at an underground food co-op in Washington, D.C. One night while I was bagging raisins, I noticed that a woman was staring at me. Finally, she stepped forward and said, "Michelle? Michelle Golden?" "No," I said, "I'm not Michelle, but do you mean Michelle Golden from Madison, Wisconsin?" and she said yes, that was exactly who she meant. I told her that I knew Michelle and that many people had mistaken me for her. A few years later, I moved to the West Coast. One Saturday morning as I was walking in downtown San Francisco, a woman approached me. She stopped in her tracks, looked me up and down, and said, "Michelle? Michelle Golden?" "No," I said. "But what are the chances of your making the same mistake twice in your lifetime on two different coasts?"

BETH KIVEL
*Durham, North Carolina*

# A FELT FEDORA

A felt fedora always covered my father's short brown curls. He wore a gray one for work — sometimes small kernels of wheat mingled with drops of tractor oil nestled in the brim. He had a brown one for dress and a beige one for leisurely Sunday drives or taking in a Roy Rogers movie on a warm summer evening. We never went to the movies except in the summer, maybe because the days were long and hot or because the nights took too long to come or because the cool darkness of the Star Theatre beckoned to my father after he had been working the dusty, dry land.

My father never went anywhere without one of his hats. They hung outside the back kitchen door on pegs, lined up in a row. Same size, same shape, same smell — a mixture of Old Spice, Lifebuoy soap, and a touch of the Brylcreem he used to tame his unruly hair.

He never wore one inside, but when he was outside it was on his head or in his hand. He'd tip it when greeting a lady and take it off when entering a building, even the post office. His manners were impeccable, but he wasn't comfortable without his hat. My mother made him leave it in the car when we went to the movies; he would have preferred holding it in his lap.

Many years later, my brother and I and our families were with my mother and father in a department store in Portland, Oregon. We were trying to help my father find a new hat. He tried them all on: wrong size, wrong color, brim too narrow, band didn't match. This went on and on, and the salesman was losing patience. My father finally found the perfect one and with a huge grin showed it to my mother. We all breathed a sigh of relief, until she looked at it and said, "Ted, you old fool, that's your own hat!"

JOAN WILKINS STONE
*Goldendale, Washington*

# MAN VS. COAT

The first and only time we met was in an upscale bar on a cold November night. I'd answered her ad in the personals column: ". . . would like to meet a self-assured man in his mid-thirties to early forties, a man who likes walks in the park and talks in the dark . . . etc." There was a simple, lilting quality to her writing that appealed to me.

She was a tall, slender brunette in her mid-thirties. She was engaging and made good eye contact when she spoke. She was both pretty and smart, and I liked her immediately. I definitely wanted to see her again. Even better, I sensed no reluctance on her part to see me again. If only I could manage the rest of the evening without a faux pas or mishap.

As we got ready to leave, she was first to put on her heavy winter coat. She adjusted her scarf and fitted her driving gloves to her long, elegant fingers. Once ready, she stood there, patiently waiting for me.

I lifted my parka from the back of the bar stool and, firmly gripping the collar with my left hand, inserted my right arm into the right sleeve. With the coat half-on and half-off, I stretched my left arm to the rear in order to catch the left sleeve. But somehow my target eluded me. I tried again, and once more I missed. More determined than ever, I intensified my efforts.

Completely absorbed in what I was doing, I didn't notice that my body was beginning to twist in a counterclockwise direction. As my body twisted, the coat twisted, too: the sleeve remained the same distance from my thrusting hand. I could feel beads of sweat beginning to break out on my forehead.

It was as if the sleeves had grown closer together during the last couple of hours. I grunted and groaned as I struggled to gain the upper hand or, more accurately perhaps, the upper sleeve. How could I have known that I was in the clutches of my own undoing? With all this twisting, my legs were beginning to corkscrew.

No man can remain upright while twisting and stabbing backward at a moving sleeve. I began to lose my balance. Slowly, I sank to the ground. Lying there in a heap with my coat partially covering me, I glanced up at my companion. Neither one of us said a word. Never before had she seen a man wrestled to the ground by his own coat.

MEL SINGER
*Denver, Colorado*

# THAT'S ENTERTAINMENT

The summer before my senior year of college, I rented a place at the Jersey shore with some friends. One Tuesday night at about 9:30, I walked out of the house and went down to the beach. No one was around, so I pulled off my clothes, left them in a pile, and dove into the surf. I swam around for twenty minutes and then rode a wave back to the shore.

When I came out of the water, my clothes were missing. As I stood there pondering what to do, I heard the sound of voices. It was a group of people walking along the beach — and all of them were walking in my direction. I decided to make a dash for it and run back to the house, which was fifty or sixty yards away. I could see that the door was open, or at least that light was coming out of the doorway. But as I ran closer, I realized at the very last second that there was a screen. I ran right through it.

Now I'm standing in the middle of a living room. There's a father and two little kids sitting on a couch watching TV, and I'm in the middle of the room without a stitch on. I turned around and ran through the busted-up screen door and tore back down to the beach. I went right and kept on running and eventually found my pile of clothes. I didn't know that there was an undertow. It had carried me about four blocks from where I had gone into the water.

The next morning, I walked the beach looking for the house with the broken screen door. I find the house, and as I'm walking up to knock on what's left of the door, I see the father inside, walking toward me. I start stammering and finally manage to say, "You know, I feel really bad about what happened, and I want to give you some money for the screen door."

The father cuts me off and very dramatically throws up his hands and says — "Honey, I can't take anything from you. That's more entertainment than we've had all week."

NANCY WILSON
*Collingswood, New Jersey*

# THE CAKE

I was fourteen and my brother was sixteen when we went with our parents to my cousin's graduation party. Getting out of our house to go to a family function was always fraught with tension and screaming. My father hated going anywhere. He didn't mind being places once he got there, but he hated the going and getting ready part. He had yelled at my brother and me most of the morning for being teenagers and smirking and grunting the way teenagers do. My father was a strict disciplinarian who could, if provoked, use his closed fist on us. Not that it scared us, but you had to gauge very carefully how far you wanted to provoke him and make sure that you were ready to face the consequences.

My brother and I fought often with each other: vicious, face-punching rows that scared the local kids from messing with us, although we rarely fought with anyone else. As if fighting was an intimate gesture reserved for the people close to you.

The party was held in Guttenberg, New Jersey. We had come from the Bronx, and my brother and I stood against a wall between the kitchen and the living room, waiting for the cake to be cut so we could get this over with and go home and sulk in our rooms. We stood against the wall like two clumps of wet paper towel that had dried and now looked like some plaster deformity growing out of

210

the Sheetrock. There were young children there, too. They were running in and out of the rooms shrieking and laughing in anticipation of ice cream and cake. We were beyond that kind of excitement, my brother and I. We were being cool. Then, one of the boys, with teeth in different stages of falling out and coming in, darted to the graduation cake and stuck his head out over the professionally sculpted icing. "Look at me! Look at me!" he yelled. I saw my brother grit his teeth and clench his fist. I knew what he was thinking, and with a silent nod of the head I dared him to push those uneven teeth into the cake. He smiled through his clenched jaws and shook his head. We both knew the consequences.

The shrill boy knew them, too. He darted over to my brother and taunted him to do it. Then he darted back over to the cake and taunted him again. My brother shifted his weight and unstuck himself from the wall, ready to make the move I so desperately wanted him to make, and as he made that little shift in posture, my father entered the room and went into the kitchen to pour himself a drink. He was still carrying on a conversation with someone in the room he had just left, talking in a loud voice through the cigar that was perpetually stuck between his teeth. The boy noticed my brother frozen next to the wall and taunted, "I'm over the cake. I'm over the cake. . . ." My father entered the room on his way back from the kitchen, and with one quick glance he sized up the situation. He saw what my brother's intentions were, and he understood who those intentions were directed at. My father swiftly stepped over. Using

211

the same hand that held his smoking cigar, he thrust the boy's face deep into the green icing of the cake, stifling his taunts in midshriek. Then, barely breaking stride, my father went into the living room to continue his conversation.

My father and I have had our differences, but I will always remember him for that.

I will always love him for that.

G.B.
*Ringwood, New Jersey*

# RIDING WITH ANDY

Andy lived on his motorcycle. It was his sole means of transportation, and he transported a lot. This was back in the '50s, before cruisers with tail trunks, capacious saddle bags, and fairings with storage pockets, and he carried everything in his clothes. In all but the steamiest weather, he wore a large riding suit that covered a leather jacket that covered a sweater that covered a flannel shirt that covered a pair of long johns. His many pockets were filled with all kinds of stuff, and for larger stuff he had a beat-up saddlebag. Although he wasn't fat, this regalia made him look like the Michelin tire man.

Andy lived near the Bronx Whitestone Bridge in New York and worked as a railroad-crossing gate-keeper far out on Long Island. I would see him on weekends at the local Triumph and BSA shop and at scrambles and road races. Sometimes, though, he would show up at my house on weekday mornings on his way to work and have a cup of coffee while I ate breakfast. My mother was never happy to see him, although she was gracious and hospitable. She especially disliked being addressed as "young lady" when she met him at the back door on his morning visits. Although she could be abrupt and gruff, she classified him as someone in need of help and kindness. Andy was in his thirties. He had an intent and crazed way of looking at you, and his voice had a blue-steel whine that made people turn their heads.

After a few visits, Andy began giving me rides to school. I attended a Catholic high school eight miles away that was completely off his route to work. I was delighted to arrive in front of the school on Andy's Triumph Tiger rather than on a school bus, even though Andy would take curves so fast he dragged his foot pegs.

One day, when we arrived at the high school, I realized that I had forgotten my bag lunch. Andy said, "That's too bad." I thanked him for the ride, and he left. Twenty minutes later, my mother heard a knock at the back door. When she opened it, Andy said, "Good morning again, young lady. Jim forgot his lunch." My mother led him into the kitchen and found my lunch on the counter and handed it to him, thanking him for his kindness. Whereupon he sat down and ate it.

JIM FURLONG
*Springfield, Virginia*

# SOPHISTICATED LADY

I was eighteen years old and attending the University of Wisconsin when my younger brother was awarded a music scholarship to St. John's Military Academy. On a beautiful fall afternoon, he was scheduled to perform in his first concert. Orders had been issued from home that I would be attending the event. My parents arranged to pick me up in front of Langdon Hall at 11:00 A.M. and drag me along to Delafield with them. The thought of sitting through a high-school band concert was definitely not my idea of a good time.

While we were waiting for my brother to arrive in the main reception area, I decided to play the experienced, charming, and sophisticated older sister. I would really impress those young whipper-snappers. Impatiently floor-tapping my three-inch heel, I struck a bored pose, interjecting a few yawns and deep sighs, to show these little soldier-playing boys in red sashes that they did not impress me.

Still waiting for my brother to appear, I excused myself to go to the ladies' room. I returned a short while later to the snickers and grins of everyone in the room. Stuck to my shoe and trailing behind me with every sophisticated step was a forty-foot stream of toilet paper.

JOAN VANDEN HEUVEL
*Madison, Wisconsin*

215

# MY FIRST DAY IN PRIEST CLOTHES

It was a beautiful, sunny day in late October, and I had a dentist's appointment. I was not a priest; I was a seminarian, a member of a religious order. I was about two months past the vow day when I had become a full-fledged member of the order. I would be a priest some day, but not for several more years. In the seminary, we wore cassocks: long black garments cinched at the waist and made of serge (very warm in the summer!). After vows, when we went out in public, we dressed in the traditional Roman collar and black suit of Catholic priests. I had never done this before and had not yet worn my collar and black suit. But on this sunny October day, I had to keep my dentist's appointment.

So it was my day to go public with the collar.

I must say, I never looked better than I did then. I was twenty years old. I had been on the chubby side in high school — you know, "husky" sizes in the boys' section. However, in the novitiate (our first two years of training), I had been encouraged to observe fast days strictly. There went the baby fat. I was slim and trim and I felt great. In all modesty, I looked a little like a young Pat Boone. I was only a little bit aware of this at the time. I was not in any way encouraged to think that I was cute or handsome. There were no girls, no dating, none of that. Still, when I actually put on the Roman collar and a surprisingly well-fitting black suit, I was pretty impressed with myself. But going out into the world! That was a pretty daunting prospect, and I felt very self-conscious. To get to the dentist, I took a bus, which made my feeling of exposure all the more intense. I was dropped off about half a block from the dentist's office and found myself walking along a city street. As I nervously and so very self-consciously made my way along the sidewalk to the office — dressed so strangely for the first time, looking like a priest, but not at all a priest — along came five or six small kids, running, dancing, laughing. They were dressed up in costumes! A ghost, a witch, a bear . . . they were coming from a school Halloween party. My first day in priest costume, and it was Halloween. We were all in costume.

EUGENE O'BRIEN
*Hubbard, Ohio*

# JEWISH COWBOY

I was having one of those moments high-school teachers live for. The class was silent, listening with rapt attention to one of their classmates give his sociology report. The students had chosen to investigate a particular aspect of their cultural heritage, and Bruce had focused on Judaism, the religion to which he had converted at the age of ten. He was demonstrating the rituals of devout prayer to his classmates, something only the most daring teenager could pull off without embarrassment.

Bruce was a tall, handsome senior. The paragon of cool, his peers listened to him whenever he deigned to speak. Standing before the class, he explained that donning the tefillin was a sacred act and must be performed in complete silence. To my pride and amazement, the entire class sat still, practically holding its collective breath. Bruce prayed and slowly wound the thin black strap around his arm, then deliberately placed the other strap over his forehead. I could never have imagined such complete and reverent respect inside a public school. When he was finished, the students asked questions in subdued tones. Bruce answered with professional patience, then returned to my office to remove the straps in private prayer. I was filled with renewed faith in the American Teenager, and for a week I repeated this story of religious conviction and adolescent self-confidence

218

to anyone who would listen.

The following year, Bruce came back to visit the school just before Thanksgiving break, as many recent graduates do. I overheard him telling a bunch of admiring kids how he'd deferred going to college for a while and was riding rodeo somewhere in the South instead. He'd developed a distinct drawl and was leaning against the doorway in his blue jeans, a bandanna casually stuck in the back pocket. He talked about riding bulls as if he'd been doing it all his life. When the other students had gone on to class, my curiosity got the better of me, and I pulled Bruce aside.

"Bruce," I asked, "I just want to know, how do your cowboy buddies react when you leave the rodeo to keep the Sabbath?"

"Oh no, ma'am," he said. "I gave all that up. I'm born-again now."

JENNIFER PYE
*Rochester Hills, Michigan*

# How to Win Friends and Influence People

In order to build a housing project in Fort Lauderdale, the plans have to be approved by the city building department and an architect from the hotel and restaurant commission. Rick Reiley was that architect, and I had an appointment with him early one morning. Running late, I drove up the right lane past a dozen cars waiting for a traffic light in the hopes of puffing out in front when the light changed. As luck would have it, the first car in the line was a police car, and there was a sign that read, "Right Turn Only."

I turned right and became hopelessly lost in a maze of one-way streets and canals. I never like being late, and I was paying more attention to finding my way back downtown than to the road. That's when I felt a hard bump. I stopped and saw a large dog, apparently dead, in back of my car. I ran to a house and rang the bell, but no one answered. I ran to the next house and rang that bell, and a young woman in a tennis outfit opened the door. "I've killed a dog and I need to call the police," I said. "Can I use your phone?" I asked.

She looked out and said, "That's my dog."

After I had called the authorities and calmed the woman down, she asked if I would like a cup of coffee. I accepted and sat down in the kitchen.

There was a Dale Carnegie book on the table, and I asked her who was taking the course. I managed the area for Dale Carnegie and knew everyone who enrolled. "My husband," she said, and when I asked who he was, she answered, "Rick Reiley."

Great, I thought. I need this man's approval, and I've just killed his dog.

I explained to Mrs. Reiley that I had an appointment with her husband and asked her to please call him and explain why I was late. I got back in my car and arrived at city hall a few minutes later. As I walked toward Rick's office, I saw him coming down the hall with a scowl on his face. When he reached me, he grabbed me in a bear hug and said loudly, "You've done us a great favor, Jerry. Our dog was old and blind and had cancer, and neither my wife nor I had the courage to put him to sleep. Thank you so much for what you've done."

JERRY YELLIN
*Fairfield, Iowa*

# YOUR FATHER HAS
# THE HAY FEVER

My father is obsessed with his nose, slave to it. In his mind, he believes God created the nose as a joke around the office and forgot all about it in the rush to finish up the universe before Sunday. His day off. My father and God have a lot in common: God has the fate of all existence on his shoulders, Dad has hay fever. Dad figures it comes out about even. "He doesn't want hay fever. Believe me." Not a moment goes by when our household is not preoccupied with Dad's nose. How could it possibly be otherwise? It's like some kind of malicious presence that lives with us. Any little diversion we plan — an afternoon drive to the Dairy Queen, a game of Monopoly after supper — Dad's nose vetoes. And those we do manage to get under way while Old Faithful slumbers are invariably aborted when it awakens, like a cross wasp pinned to my father's face. We cut the picnic short or leave the movie and go home to follow Dad around the house, in search of his inhaler or nasal spray, like five ghouls patrolling their rooms as Dad leads the way with the litany, "My nose, my nose, my nose," as if that were the object of our search. Anyone looking in the window would be a fool not to call the authorities.

He stands at the bathroom lavatory, both nostrils clogged beyond sanity. His arsenal is set out before him: nasal spray, nasal drops, nasal plugs, nasal cream, Vicks VapoRub, camphor oil, olive oil, motor oil, 3-in-1, Liquid-Plumr, Drano, blasting caps. He has developed combinations requiring EPA approval, industrial permits, evacuation of the neighborhood. I stand at the door and watch as he mixes his snake oils, administers them, then waits for the miracle, absolutely still, as if he's listening for faraway hoofbeats, the cavalry, coming to save him from his own nose. Invariably, the bugle never sounds, the army never arrives.

"My nose."

Sometimes it's a statement of resignation. Lying on the couch with his handkerchief on his belly, handy, you know, he groans, "My nose." Other times, it's a declaration of war, especially when he is trying to do something that requires concentration, like repair the lawnmower. He squats beside the machine, threading a screw the size of a flea, his eyes watering, face crimson and swollen. Suddenly, with no more warning than would accompany an alien invasion, he slings the screwdriver across the yard and leaps to his feet, digging into his hip pocket for his handkerchief as if it's a scorpion stinging his butt. He blows. He lifts his countenance to the heavens. He bellows, "My nose!"

I am six years old. Dad is trying to get the chain back on my bicycle. I am such a delinquent for allowing it to come off in the first place. Dad grumbles. I see a drop of clear liquid descend from his nostril and hang there like a pendant an aborigine might wear. I silently retreat a few steps. He sniffs, wipes with his sleeve, sniffs again, grumbles a curse to the creator of such an inanely designed apparatus as the human nose. He blinks his eyes rapid-fire, yanks on the chain a couple more times for show. And then the nose is in control. Dad roars like a wounded grizzly, snatches the bike over his head, and heaves it down the driveway. Out comes the scorpion. He blows. Birds take flight, small mammals urge their young deeper into their burrows, folks all over town look at their watches and wonder why the noon siren is blowing at 10:25. The blast echoes off the water tower to accompany his anguished cry. "MY NOSE!!!"

My mother talks to her doctor about it. She misunderstands him and tells everyone, "Jerry has a deviant septum." She brings home brochures, puts them in his lunch box. As if he needs reminding.

It is the summer of my ninth year, and we are vacationing in Florida. Mom wants to visit Cypress Gardens. Dad is reluctant. "What about my hay fever?" Mom opens her purse: inside is enough Contac and Triaminic to fill a beanbag chair. Interstate transport violations and border seizures flood my mind. I picture the five of us assuming the position along the side of the highway, traffic slowing to a crawl, the contents of Mom's purse strewn on the ground, photographers taking pictures of the stash.

We go on to Cypress Gardens. Before we have parked the car, Dad is well on his way to being included in the Hay-fever Hall of Fame.

"My nose."

Mom breaks out the medicine. "Here, take

these." She even has one of those plastic collapsible cups and a thermos full of orange juice. She really wants to see Cypress Gardens. "They won't help," Dad says, gulping them anyway. They don't.

I remember it as a day of wrath and embarrassment. Dad's nose was in total control of our itinerary. Mom and us kids wanted to see the ski show; Dad's nose wanted to go home. We wanted to eat lunch in the picnic area beneath the weeping-willow trees; Dad's nose threw a fit and asked us if we were all out of our minds.

I walk the winding paths, head down in shame, as Dad heckles the groundskeepers. "Keep it up. Kill us all! You probably never had to use a vaporizer in your life!" He approaches total strangers and asks if they have a pocketknife on them. "My nose!" he wails, to the strangers' complete horror. "Remove my nose from my face! Just lop her right off. I'm dying here. Put me outta my misery."

TONY POWELL
*Murray, Kentucky*

# LEE ANN AND HOLLY ANN

When I was a senior in high school, I was chosen to sing in a statewide choir at a national music educators convention. There were several hundred students, so we all had seating assignments. Three charts were posted in different locations. On two of the charts I was placed in one seat, and on the other I was one row and one seat forward. I was confused by this and went to the seat that had been on the two charts, assuming the third was a mistake. Partway through the first day of rehearsals, I heard someone yell, "Heflebower!" I turned around and didn't see anyone I recognized, but a young blond woman responded to the call. It suddenly dawned on me that I had encountered something I had never encountered before: another Heffelbower. She was named Lee Ann Heflebower, and I was named Holly Ann Heffelbower. No wonder the seating charts had been switched. We got to know each other, dutifully exchanged one Christmas card, and then lost touch.

Seven or eight years later, I was still living in my hometown, in an apartment building called the Holly. On Valentine's Day, I came home to check my mail before going to the funeral of one of the members of my church choir. I put my key in the mailbox, and it didn't work. I looked at the mailbox, and it said "Heflebower," and I tried the key again. It wouldn't turn. I looked at the box again, and it still said "Heflebower." But so did the one to the left of it: "Heffelbower." I put my key in the other one, got my mail, and rushed off to the funeral. When I got home, I discovered that Lee Ann had moved in across the hall from me. She had just come back to Lincoln from Ohio and had rented the only place she could find that allowed cats. This time we became the best of friends and eventually became roommates. Two years ago, I sang at her wedding.

HOLLY A. HEFFELBOWER
*Lincoln, Nebraska*

# WHY I AM ANTIFUR

Uncle Morris had eyes the color of Windex. He wore pinky rings and fedoras and cashmere topcoats to die for. He smelled of bay rum and Cuban cigars, a combination even my seven-year-old self found intoxicating. He could tell a great story.

In his youth he ran away to Toronto and for a short time pursued a career as a professional wrestler under the name of Murray. There he met Aunt Faye and Aunt Rae. Uncle Morris could not say no to women and seldom tried. So he married them both.

Aunt Rae was so unlikable even her own babies found her irritating. She had a daughter with Morris who looked just like Whitey Ford and wouldn't speak to either of them from the day she was born.

With Aunt Faye he had twin boys named Erwin and Sherwin. Supposedly, one was brilliant and the other "slow," but we never knew which was which. Forbidden to ask outright, my brother and I spent hours devising subtle tests that would reveal their true natures, but never with any conclusive results.

The two women lived in separate apartments on either side of town. They knew about each other and, no doubt because of Uncle Morris's charms, they both decided to live with the arrangement. Uncle Morris put a great deal of time and money into keeping Faye and Rae happy. It wasn't an easy task.

There were items of jewelry, up-to-date appliances, and wall-to-wall carpeting that had to be bought in batches of two. But more than anything, in those cold Canadian neighborhoods, both women wanted fur coats. Uncle Morris could only afford one. Thereafter, much of his time was spent driving the coat back and forth to opposite sides of Toronto so that Faye and Rae could each make use of it.

It was especially hard in the winter. The fur got around more as a coat than it had as a mink. This began to take its toll on Uncle Morris. Combine the pressures of the coat with a lifelong diet of pastrami and red pop, and a heart attack seemed almost inevitable.

In the short space of time during which Uncle Morris rose from the table clutching his chest and actually hit the floor, the coat disappeared. The family was instantly and irrevocably divided. A vast Gordian knot of relatives sifted into two camps. One thought Faye had the coat, the other, Rae.

Lies were told. Truths were told. The lies and the truths were equally damaging. There was yelling. There was crying. There was the stealing of knickknacks. The coat was never seen again.

Years later, I was helping my mother clean out a basement storage area. "What's this?" I asked, as I pulled out what appeared to be a moth-eaten bear suit from the depths of the closet. I heard a damning silence and breathed in unmistakable odors of mothballs and Shalimar. I looked at my mother.

There was a distinct lack of eye contact. "Oh, God," I gasped, "this is Faye and Rae's coat! You took it! It was you!"

My four-foot-ten-inch mother flew across the room with surprising strength and ferocity and pinned me against the wall. She grabbed my shirt and hissed, "You must never tell."

"Take it easy," I whined, "if you kill me, you'll be left with just my brother."

Ever practical, she eased her grip and turned to the matter at hand. "What should we do now?" she asked. I didn't know. If she confessed, they'd kill her.

I picked up the coat. It was so huge and heavy — Faye and Rae had been big women. I tried it on and turned to look in the mirror. Just then, my two-year-old toddled into the room. He took one look at me and screamed and screamed and screamed until I took it off.

FREDDIE LEVIN
*Chicago, Illinois*

# AIRPORT STORY

My friends Lee and Joyce live in North Shrewsbury, Vermont, about a four-hour drive from Logan International Airport in Boston. Back in the 1970s, an uncle of Joyce's died in Chicago. She decided to drive to Logan and fly to the funeral.

She drove east across the Green Mountains, then absentmindedly turned left instead of right and drove the wrong way for half an hour before she realized her mistake. A little panicked about being late, she turned around and hurried across Vermont, then across a corner of New Hampshire, and was now only about a half-hour's drive from Logan. She saw a big exit sign for the airport and pulled off. She kept following signs pointing toward the airport and finally arrived — at a big grassy field with a couple of hangars. She had been following signs for the local airport in Manchester, New Hampshire.

Now she really had to hurry to make her plane. She raced back onto the highway, south into Logan, ran out of the parking lot, and begged the passengers at the ticket counter to let her go first because her plane was about to leave. They let her run to the next agent. She told him that she needed to get on the next flight to Chicago, pulled out her checkbook — and discovered that there were no checks left in the book.

The only credit card she had was for a gas-

231

station chain.

All the money she had was a single dollar bill. There was no way she could buy a ticket.

Disconsolate and ready to cry, she decided to take her last dollar bill and call her relatives to tell them that she would have to miss the funeral. With tears welling up in her eyes, she saw a machine where she could get change for the pay phone. She put her dollar in — and out came two tickets to the Massachusetts state lottery. She'd put the dollar in the wrong machine. As the tears began to roll, a man who was walking by patted her on the shoulder and said, "Don't worry, lady. Best buy you ever made."

Now all Joyce wanted was to be alone so she could cry in peace. She went into the ladies' room.

All the stalls were pay toilets.

I don't care, she said to herself. I have no pride left. I just want to be alone to cry. She got down on her hands and knees and started crawling under the metal door.

Halfway through, she heard a woman's voice say to her, "Sorry, honey. This one's occupied."

RANDY WELCH
*Denver, Colorado*

# TEARS AND FLAPDOODLE

It was August in Louisiana and time for my father's annual party for his interns. The air was still and swollen with moisture. I cleaned fish that would eventually be one of the ingredients in a gumbo. My father didn't spend much on the food for this event; the bulk of the money went into buying liquor. The fish scales stuck to the bottom of the aluminum sink and gleamed like mica chips.

In all the years I lived at home, I never saw any of my father's trainees express an opinion that differed from his. He was not a man to cross or challenge. I watched him through the window, his Mr. Pickwick silhouette rocking slightly as he waited for his young doctors to arrive. Something caught his attention, and he looked down intently, making small circles in the air with his drink glass. Dr. Hauser showed up early; I watched him as he fidgeted around his mentor. When the other interns arrived in a slow procession down our oyster-shelled drive, they found the two of them standing under a three-tiered birdhouse for martins. My father had heard that martins could cut the mosquito population in half, and so he had put up this miniature high-rise building for them.

One of the baby birds had fallen out of the house and was lying on the ground, its beak opened slightly. My father studied it, becoming quite maudlin as he finished his second gin and tonic. He shook his head sadly and made a sound with his tongue. It didn't surprise me when I heard him order Dr. Hauser to put the dying bird back in the house with its mother.

Dr. Hauser looked at the fifteen-foot-high birdhouse, then down at the bird.

"Do you have a ladder?"

"Oh, hell, Hauser, just shimmy up the pole."

Dr. Hauser made a few feeble attempts at climbing the pole, bird in hand, while the rest of the doctors stood in a semicircle, glad they'd arrived late.

My father came inside, refreshed his drink, and then went back out. He stood under the birdhouse for a moment, the ice clinking in his glass.

"Put the car under the pole, then climb onto the roof."

"*My* car?"

"Certainly," my father said.

So Dr. Hauser drove his car under the birdhouse. His weight made scalloped dents as he stepped onto the hood of the car and then onto the roof. He was still about a foot and a half short of the birdhouse.

"Guess it can't be done," he said, cradling the small bird.

"The hell," said my father.

My ten-year-old brother, Matt, arrived on the scene pushing a mower. His khaki shirt was darkened with sweat; little blades of grass stuck to the cuffs of his pants at odd angles.

"Matt," said my father, "get on Hauser's shoulders."

My brother swatted at a mosquito, then moved

obediently toward the group of interns. Dr. Hauser climbed up onto his car, and my brother managed to get onto his shoulders. They made an odd twosome wobbling on the car roof, the marsh reeds undulating in the background. The martins chirped loudly as they circled the house, swooping and diving at the intruders. Another doctor gingerly handed the bird to my brother, who was within a breath of the small opening. He leaned forward. As he did, he toppled; they toppled. Matt first, then the doctor, and finally the bird.

There was a dull thud as they hit the car, then rolled onto the shells.

"Christ!" Dr. Hauser shouted.

"Dad! My arm!"

My brother's arm looked askew, bent as if it didn't belong to him. He put his other arm over his face to hide his tears; the oyster shells had cut into his flesh.

The doctors surrounded them immediately, and one ran into the house to find a splint for Matt's arm. Another rushed to his car for a first-aid kit. Two doctors attended to Dr. Hauser.

"Don't move, Don," one said. "I think we'd better call an ambulance."

Through all the commotion, my father stood still, his attention fixed on the spot where the bird had been flattened onto the oyster shells.

"Poor little goddamned birdie," my father said as he poured himself another gin. "Poor little goddamned birdie."

ALICE OWENS-JOHNSON
*Black Mountain, North Carolina*

# THE CLUB CAR

When I was a young sailor, fresh out of boot camp, I was granted a two-week leave. I decided to go to Miami to visit my father and sisters and boarded the train in Norfolk, Virginia. After a couple of hours, I was starting to feel hungry, so I left my seat and walked the length of the train to the club car. It was a lively place, I discovered, clearly the only game in town. I gobbled down a ham-and-cheese sandwich, drank at least two bottles of Coke, and then sat around for an hour or two trying to look cool as I thumbed through some magazines. That was my first visit. The next day, I went back, prepared now with a paperback novel that someone had given me to read. *God's Little Acre*, I remember. This time, the club car was virtually empty, and I had my pick of the seats. I chose to lounge in one of the two circular booths at either end of the car. Each had a Formica-topped table in front and was equipped with comfortable vinyl cushions. I put my book down on the table, went to the bar and ordered a large cup of coffee and a Danish, then returned to the booth. Thus ensconced, I devoured the Danish and began my reading.

Behind the booth was a stainless-steel heating grate perforated with round holes. After each sip of coffee, I would put the paper cup back onto the table and throw my right arm over the back of the booth, stretching it out in a resplendently suave

236

manner. My fingers began tapping on the heating grate. And then I slipped a couple of them in and out of the holes. Leaving my fingers in the holes for the nonce, I concentrated on my reading. Then, ready for another sip of coffee, I pulled my right arm up, and, incredibly, my fingers wouldn't come out. They were stuck in the holes.

This is ridiculous, I said to myself. This isn't happening. I tried and tried, but my fingers wouldn't come out of the holes. The car began filling up with new arrivals. At one point, a group of four people asked if I was finished with the booth because they needed the table to play some cards. I told them about my predicament. They were astonished but very sympathetic. Attempts to free my hand then ensued. First, the application of an ice pack; then some cold cream; then the talking cure: "Stay relaxed, stay calm, breathe deeply!" Nada! A contingent of the train's crew then arrived on the scene. One of them was toting a canvas bag filled with tools. They proceeded to dismantle the booth, quickly exposing the heating grate. Then they unbolted it, and there I was in the middle of the club car in my now-rumpled dress blues attached to a six-foot-long piece of stainless steel. Even then, my fingers wouldn't budge. They were visibly swollen now.

Eventually, the train stopped and I was taken off and driven to a hospital emergency room, grate and all. A perplexed intern did his best to deal with the situation, but to no avail. I then wound up in the basement of the hospital, where a maintenance man very carefully hacksawed the grate from my hand. Immensely relieved, I thanked him from the bottom of my heart.

The next day I was in Miami, none the worse for wear.

JOHN FLANNELLY
*Florence, Massachusetts*

# BRONX CHEER

Al used to stand outside with his golf sweater on, always looking to play golf. So I went over and talked to him. He said, "Are you ready to play golf?" I said, "Not really. How about a game of pool down in your cellar?"

So that's what we did. We went downstairs and started to play on this big table that covered half the basement, but next to the pool table there happened to be a wood column that supported the floors above. Every time I tried to use one of those long pool sticks, it would bump into the wood column.

I said to Al, "I can't make this shot because of the column." Al said, "Why not cut the sticks?" I said, "That's a good idea," and so that's what I did.

Then I had a better idea. I said, "Al, maybe we should eliminate this column and put a steel beam in there instead." He said, "That's a great idea."

So Al and I and the kids got into my station wagon and drove to 138th Street and Morris Avenue to pick up this twenty-two-foot steel beam for the house. The beam was so long that it stuck out of the station wagon. It kept hitting the street, bouncing up and down, and sparking and smoking. After a while the kids were yelling, "Hey, Daddy, look! The beam is on fire!"

Al and I both looked, and sure enough we had

to stop and cool it off. Once we got to the house, we put the beam in the driveway. Then we said, "How are we going to get this big beam into the house?"

I said we had to cut a two-foot hole in the concrete wall. Then we'd be able to slide the beam in under the ceiling of the basement.

So we chopped the hole. I said to Al that before we put the steel beam in, we had to support the rest of the house with jacks and supporting wood columns. We didn't want the house to collapse before we took out the old wood column.

We worked until midnight. We were tired and exhausted by then, so I went home. The next morning, around six o'clock, I got a call from Al. "Help!" he said, "I think there's something wrong. There's water coming down the steps, and the kids are yelling that they can't open the doors to the bathroom and the bedrooms to get out."

I ran across the street, and there's Al with his golf clubs and his golf sweater, standing in front of the house and yelling at the kids, "Turn off the water! Don't flush the toilet! Your mother's downstairs on the table holding up the chandelier and ceiling with her hands!"

Sure enough, when I went into the house, that's exactly what I saw. Arlene was up there on the table, trying to keep the chandelier and ceiling from falling down. Al then ran upstairs and opened the doors for the kids to let them out. I ran downstairs into the basement and shut off the water. When I turned around, I saw squirrels jumping in through the hole we had cut in the wall. The short, cut-down sticks were still on the table, and it looked like they were playing pool with them.

When I got upstairs, my wife was there, yelling at me that it was our anniversary. We have reservations in Canada, she says, did I forget? Hurry, hurry, we have to go.

I looked at Al and then at Arlene, who was sopping wet, and at Al Jr. sliding down the banister, and at Keith coming down the steps backward on his knees, and he was sopping wet, too. Upstairs, the girls were yelling, "Where's my clothes! My clothes are all wet!"

So I yelled out at the top of my voice, "STOP! Let's get Arlene off the table, and let's try to clean up this mess so Al can go play golf."

I said to him, "I have to go on my anniversary trip, but when I come back, I'll try to put everything together again."

When I did come back, of course, Arlene had already put some Sheetrock on the ceiling. She asked me to plaster it and then paint the rest of the house, and that's what I did. But I still wanted to know what had happened, and Al said to me, "Just before you came that day, I had a carpenter come in to shave and cut the doors to fit the sagging house." I hadn't known about this so, quite naturally, when we leveled off the house without jacks and supports, we straightened it out, and that's why nobody could open the doors.

You have to understand that this was not a normal house. It looked like something from that old comic book *The Old Lady That Lived in a Shoe*, with forty kids looking out the windows. But, of course, that didn't bother Al. He would say to Arlene, "Don't forget to plaster and paint the walls. And don't forget to pick out the color and feed the kids before bedtime. I'm going to play golf." She would say, "Okay," but somehow, whenever she said okay, out popped another kid. There were kids all over the place.

JOE RIZZO<br>
Bronx, New York

# ONE DAY IN HIGLEY

One day, when I was a young CPA, I visited a client at his farm near Higley, Arizona. While we were talking, we heard something scratching on the screen door, and he said, "Watch this." He went to the door and opened it to let in a rather large bobcat. He had found this bobcat in an alfalfa field just after it was born, and the animal had been part of the family ever since. When he opened the door, the cat ran into the bathroom, jumped up onto the toilet, and squatted over it to "do his job." When the bobcat had finished, he leaped down to the floor, stood on his hind legs, reached up, and flushed the toilet.

CARL BROOKSBY
*Mesa, Arizona*

# STRANGERS

# Dancing on Seventy-fourth Street

Manhattan, August 1962

A hot afternoon, my third day here. The studio apartment is scorching. With a hammer and screwdriver I chisel paint from the only window. Then, with one great shove, I push the jamb to the top and turn my head toward the unbroken line of brownstones.

Next door, neighbors are fanning out to the stoops, where a brown-skinned infant curls its lip and arches its back before mama offers her nipple. In turquoise pants and clear plastic pumps, she sits cross-legged, dangling her shoe from her toes, a newspaper between her and the hot cracking cement. While the newborn draws its milk, mama alternates between a thin cigar and a bottle of cerveza.

Papa in his undershirt swaggers out with a radio in one hand and a toddler dragging a broom in the other. The tot begins sweeping the stoop but changes its mind and strums the bristles instead. Kitchen chairs are being carried out, along with six-packs of Tab, 7Up, and Rheingold.

I'm getting a whiff of black beans and saffron rice steaming from the hibachi under the stairs. Mama ties back her brash red hair, plops the baby in a box from Gristedes Market, and slowly begins to twirl, her hands on her waist. She stops, slinks over to her man, and, with her knee, nudges his thigh. Grinding to the sounds of the Caribbean, the pair dodge, plunge, twist, and swerve. The child accompanies with a wooden bowl and spoon; his father smiles in approval — flashing a gold incisor. Bongo players expand along the pavement while the new one sleeps in a cardboard box.

And I, a girl of twenty, a year out of Nebraska, watch transfixed. Suddenly, papa with the flashing incisor looks up from the pandemonium to my window.

"Hey muchacha!" he yells to me. "You got a smoke?"

CATHERINE AUSTIN ALEXANDER
*Seattle, Washington*

# A CONVERSATION WITH BILL

My wife and I had moved to southern Maryland, where I was studying marine ecology at a university lab on Chesapeake Bay. The town we settled in was quite small and rural. Downtown consisted of just a few enterprises: a general store, a liquor store, and a barber shop, among a handful of others. There was one bar, and if I didn't have any Friday-night plans, I would often drop in for a pint or two of beer and perhaps a game of pinball. The bar had a group of loyal regulars, local men who worked on the water as fishermen, or at the nearby power plant, or for construction companies that built houses in the area. I didn't really fit in with them, but I loved hearing their fishing stories. I marveled at their descriptions of the old days on the bay; mysterious images would come to me while I listened. This particular group was nicknamed the "ciderheads" by some of the bartenders, and they always occupied the same end of the bar, near the front door.

It was December 24, and I found myself temporarily alone at the bar, sipping a pint of Guinness stout. I was thinking about our plans for the next day, when my wife and I would be driving up to Connecticut to spend the Christmas holiday with my family. After a while, I noticed that Bill, one of the men from the ciderhead group, was beckoning me into conversation. Bill and I had seen each other dozens of times over the past two years, but we had never spoken. We had one of those silent agreements between people who choose not to interact but who respect each other just the same.

So I was somewhat surprised when he started talking to me. It was quite spontaneous. After an initial, polite introduction and some small talk, Bill launched into a long narrative that covered much of his life's history. He was in a jovial mood, having already had a few drinks, and made a point of telling me that he was a fisherman. He emphasized his love for the bay and his fascination with its ecology. He described his new fishing boat in exquisite detail and how he had just taken it out of the harbor for some repairs. We got around to talking about Christmas, family holiday plans, and the like. He told me that he and his grandmother shared the same birthday, and that they still celebrated together, despite her advanced age. More and more, he was opening up his life to me, letting me into the cracks and crevices that are usually barred to strangers. I was somewhat astonished by all this, but it was a festive time of year and I didn't mind the opportunity to really get to know Bill.

Our conversation lasted about thirty minutes. He finally looked at his watch and told me that he had to be getting on home — his wife and kids were expecting him. He put his arm around me, gave my shoulders a tight squeeze, and told me how great it was to talk to me and that we certainly needed to talk more often. I agreed and shook his hand, and we said good-bye.

I sat back down at the bar. By this time, my friend Carl had come in. I asked him if he knew

Bill and if he had any clue as to why he might have chosen to befriend me. Carl couldn't offer any answers. He just said that Bill had always been a bit quiet.

Of course, one's sense of time is often shaky, especially in bars, but it seemed as if Bill had only just walked out the door when I noticed that the bartender had broken down and was in a helpless state of sorrow. The din of the crowd subsided, and people were whispering. Obviously, something terrible had just happened. It turned out that Bill had been in an accident on his way home. His speeding pickup truck had left the pavement and careened into the dense hardwood forest. He had been killed instantly.

This news sent me into a state of shock. It's almost impossible to describe how stunned I was. I told Carl that I was probably the last person Bill had ever talked to. We had never talked before, and he had told me so many things about his life, had put in so many tiny personal details. It was almost as if he had known that something was going to happen to him.

After a while, I had to get outside, away from Bill's grieving friends and relatives. I stood in the parking lot with Carl, and several police cars went by, apparently returning from the scene of Bill's accident. Following them was a tow truck carrying away what was left of Bill's pickup. The crushed windshield resembled a crazy spiderweb, sparkling under the streetlights. The body of the pickup was all twisted from the terrible force of the crash. The wrecker paused at the intersection for a moment, and then it continued on its way.

We stood there in silence, watching until it was swallowed up by the darkness beyond.

JOHN BRAWLEY
*Lexington, Massachusetts*

# GREYHOUNDING

It was late May or early June when I boarded the bus in Reno. The year was 1937.

I stopped at the first empty seat. "May I . . . ?" I asked. The person sitting in the window seat shot me a look that said she'd rather not have company but then she nodded her assent. She was an old woman (though probably about ten years younger than I am now), with a stately presence and expensive clothes — well-heeled, as we used to say. Not your usual Greyhound type. I wondered why she chose bus travel over the luxury of a Pullman. After a while, I dared to ask.

The vehemence of the reply almost knocked me out of my seat. "I want to see the country while there's still some of it left! Because there won't be anything left when this man Roosevelt gets through with it!"

I loved FDR, but I said nothing. Roosevelt haters never listened to logic. Besides, I didn't feel up to arguing just then.

I'd been in Reno for what was the usual reason at the time: a divorce. Now, on the Greyhound bus, I was feeling a clashing mixture of joy and shame. Joy because I was free, and shame for having made a ridiculous marriage in the first place. I was twenty-three.

My traveling partner got off at the next city. She said she would relax for a day or two and then

253

carry on with her farewell inspection of America. I moved into the seat by the window, and a large woman sat down next to me. Immediately she went to sleep. She snored for the rest of the ride.

How did Jean and I find each other? At a rest stop, of course. On a long bus trip, nothing was more welcome than those rest stops. As we pulled into one, the driver would call out, "Folks, it's ladies to the right, gents to the left. We take off again in fifty minutes." Behind him passengers would stir and murmur in anticipation.

Inside the bus passengers were isolated, two by two, but at a rest stop we could mingle. Some of us took brisk runs back and forth, while others stood around eating hot dogs from the food stand. And we all remained upright for the whole break to soothe our aching, sat-upon bottoms.

At one of these stops I noticed a girl about my age laughing at the same thing I was laughing at. Shared laughter is a foolproof introduction, and we struck up a conversation. Jean was a small brunette with an engaging smile. I was taller — too tall, I thought — and my hair was light brown. We were probably both wearing seersucker dresses, cool and pre-rumpled, with full skirts and hems at midcalf (slacks for women were years away).

Jean told me that she had been living in California with an aunt and going to college. Now she was heading home to Pennsylvania. I told her that I was out of school and thinking about starting a career.

When we got back on the bus, we finagled a couple of switches and got seats next to each other. Side by side, we read this new magazine,

*Time*, and Thomas Wolfe, the *real* Thomas Wolfe. We took turns by the window, groaning about the terrible heat. Looking past the driver through the wide windshield, we could see the two-lane highway dissolving into shimmering mirages, cool lakes we'd never reach.

We talked. And laughed. And talked. Sometimes, we slept. We sang quietly so no one could hear us, harmonizing "Old Mill Stream" and "Stardust." I learned that Jean had never been truly in love — she'd only had crushes. She wanted to be a teacher because, as she put it, "If you can teach, you can do anything."

I told her about the divorce. She was startled but accepting. I began to realize that this younger woman was remarkably well adjusted, whereas I felt scattered and flailing.

Over the long haul, the bus riders tended to get itchy and stinky and crampy and cross. Jean and I decided that we needed time off, and we spent a night in Omaha, Nebraska. There, we walked up and down beautiful hills in the shadows of great mountains. In Omaha, I learned that breathing could be a sensual pleasure.

We bused out again the next morning, and the rest of the trip was a breeze. When we reached Jean's Pennsylvania terminal, we vowed to keep in touch.

And the extraordinary thing is that we did. For sixty-two years, we wrote to each other once or twice a year, coast to coast. Jean suddenly fell in love with a GI she had known for nine years. They got married and moved to Southern California. I remarried, doing a better job of it this time.

Early in 1999 my friend suggested a reunion. I hesitated, thinking such an old friendship might be safer left in memory. But Jean insisted, and I'm glad.

We met for an August weekend, two octogenarian widow ladies, one short and one tall, neither stout, both still woman-shaped, our well-trimmed hair going gray to white. We were both still quite good-looking, I thought. Between us, we had had three heart attacks, one small stroke, three cataract surgeries, a thyroid deficiency, emphysema, arthritis in countless joints. We took our pills companionably, both kept eyeglasses at the ready, and we walked deliberately but without props. Neither one of us required a hearing aid.

We talked and laughed for two days straight, comparing our lives and times. I talked about my two sons, of whom I am greatly proud, and about my career, of which I am not; it fizzled after a few flashes-in-the-pan.

Jean had achieved real distinction. She had founded and directed a service to help retired people find new ways to stay useful. She was chosen for a national committee that studied older people all over the world. She had traveled to China, Russia, and South Africa.

At our good-bye dinner on Sunday evening, a question arose: If we were given the opportunity to live our lives over again — exactly as we had done, with not even the tiniest changes allowed — would we?

Jean said yes. I said no.

We looked at each other.

"What does that signify?" she asked.

"Must it signify something?"

"I think so," she said.

"That you liked your life."

"Maybe," she said, "and maybe that you don't give yourself credit for yours."

"Maybe . . ."

Later, we raised our champagne glasses and toasted the world. We toasted our reunion and pronounced it good. Then we parted without any nonsense about having another, and with love.

BETH TWIGGAR GOFF
*West Nyack, New York*

# A LITTLE STORY ABOUT
# NEW YORK

In 1979 I was living on the Upper West Side of
Manhattan — at 47 West Eighty-fifth Street, between Columbus and Central Park West. It was a
transitional neighborhood in those days. The west
side of Columbus Avenue was still lower-class, but
across the street it was rapidly becoming chic. Poor
people lived shoulder to shoulder with young pro-
fessionals in an uneasy sort of peace.

I managed on my meager income because I had
lived in the same place since 1976, and it was a
rent-controlled apartment. The building was an
old brownstone that had been hacked up into a
grid of narrow efficiency units. One was a two-
bedroom — the so-called penthouse — and another the only garden apartment: a weedy, cat-
smelling area out back filled with plain trees. The
landlord was a testy, balding man in his forties,
Mr. Yablons. He was always hatching schemes to
drive out his tenants so he could turn the building
into a pied-à-terre for himself and his mother.

He and I had a continually deteriorating relationship. My finances were a mess, and I was usually late paying the rent. It got to the point where
he would only accept cash from me, so when rent
day came around, I would have to cash my pay-
check and carry the money over to his fancy-

schmantzy office on the Upper East Side.

I was always trying to incite mutiny among the tenants. Whenever the landlord pulled one of his outrageous stunts on us, I would organize an indignation meeting in my apartment. We would drink a lot of white wine, blow off steam, and generally have a good time.

I loved being in New York in the summertime. It was hot but quiet and empty. During the week I would walk the mile or so downtown to my job at the theatrical actors' union, enjoying the shady, deserted streets and the different neighborhoods that I passed through — from Central Park West and its grand old apartment buildings to the patchwork of Broadway with its Cuban-Chinese takeout joints and Jewish delis. At night, I would sometimes drag my mattress up to the roof and lie on my back, listening to the city noises and cooling off in the breeze. Or my cat and I would go downstairs in our bare feet and sit on the stoop, where I'd drink a couple of Budweisers with the other tenants, listening to the sounds of Eighty-fifth Street. It was a quiet, slow-moving neighborhood in those days. Elderly women planted folding chairs in the entrances of their buildings and sat fanning themselves. Everyone opened their windows wide for air circulation, so we could hear babies crying and couples arguing and televisions blaring. Elliot from the second floor would practice jazz numbers for his club gigs, sometimes until after midnight.

On one hot Thursday evening during rent week, I came home early with my pocketful of cash and two large paper sacks of groceries in my arms. All I wanted to do was get home, drop the heavy bags, and turn on my floor fan. No one was out on the stoop to help me, so I opened the outer door with my foot and sidled in next to the mailboxes. I was dimly aware that someone had come into the building behind me, but I was distracted as I shifted the bags around in my arms so I could reach my key and turn the lock of the inner door.

I was walking through the foyer when I heard a voice say to me, "Give me all your money."

The meaning of the words hardly registered. I turned around and was starting to say something when I saw him: a tall, heavyset man holding a long knife.

I stared at him.

He said, "Give me your money."

I heard my own voice answering, "Are you crazy? I just went to the store. I don't have any money." It didn't make any sense, and I couldn't believe that I had said it. I'm sure he couldn't either.

"Give me all your money — or I'll cut you," he said.

I thought, how can I pay the rent if I give him all my money? I can't give him my money. I need it.

"No," I said. "Go away."

He looked confused. After all, I was a helpless female, and he was a big, tough-looking guy with a knife.

"Give me all your money," he repeated, but with less conviction.

"Get out of this building!" I retorted.

"Give me —" he began again.

"Didn't you hear me?" I cut in. "Get out of

260

here. Get out of here now."

Suddenly he glanced up the stairs. "Well," he said, "okay." And he slipped out of the building just as smoothly as he had entered it.

For a moment, I stood there in a daze, and then my knees began to shake. I put the grocery bags down on the floor and ran upstairs as fast as my wet-noodle legs would take me. I pounded first on Elliot's door, but he didn't answer, so I ran up two more flights to Robert's apartment. Robert was a cameraman for a TV station, so he tended to have odd times off. He answered the door.

I started babbling, explaining as quickly as I could what had happened and begging him to walk to the police station with me. It was only a couple of blocks away. But Robert said no, the police wouldn't be interested. The man hadn't robbed me, after all, and they probably wouldn't believe my story. I had to agree with him there — it was starting to sound unlikely even to me. Then Robert went into his bedroom, and I followed. He opened the top drawer of his dresser and pulled out a handgun. He looked excited.

"What do you plan to do with that?" I asked.

"I'm not planning to shoot anyone," he said. "I just want to scare him." He told me that we were going to go outside together to see if I could identify the would-be mugger. I know I wasn't thinking clearly at that point, because I obediently followed Robert out of his apartment, down the stairs, and onto the street. But once we started to walk around the neighborhood, I realized that I probably wouldn't be able to identify the man. Robert seemed quite disappointed when we turned around and went back inside.

I couldn't figure out why the man with the knife had given up so easily. It couldn't have been that my short, curly-headed, round-faced, pink-cheeked self had intimidated him. Who or what had made him turn around and leave? Was it his conscience? An angel? Old lady Yablons? I paid my rent promptly the next day.

Years later, after I moved to Wisconsin, I heard that Robert had become quite depressed and would spend long hours alone in his bedroom with the door locked. According to what I was told, he still had the gun.

DANA T. PAYNE
*Alexandria, Virginia*

# MY MISTAKE

I was driving day shifts for a yellow cab company in Dayton, making a meager hourly wage. It was the summer of 1966, the city was in the grip of a heat wave, and everyone was irritable, including me. On this afternoon, I was sitting at a downtown cab stand in front of the Biltmore Hotel, a large, elegant place that was just slightly past its prime. I had all the windows rolled down to catch any slight breeze in the still air. I was hoping to get an airport run.

Instead I got a call from the dispatcher. Over the radio, he told me to go to Wilkie's newsstand and buy a *Racing Gazette*. Then I was to stop at the Liberal Market downtown and pick up six bottles of Schoenling beer, a small shaker of goldfish food, and a box of White Owl cigars. No substitutions were permitted, and I was to use my own cash to pay for the goods; the customer would reimburse me, so I was to save the receipts. He then directed me to deliver the goods to apartment 3B at an address on Third Street, which I recognized as an apartment building in a deteriorating neighborhood.

I protested, not wanting to lose the chance for an airport run — but also not wanting to lay out money from my own cash supply, because I was afraid I might not be able to collect or, worse, that I was being set up for a robbery. The dispatcher, now growing impatient, told me that this man was

263

a regular customer, that there would be no problem with payment, and that I should get moving or bring the cab back in to someone who would. Since he put it that way, I got moving.

Privately, though, I cursed the customer. I figured he must be some kind of welfare bum who was too lazy to feed his own goldfish and to procure what he needed to satisfy his own vices. It infuriated me to run these errands for someone who, judging from where he lived, couldn't possibly have enough money to pay me.

I drove to Wilkie's and bought the *Racing Gazette*, then down the street to Liberal's for the goldfish food, beer, and cigars. Then I drove up to the customer's address. It was an old 1890s four-story dark-brick apartment building in nearly livable condition. I entered, smelling the stale tobacco smoke, bacon, and mildew that are always present in such places. When I reached the third-floor hallway, I knocked on the dark hardwood door of apartment 3B. There was no immediate answer. I could hear something moving across the floor, but it wasn't footsteps. Finally, the door opened, but I saw no one. No one, that is, until I looked down.

There, sitting on a small plywood platform and looking up at me, was a man. He had a slight build and thinning black hair, and he was wearing a white T-shirt and gray wool pants with a thin black belt at the waist. He had only stubs for legs — about as long as my hands.

He was a double amputee who moved about his one-room apartment by propelling himself on a small platform across the bare wood floor. He held a rubber cylinder in each hand to push himself along. They were almost as big as mallet heads, with rubber rings on top for handholds.

The man was polite and very grateful for my services. He directed me to put the beer in a small Frigidaire, a relic from the late 1940s, and to leave the cigars on the kitchenette table. The goldfish were in a bowl there, and he asked me to feed them. Then he asked me to put the *Racing Gazette* on an old glass coffee table in front of the worn couch.

I did everything he asked gladly. I wasn't feeling irritable anymore.

When I set the *Racing Gazette* down on the coffee table, I noticed an open velvet case that looked like a jewelry box. As the man rolled over and reached for the money he was going to pay me with, I looked inside the box. Inside was a slightly tarnished medal — a Purple Heart. It was almost certainly from World War II, since the man seemed to be in his midfifties.

Guilt began to creep over me as the man paid me for all the supplies and the cab fare. Then the guilt settled in when he gave me a generous tip, much more than I would have made on any airport run.

The man was a quiet sort of person, obviously not in need of companionship. Once our business was done, he showed me out. He had long ago reconciled himself to his condition and to the sacrifice he had made. He had no use for sympathy and didn't offer any explanations. I would make that run many more times until I moved on, but I never learned the man's name and we never be-

265

came friends in spite of our regular contact.

Unfortunately for me, I would be more than twice the age I was then before I learned that pre-judging people makes one wrong about most things most of the time.

LUDLOW PERRY<br>
Dayton, Ohio

# No Forwarding Address

After I graduated from college, I moved in with my friend Tom and his three roommates in Somerville, Massachusetts. It was a two-story house that had been rented for years to various students.

Tom was a childhood friend, but we hadn't spent much time with each other since high school. As kids, Tom and I had filmed a comic documentary tour of my father's farm in Maryland. Now, in Somerville, we decided to videotape snippets of our life in that house. Along with ample commentary, we shot each of the five roommates' rooms, the kitchen, my basement painting studio, the backyard, the bathroom, and various and sundry details of slovenly bachelor life.

Many transitory students had lived in the house over the years, and we had collected a pile of mail intended for them. In fact, it was a *huge* pile of mail. We kept it in a large paper shopping bag at the top of the stairs. In it were letters, bills, and junk addressed to at least eight different people. Who knows why we were saving it, since we never bothered to forward it and no one ever showed up to claim it. We had never even seen or heard from any of these former tenants.

At one point during our hour-long video tour, Tom zoomed in on our mail collection, and I pulled out an envelope at random. I announced the addressee's name, Robert Jaffe, tore it open, and then read the contents. It was a generic junk-mail letter, but I improvised for comic effect.

We moved the video tour on to the kitchen, and I filmed Tom preparing his specialty meal, spaghetti and salad. Then the doorbell rang. I handed Tom the camera, which he kept rolling, and I ran downstairs. At the door was one Robert Jaffe, stopping by for the first time since he had lived there, to see if any mail had been delivered for him, and to see if anyone had bothered to save it.

JOSH DORMAN
*Brooklyn, New York*

# THE NEW GIRL

It was a hot, bright day. Everything was burning —
the roofs, the shrubs, the asphalt, our bike seats,
our skin, our hair. Allison's father was watering the
lawn, and Allison and I rode our bikes over the
soggy grass and through the whirling water that jet-
ted out of the sprinkler.

I lived on Prospect Street then. I was eight and
Allison was ten. We were the only kids on the
block, so we were best friends by default. I looked
up to Allison, even though I didn't share her interest in Barbies and Hall and Oates. During the
summer, we spent a lot of time riding our bikes,
playing Clue, and pretending to be married. But I
don't think she liked me very much, and I don't
know if I liked her either. I also don't remember
what we talked about most of the time, but this is
one conversation I can't forget.

As we rode, our bike tires scored the lawn with
deep muddy wounds that would never completely
heal. Four years later, when my parents and I
moved away, the scars in the ground were still
there.

I was the first to see the younger girl standing in
the middle of Prospect Street, straddling her bike,
watching us. I heard someone laughing when I almost collided with Allison, I looked up, and there
she was.

I smiled. She smiled back.

Prospect Street was in a white, lower-middle-class neighborhood. Most of the houses were about seventy years old, of simple, sturdy design. There were a few thick trees with gnarled trunks, but mostly there were short, squat shrubs that provided little shade. The girl, dressed in kelly-green shorts and a T-shirt, looked small against the plainness of the road, but her smile was expansive. The house across the street from Allison's had been sold the week before, and I guessed the girl must have moved in there with her family.

As Allison came out from under the arc of water, she looked at me. Then she stopped her bike and turned to see what I was grinning at. As I said hi to the girl, I heard Allison say, "Get out of here, nigger," with such contempt that I froze, my smile still glued on my face.

The girl kept smiling, too. Allison swung one leg over her bike seat and faced the girl. Holding her bike with one hand, Allison pointed to the house across the street with the other. "I said get out of here, nigger, or I'll beat you up."

The girl's smile disappeared. I also stopped smiling and looked at Allison. Her eyes were drawn into slits, and her long hair was dripping with the water that shot against the small of her back every time the sprinkler swung in our direction. The sunlight was burning in the strands that had come loose from her ponytail, giving her a sort of halo. The water hit me between my shoulder blades, pushing me forward with each blast.

I turned back to the girl and twisted my mouth into a sneer, trying to imitate the hatred I had seen on Allison's face. I avoided the girl's eyes.

The girl said, "I thought maybe we could play. My name is —"

Allison spat back, "I don't play with niggers."

I watched the girl roll her bike across Prospect Street and dump it on the lawn of her house. She shuffled up the porch steps, her head down, her chin quivering, and disappeared into the house. After a few moments, the curtains of one of the windows parted a bit — not so I could see a face, but just enough to feel the hot eyes of the little girl's mother. I remember it all so clearly: standing there with my bike, watching the rose-colored curtains of the house across the street parting, the large brown hand pushing them open just enough to let someone inside peer out.

"Who was that?" I asked Allison, watching the hand lower out of sight and the curtains drift back together.

"Who cares," she said. "They moved in last week, and Mom says they're going to ruin our house."

"How are they going to ruin your house?"

"I don't know. I don't want that black girl any-where near me, though," she said.

And here's what I said back: "Niggers are stu-pid. Maybe they'll move."

We rode our bikes up and down the lawn for a little while longer, but I felt the house across the street as if it were a living, watching presence. I kept thinking of the hand parting the curtains. I kept expecting the younger girl's mother to emerge from the house and demand that we apol-ogize to her daughter. But that didn't happen. As

271

the sun began to set and I rode home for dinner, my stomach was twisted in a tight knot.

Afterward, from time to time, I would see the little girl in her front yard, playing with friends, but I never spoke to her, and I never said I was sorry. I was usually with Allison. All through the summer, the knot in my stomach swelled and grew tighter until it became impossible to untie. When the girl and her mother moved away a few months later, I hoped the knot would disappear. It didn't.

This happened twenty years ago, but I still think about that afternoon almost every day. I never spoke to Allison after my family left Prospect Street, but I hope she thinks about the little girl as well. And I hope more than anything that the girl and her mother have forgotten about me, but I know they haven't.

MARC MITCHELL
*Florence, Alabama*

# THE ICEMAN OF MARKET STREET

For three years in the early '70s, I was a trolley-bus driver for the San Francisco Municipal Railway on the #8 Market. Market Street is a major thorough-fare, and a cross section of society travels up and down it every day. I drove at night, coming to work at the beginning of rush hour. My first few trips consisted of carrying office workers from the finan-cial district to the residential area just west of down-town. Later in the evening, the riders were less diverse: night workers, pleasure seekers, and the Market Street "regulars." The regulars were people who lived on or near Market Street, almost without exception in residential or transient hotels. The largest of the welfare hotels was a colossal building known as the Lincoln. It was situated near the foot of Market Street, a block from the waterfront.

The Lincoln Hotel was a five-story building with about two or three hundred small rooms. I went there once to visit a friend who was down on his luck. This is not his story, but my memory of the building stems from that visit. Upon entering the narrow foyer, you were confronted by a small, wire-mesh cage. Inside the cage was a bored clerk who handled infrequent transactions. To the right of him was one of those ancient elevators without glass or solid walls — another cage. To the right of the elevator was a long, narrow hallway with a staircase at either end. The bare wooden floors had trails worn into them by years of use. The walls were lined every few feet by doors that opened into small, cell-like rooms that constituted the private quarters of each resident.

A lot of different kinds of people lived in the Lincoln Hotel. Some were transient, sent there by the welfare department for emergency housing. A few were parolees from the prison system. The majority, however, were long-term residents of months and years; mostly single people who managed to pay the modest rent with pensions, social security, and disability checks. A few worked at menial jobs for subsistence wages. Most were middle-aged to elderly. Almost all had one characteristic in common. They had dignity. Their means were limited, their futures were generally bleak, but they comported themselves with dignity and were usually kind to each other.

In the latter part of the evening, I had a small number of regular passengers who got on and off at the same places at the same times each night. One of these was a black man who appeared to be about retirement age. He was thin, slightly smaller than average, and moved with quick, sure movements. I would describe him as "wiry." Since he kept to himself and initiated no conversation, I might not have noticed him. Every Friday night at 11:20, however, he boarded the bus carrying a huge heavy-duty green garbage sack slung over his shoulder. It rattled and clinked. It was the size of Santa's bag, carried by a small, wiry, urban Santa Claus. I was curious to know what he was up to

274

but chose to respect the fellow's privacy. He boarded at Seventh Street and alighted at Main Street, the stop closest to the Lincoln Hotel.

With each successive Friday night, my curiosity grew. After four or five weeks, I decided to venture an inquiry. As he boarded the bus and proffered his transfer, I asked, "Do you mind if I ask what you're carrying in that bag?" "Ice," he replied. "Ice?" "Yes, ice."

This was clearly not a loquacious man. I said nothing further, expecting him to offer an explanation. The Market Street regulars are usually lonely people and are quick to open up when someone expresses interest in them. This fellow said nothing further. I was too confounded to pursue the conversation. A few moments later, he was stepping off the bus with his rattling, clinking cargo.

By the middle of the following week, I had resolved to seize my next opportunity to unravel the mystery of the Iceman of Market Street. I became anxious. What if he never appeared again? Would he become one of life's mysteries, never to be solved? All day Friday I anticipated our rendezvous.

Finally, as I approached the Seventh Street stop at 11:20, I saw him waiting there with The Sack. As he stepped on board I greeted him, "Hello." "Hello," he replied. Apparently our terse conversation last Friday had established recognition. I pursued the opening. "Is that ice in the bag?" "Yes," he replied.

Abandoning all reticence, I confessed my great curiosity as to his purpose in carrying a huge sack of ice. He told me his story. He worked at the University of San Francisco, in the kitchen of the cafeteria. He was the cleanup man who mopped the floor and dumped the garbage. On Friday the kitchen shut down for the weekend. To conserve energy, the school disconnected the freezers. Since all the ice would melt over the weekend, he was free to take as much as he wished.

Almost every job has its fringe benefits. Culinary workers get free food. Teachers sometimes still get apples. Clerical workers are never short of paper clips and rubber bands. This worker was allowed all the frozen water he could carry off once a week.

At this point, Dear Reader, you are probably thinking what I was thinking at the time — that it was an absurd acquisitiveness that led him to lug this obviously heavy burden every Friday night. I was wrong. He explained further that he lived (as I had suspected) in the Lincoln Hotel. In his room he had a large ice chest that would keep the ice through the weekend.

Many of the other residents in the hotel received weekly checks and could sometimes afford to invest in a pint of whiskey. They were welcome to stop by his room for some free ice. Often he was offered a drink. He sometimes accepted; not always. It was obvious from his manner that he was no drunkard. Frequently a small group of his neighbors would gather — pensioners, the disabled, the unsuccessful — to share his bounty and he to share theirs.

He had a role in society at the center of a fellowship. He carried ice that would soon melt and pass

276

away. While it melted people came together to share ice and drinks, company and good cheer.

Times change.

Today the site of the Lincoln Hotel is occupied by the Federal Reserve Bank building.

R. C. VAN KOOY
*San Francisco, California*

# ME AND THE BABE

It was a Saturday in the summer of 1947. The next day, an old-timers baseball game would be played before the Indians game at Cleveland's old Municipal Stadium. I had just turned thirteen. As I often did on Saturdays, I accompanied my father to his patent-law office downtown to putter around with the inventions that lined his office shelves.

At noon he sent me across the street to the Hollenden Hotel coffee shop to pick up some sandwiches for us. As I entered, I immediately recognized Babe Ruth. The real Babe, the legend himself, bigger than life. He was sitting with two other men at a table.

I was too nervous and excited to think. I had no pen and paper with me, so instead of approaching him and asking if *he* had a pen, I bolted out, ran back across the street, and flew up the four flights of stairs to my father's office.

"Dad," I yelled, "I just saw Babe Ruth! Give me a pen and paper!" He became just as excited as I was and jammed his pen and a loose-leaf sheet into my shaking hand.

A minute later I burst through the coffee shop doors. The Babe was still there, sitting alone now and lingering over his newspaper. I hurried over to him and squeaked, "Mr. Ruth, can I have your autograph?"

He turned to me and smiled. "Sure, kid," he

said. And then, as he scrawled out his familiar, beautifully Spencerian signature for me, he added, "You shoulda been here five minutes earlier, kid. You coulda got Ty Cobb and Tris Speaker, too."

SAUL ISLER
*San Rafael, California*

# LIVES OF THE POETS

In 1958, while still a student at Indiana University, I began driving to New York City over vacations and holidays. Like countless aspiring artists before me, I "knocked on doors." Allen Ginsberg came to the door of his Tenth Street flat and said that he would talk with me if I bought him a hamburger. I did, downstairs at the luncheonette, and he talked nonstop for an hour about Shelley and Mayakovsky. Then he told me to go meet Herbert Huncke and say that Allen had sent me. I knocked and was met by a pale, gentle-looking man who invited me into the living room, where several people were silently camped out on battered furniture. "We're cookin' a poem, man," Huncke said, "com'ere." He led me into the kitchen and opened the oven door. There it was! A typed poem on a sheet of paper turning brown around the edges in a 350° oven. Huncke closed the door and shuffled back to the living room. I followed him. Everyone was still silent. After hanging around for a few moments, I decided that I wasn't hungry and slipped out.

CLAYTON ESHLEMAN
*Ypsilanti, Michigan*

# LAND OF THE LOST

I teach at a university, but in one of my previous lives I was an actress, doing mostly guest appearances on television shows. In the 1970s I was once in an episode of the Saturday morning children's show *Land of the Lost*. I played a grown-up version of the little girl on the show, coming back through time to warn her that she was in danger. We both had long blond hair and I wore a flowing green dress.

About five years later, I was traveling in Burma. Tourists were only allowed in the country on a seven-day visa. The plane from Bangkok flew in on Tuesdays, and I saw few Westerners as I traveled from Rangoon to Mandalay to the Shan States. Other than Rangoon's wide boulevards — relics of British colonialism — Burma seemed untouched by Western influence or the trappings of the modern world. The beauty of Burma and the gentle friendliness of its people entranced me.

One afternoon I was walking through the Shwedagon Pagoda, with its monks in crimson robes, its gold statues of Buddha, and its constant stream of visitors, families, and pilgrims. The smell of incense was everywhere. I had stopped to admire a Buddha when an older gentleman came up next to me and began telling me about the statue. His English was perfect. He was obviously very learned, and I was drawn in by the story he was telling. He said to call him Dr. P., since his last name was very long. Several hours slipped away as Dr. P. told me about history and politics, the teachings of Buddhism, and the spiritualism and fatalism of the Burmese people.

Then he interrupted himself. "It's lunchtime," he said, and he invited me to accompany him to his house to meet his family. Of course I went.

Dr. P.'s wife greeted us graciously at the door, and we entered his house, which was filled with his children and grandchildren. One granddaughter, about eight or nine years old, seemed to be studying me. Finally, she said something in Burmese to her grandfather.

"My granddaughter says she has a picture of you," Dr. P. said to me.

I smiled indulgently at her. "Oh, does she?"

"Yes," he said, "she would like to show it to you."

The child slipped out of the room and returned a minute later with a plastic toy called a View-Master, which displays three-dimensional images from slides mounted on cardboard disks. I had seen one years earlier in a gift shop at the Giant Redwood Forest. The child handed me the toy. When I put my eye up to the glass lens, I was stunned: I was looking at a picture of myself, wearing the flowing green dress on the set of *Land of the Lost*.

Dr. P.'s son had worked as a sailor on a merchant ship. When the ship had landed in New York, he had bought this toy for his daughter, and it just happened to come with pictures from my episode of *Land of the Lost*. Then I happened to travel to Burma and happened to meet Dr. P., who happened to bring me to his home, where his granddaughter happened to recognize me. I was flabbergasted.

But the most astounding thing of all was the reaction of the family. They weren't surprised in the least. Since they had my picture, they thought it perfectly natural that fate should bring me to their door.

ERICA HAGEN
*West Hollywood, California*

# RAINBOW

One bitter winter night when Cochran was about thirteen and Jennie six, I took them to the local ice-cream parlor, one of the few places in our town where college students and locals manage to coexist peacefully, sometimes even cordially. I didn't realize it was fraternity initiation week at the college until, out of the icy night, a young man appeared in the doorway, teeth chattering, clad in nothing but maroon bathing trunks and a filthy white T-shirt covered in bright arcs of mustard and catsup. His hair was sprinkled with chopped onions, and something like syrup or molasses had been poured over his head and was drizzling down into his face and dripping from his earlobes. Standing in the open doorway puffing haze with every breath, this sorry sight announced to the eight or ten tables of customers and the two women behind the counter that he had to find a girl who was willing to go back to his fraternity and dance with him for five minutes, and wouldn't someone — please . . . ?

Every woman in the place stared aghast, squirming uncomfortably, giggling, looking away. The waitresses in their white uniforms practically screamed in unison that they couldn't leave the ice-cream parlor unattended. The miserable fellow then began to cruise from table to table, but no one wanted to meet his eye. It was impossible to look at him without feeling disgust.

Finally, he got to us. "Ma'am?" he said to me, eyes pleading. I could hardly bear to be near him. But suddenly a thought hit me. I leaned down and said to Jennie, "Would you like to go to a fraternity party? It's a kind of dance."

Jennie's green eyes lit up. "Yeah!" she said, breaking into a big smile. Ignoring Cochran's appalled glare, I said to the young man, "This is Jennie. You'll have to walk slow or carry her. She's retarded, and she has cerebral palsy."

Trapped animal. "But, ma'am —" he began to protest. "I'll get her dirty — I mean —" and he spread his arms to show me what he looked like, just in case I hadn't noticed.

"It's okay," I said, "she's washable. So are her clothes."

His eyes darted around frantically, but he realized that this was the only chance he was going to get to make it into the fraternity of his dreams. So I stuffed Jennie into her hooded jacket, and he hoisted her onto one hip, mashing her against the garish clots of condiments on his chest. Then he carried her off into the darkness.

Now I had to contend with Cochran. Always Jennie's fiercest protector, he had been stopped from preventing this disaster only by his larger-than-life sense of propriety. His blue eyes were huge and terrible over his Oreo sundae.

"Mother!" he whispered (he called me that only when he was angry). "You didn't even get his name! You don't even know what fraternity he's going to! Do you have any idea what they do at fraternities? What if he doesn't bring her back?"

"Oh, don't worry," I said with artificial cheer, suddenly realizing how irresponsible I had been. "He'll bring her back."

But my heart sank. Cochran was right. It had been more than a quarter of a century since my honeysuckle days as the sweetheart of Kappa Sig, and I had no idea what went on in fraternities today. Jennie is one of God's innocents, a child who once described a stranger as "a friend I don't know yet." Anyone could take advantage of her. Oh God, why hadn't I stopped to think? I sat watching my root-beer float turn into a polluted lake of foam. Before long, it had become a metaphor for my careless life. My mind tortured me. I saw the headlines in the newspaper: LOCAL CHILD KIDNAPPED . . . SEX MANIAC POSES AS COLLEGE STUDENT . . .

I wondered how many of us in Sweet Things could give an accurate description of the young man to the police. I thought he was maybe five-nine, and I thought I recalled that his hair was a sort of brownish blond. Or was it blondish brown? . . .

"They'll be right back," I assured Cochran.

And soon they were. The young man, already looking a lot less miserable, plopped Jennie down in her chair, thanked me with a jerky, truncated bow, and once again disappeared into the night, leaving behind only his unique perfume and a few bits of diced onion bobbing in my float.

"Jennie!" I exclaimed in delirious relief. "Did you have a good time?"

"Yeah," she said. "We danced, and they had

loud music, and it was great. And Mama? Cochran? Did you notice? *He had a rainbow on his shirt!*"

KATIE LETCHER LYLE
*Lexington, Virginia*

# RESCUED BY GOD

I am a seventy-three-year-old woman. For the first fifty-five years of my life, I suffered from severe anxiety attacks. I lived in fear that I was either going to die of a heart attack or go stark raving mad. Somehow I managed to get married and have five children through it all, but no doctor had been able to diagnose my problem.

I finally began reading articles about panic attacks in 1981, and I was very relieved to discover what the problem was. With a lot of help from family and friends, I began venturing out into a world that had terrified me all my life. Then, a few years later, I had to face what seemed to be an insurmountable challenge.

My mother-in-law had been in the hospital and needed someone to help when she came home. I lived in Chicago, and she lived in Santa Monica, California. I had flown on several business trips with my husband by that time, but this was going to be my first solo flight. My husband upgraded the ticket to first class, assuring me that I would really like it. My anticipatory worry was overwhelming. I had nightmares about going insane and demanding that the pilot land and let me off the plane.

I was shaking so hard when I took my seat that the flight attendant asked if I was all right. I had a very nice seat partner, who told me that the in-flight movie was excellent, and once the movie started, I became totally absorbed in it. We flew into a terrible thunder-and-lightning storm, and I became aware that my seat partner was absolutely paralyzed with fear. I wound up assuring him that we would be just fine because my husband was a B-24 pilot in World War II, and he had told me that planes were so well insulated that they could withstand lightning hits. We landed safely, and I was feeling very elated at having handled the flight so well.

I stayed in Santa Monica for several weeks, and then the time came to begin thinking about my flight home. By my departure date, I was once again a basket case. I thought I would have to call my husband and have him come out to fly home with me. That wasn't an option, so once again I got on the plane. My seat was by the window in the first row of the first-class compartment. As I fought off the urge to get up and run off the plane, I decided to say a prayer. It went something like this: Please, God, help me, and do it now. Right now!

As I sat there with my eyes shut and my hands gripping the armrests, I heard a commotion on the other side of the first-class compartment. The flight attendants were pushing black boxes on wheels to the front of the cabin — the kind used by musicians and other entertainers. I watched as a little old man was escorted to the seats opposite mine. A young man and woman were assisting him, and he was standing with his back to me. They took his overcoat, folded it, and placed it with his hat into the overhead bin. The old man kept his scarf, placed it carefully around his neck, and patted it down on his chest. The young woman took the window seat, and as the old man turned around to face me, he gave me the most beautiful smile. It was George Burns. I had just seen him play the role of God in the movie *Oh God.*

I have prayed for help many times in my life, but God has never answered in such a dramatic way. I guess God figured I needed it under the circumstances. I have never been afraid to fly alone since.

MARY ANN GARRETT
*Elmhurst, Illinois*

# MY STORY

Here is my story, the story I tell you when I know you well enough. I am twenty-three as I write this; when these things happened, I was nineteen, on the verge of twenty.

After my sophomore year of college, I got a summer job working for the forest service in California. I didn't want to drive all the way from Georgia by myself, so I convinced Anna, my best friend of ten years, to ride with me and then fly back home. Neither one of us had ever been across the country. My father filled the car with pounds and pounds of emergency equipment for the road: an axe, a baby-blue "do-it-herself" tool set, flares, emergency lights that would last for thirty-six hours, a fancy jack, a gallon of water, a bent coat hanger (in case the muffler fell off), a small first-aid kit, and a cellular phone that could be plugged into the cigarette lighter. He spent several nights awake, thinking of ways to protect us from everything that could possibly happen to us on the trip.

We set off in early June, driving fast to get out of the Southeast. We began to relax a little when we reached the prairie edge of the western mountains and took our sweet time when we rolled into the deserts of the Southwest. I remember driving between the golden sandstone formations in the heat and Anna putting her palms flat against the wind-

291

shield and exclaiming that it felt like she was holding the sunshine in her hands. That night, we stopped in a tiny Utah town called Blanding. In the hotel, we charted out our route on the map and decided that we would wake up early, speed south through Arizona, and reach Las Vegas by the following night.

We started out just after dawn, heading south on Highway 81. It was a two-lane highway, and as soon as we left Blanding, there wasn't much to look at but sagebrush and distant red hills. I was driving, and Anna was running the video camera. Just before we turned it off that morning, I remarked on how horrific it would be to have a car accident out there — the isolation was palpable, the treeless landscape felt merciless. I was looking forward to seeing trees again.

Suddenly, there was the figure of a man ahead of us on the right side of the road. He seemed to have emerged from the low embankment and was waving his arms at us.

"Oh, Jesus," I said, thinking of my mother's talk-show stories of women being ambushed on the road, "what the hell is this?"

"Rachel," Anna said, her hand on her window, "do you see his face? Do you see that car?"

I turned and I looked. It was the last thing I wanted to see.

The man's face was half-covered with blood. About forty feet behind him was a truck, turned upside down and smashed flat in the sand. I saw bodies scattered around the sagebrush, some as far as fifty feet from the road.

Anna rolled down her window. The man said

that there had been a terrible accident and that they needed help. I pulled the car over and punched on the hazards, while Anna called 911 on the cell phone. I had noticed a sign a moment before; we were five miles north of the Arizona border. Anna asked the man how many people were down there. I heard her tell the tiny phone, "I think it's about fifteen people." There was no one else around and nothing in sight for miles. We had not seen another car since starting out that morning. When Anna hung up the phone, it was only us and them. The man said his name was Juan.

The first emergency vehicles would arrive about forty minutes later. Over the course of the morning, they would come one by one, running out of tape and backboards and room for bodies. A few people would stop to help. It was a one-car accident, a covered truck carrying seventeen Mexican immigrants that had been traveling all night. Three of them died that day, and fourteen suffered internal injuries, lacerations, and broken bones.

I got out of the car and made my way down the embankment, trembling, carrying the little water we had. As I reached the flat ground, a girl my age came running at me. She was the only woman in the group, and she had sprung up from the side of a young man who was stretched out on his back on the ground. There was blood on her face and her mouth and she had a crazed look in her eyes. She was speaking in Spanish, and she took the water from me. Her long black hair flowed behind her. I followed her back to him and knelt beside her as she poured water over his face, screaming something over and over in Spanish. I looked up for a second. Other men lay silently on their stomachs in the sand. The young man's breathing was labored and clogged, and something told me that his insides were completely broken. I ran back to the car to get our supplies.

When I reached the car and pulled out the prepackaged first-aid kit, which was about the size of two baking potatoes, I started to laugh. I unzipped it and looked at the small, wrapped gauze pads and the Band-Aids, and I was gripped by a sudden, overwhelming feeling of self-hatred. I imagined myself crawling under the car and waiting for the ambulances to arrive. This moment seemed to last, but it couldn't have. Another feeling rushed up from a different place and lifted me out of myself, and I knew that I would go down there, and that nothing I would see could make me turn away.

For the next four hours, Anna and I ran from one body to another, using Juan as an interpreter, telling men to be still or asking if they were cold. Anna and I pulled out all the towels and blankets that I had packed for the summer, tucking them around the men who were beginning to shake from shock. There were several gruesome sights. I found myself putting my face in the sand to make eye contact and moving my hands softly over backs and heads, speaking English in what I hoped were soothing tones, knowing instinctively that if you feel alone, it is easier to decide to die.

When the ambulances arrived we helped the paramedics load the men onto backboards, tried to keep the sand off the tape, and stayed with the men who had to wait on the side of the road for the next round. One man's breathing sounded nearly impossible, his eyes were like glass marbles, and his mouth was coated with blood. I positioned my face directly above his and gently rubbed his chest, encouraging him to keep breathing.

The boy who was broken died while I watched his nineteen-year-old wife screaming and pushing up on his lips and gums as if looking for life in his mouth. I sat still for a moment, stunned and paralyzed. When I understood that he was dead, I ran to another silent body turned facedown in the sand.

As I put my head down to speak to one man who was lying crushed on his stomach and whose forearm was snapped in half, I glanced up and saw the deeply lined face of an old man with long gray hair staring at me, his head resting on the sand. I scrambled to get there and shut his eyes, to get one of the sheets to put over him, to do anything for him so he was not just lying there dead and unnoticed.

There was a boy who had been thrown farther than anyone else, who was being strapped to a backboard by the paramedics. I spoke to him, smiling brightly and assuring him that he was going to be FINE! His eyes and mouth were filled with blood, but he seemed to see me and he seemed to smile back. He died later in the helicopter that was taking him to Grand Junction.

By the time all the others had been taken away, Anna and I had fallen in love with our interpreter, Juan. He was twenty-seven years old, spoke perfect English, and had a head of thick, dark curls.

As a female Navajo paramedic tended to him with Anna and me on either side, he said he was embarrassed that he had gone so long without a haircut. Anna went and got his bag out of the crushed truck, a plastic grocery bag with socks in it. He had four lacerations on the top of his head; his thick hair had helped control the bleeding. He was heading into delirium when they finally loaded him into the ambulance. When he realized that we were being separated, panic came into his eyes and he reached out to me from the stretcher.

"Where are you going?" he asked, and I had to say that we were getting back on the road. I said it because I didn't know what else I could do. I couldn't follow him into the world of the hospital. I had had enough. I was ready to return to the world of safety, to blood and bones neatly contained within bodies, to trees and comfort and mercy.

"I cannot pay you," Juan said, "but God will repay you."

The smell of the man stayed with me, despite repeated washing. I could smell it emanating from my wrists while I drove, the bitter smell of old sweat and poverty. Our leg muscles cramped up in the night from the hours of tremulous running back and forth across an incline of sand, and the sand mixed with my own sweat is still embedded in the sandals I was wearing that day.

Anna and I reached Las Vegas that night, exhausted and shaken. I wept on the phone to my father, saying over and over, "It was so awful." That was the only time I cried about the accident. One year later, I woke up in a cold sweat in the middle of the night with a voice pounding inside my head, repeating over and over the phrase, "You have seen a man die."

What is to be done with that? What is to be done with the events of that morning, swallowed back up into time as we drove away, things never to be heard of again — no segment on the nightly news, no articles in any paper we ever saw. It might as well have been a dream we both had.

What do you do with a story like that? There is no lesson, no moral, barely even an ending. You want to tell it, hear it told, but you don't know why.

RACHEL WATSON
*Washington, D.C.*

# SMALL WORLD

In the summer of 1983, I had just finished my third year of architecture school and had to find a six-month internship, I had grown up and gone through my entire education in the Midwest, but I had been to New York City once on a class field trip and thought it seemed like a pretty good place to live. So, armed with little more than an inflated ego and my school portfolio, I was off to Manhattan, oblivious to the bad economy and the fact that the city was overflowing with young architects.

I arranged a ride from Kalamazoo to New York with a former girlfriend who was moving to Boston. The morning we were scheduled to leave, I woke up with miserable stomach pains, but I decided to make the trip anyway. As it turned out, I was an awful traveling companion. I had acute diarrhea for the entire journey. I think my friend was relieved when she dropped me off at the Greyhound station in White Plains, where I caught a bus into the city.

I got a room at the YMCA on Thirty-fourth Street, the Sloan House. It was a sunny Sunday afternoon, but it was brutally hot and humid. My room faced a smelly inner courtyard and there was no air. I was a slave to the toilet and didn't dare leave the building. I lay on the lumpy cot in my room with the door ajar, knowing I should have been out exploring the city before starting all my interviews the next day.

I was in this pathetic horizontal position when there was a knock at the door. A guy about my age, with curly black hair and a backpack slung over his shoulder, poked his head through the door and invited himself in. I was a little leery but welcomed the company. He sat down on the end of the cot, and we made small talk. I told him where I was from, where I had gone to school — that kind of stuff. After a little while, there was a lull in the conversation, and after a few seconds of silence, he asked me if it was okay with me if he did some coke. I was surprised but said, "Sure." I expected to see a line or two drawn out on my desk, but instead I witnessed something I had seen only once, in a movie. He got out a bent spoon, a lighter, and a used syringe. Then he took off his belt. He explained that he was actually mixing cocaine with a little heroin. "Not just a high or low," he said, "but an elevator ride."

As he went through the steps of preparing his injection, he told me he had been banned from the Y but occasionally sneaked in when he didn't have anywhere else to go. He had dropped out of college and was driving a cab for a living. He hoped to earn enough money to buy a medallion and get his own cab. Before succumbing to his high, he looked at me through half-closed lids and murmured, "You know, my best friend goes to the University of Michigan and I think his girlfriend is from Kalamazoo." Then he blacked out, slumped at the foot of the bed.

Meanwhile, I had put two and two together. It all sounded too familiar. I knew who the girlfriend

299

was. I knew who the best friend at the University of Michigan was. A friend of mine from Kalamazoo had gone to school there, and when he came home for the summer, he had told me about one of his suitemates, a private-school boy from New York. The suitemate's best friend had been going to Vassar or one of those high-buck colleges back East. Halfway through the school year, the best friend had left school, cut off contact with his parents, and sold everything he owned to buy drugs. He had disappeared into New York City. I had always assumed the story was one of those bits of folklore you hear on college campuses.

But now, here I was inside the story, and I couldn't believe it. I hadn't been away from Michigan for forty-eight hours, I was in a huge city, and the needle in the urban haystack found me while I was incapacitated with diarrhea in a dingy room at the Y.

Every fifteen or twenty minutes, the guy would wake from his stupor. He would pick up the conversation for a little as though nothing had happened, and then he would nod out again. The first time he came to, I said, "Your best friend's name is Dave and his girlfriend is Stephanie. She and I knew each other when we were kids — we went to music camp together."

"Yeah," he mumbled. "Wow. What a small world." Then he was out again.

After he had been there for an hour or so, I was starting to wonder how I would ever get rid of him. Finally, he woke up, stretched, and packed up his backpack. He said he was off to Grand Central Station, where he would pose as someone trying to leave town who didn't have quite enough money for a ticket. That was his way of bumming change. He offered to come back later with a sandwich and asked if he could hide his needle in my room. I let him do this to get rid of him faster, but as soon as he was gone, I threw out the needle in the bathroom. After that, I kept the door closed, and the next morning I arranged to move to a different room.

I saw him again only once, from my new window facing the street.

I never landed an internship that summer, and eventually I ran out of money and had to go home. I arranged with my friend John, the one who had told me the story about the guy in the first place, to meet me in upstate New York. I spent my last dime buying my train ticket in Grand Central Station. But at least I didn't have to bum any extra change.

PAUL K. HUMISTON<br>
Minneapolis, Minnesota

# CHRISTMAS MORNING, 1949

A light drizzle was falling as my sister Jill and I ran out of the Methodist Church, eager to get home and play with the presents Santa had left for us and our baby sister, Sharon. Across the street from the church was a Pan American gas station where the Greyhound bus stopped. It was closed for Christmas, but I noticed a family standing outside the locked door, huddled under the narrow overhang in an attempt to keep dry. I wondered briefly why they were there but then forgot about them as I raced to keep up with Jill.

Once we got home, there was barely time to enjoy our presents. We had to go off to our grandparents' house for our annual Christmas dinner. As we drove down the highway through town, I noticed that the family was still there, standing outside the closed gas station.

My father was driving very slowly down the highway. The closer we got to the turnoff for my grandparents' house, the slower the car went. Suddenly, my father U-turned in the middle of the road and said, "I can't stand it!"

"What?" asked my mother.

"It's those people back there at the Pan Am, standing in the rain. They've got children. It's Christmas. I can't stand it."

When my father pulled into the service station, I saw that there were five of them: the parents and

302

three children — two girls and a small boy.

My father rolled down his window. "Merry Christmas," he said.

"Howdy," the man replied. He was very tall and had to stoop slightly to peer into the car.

Jill, Sharon, and I stared at the children, and they stared back at us.

"You waiting on the bus?" my father asked.

The man said that they were. They were going to Birmingham, where he had a brother and prospects of a job.

"Well, that bus isn't going to come along for several hours, and you're getting wet standing here. Winborn's just a couple miles up the road. They've got a shed with a cover there, and some benches," my father said. "Why don't y'all get in the car, and I'll run you up there."

The man thought about it for a moment, and then he beckoned to his family. They climbed into the car. They had no luggage, only the clothes they were wearing.

Once they were settled in, my father looked back over his shoulder and asked the children if Santa had found them yet. Three glum faces mutely gave him his answer.

"Well, I didn't think so," my father said, winking at my mother, "because when I saw Santa this morning, he told me that he was having trouble finding y'all, and he asked me if he could leave your toys at my house. We'll just go get them before I take you to the bus stop."

All at once, the three children's faces lit up, and they began to bounce around in the backseat, laughing and chattering.

When we got out of the car at our house, the three children ran through the front door and straight to the toys that were spread out under our Christmas tree. One of the girls spied Jill's doll and immediately hugged it to her breast. I remember that the little boy grabbed Sharon's ball. And the other girl picked up something of mine. All this happened a long time ago, but the memory of it remains clear. That was the Christmas when my sisters and I learned the joy of making others happy.

My mother noticed that the middle child was wearing a short-sleeved dress, so she gave the girl Jill's only sweater to wear.

My father invited them to join us at our grandparents' for Christmas dinner, but the parents refused. Even when we all tried to talk them into coming, they were firm in their decision.

Back in the car, on the way to Winborn, my father asked the man if he had money for bus fare.

His brother had sent tickets, the man said.

My father reached into his pocket and pulled out two dollars, which was all he had left until his next payday. He pressed the money into the man's hand. The man tried to give it back, but my father insisted. "It'll be late when you get to Birmingham, and these children will be hungry before then. Take it. I've been broke before, and I know what it's like when you can't feed your family."

We left them there at the bus stop in Winborn. As we drove away, I watched out the window as long as I could, looking back at the little girl hugging her new doll.

SYLVIA SEYMOUR AKIN
*Memphis, Tennessee*

304

# BROOKLYN ROBERTS

He called himself Brooklyn Roberts. I got curious about him because he wanted to remain hidden. Then I heard he was shot and killed for almost nothing.

When I was twenty-three, I got involved in a nonprofit cooperative coffeehouse that served home-baked goods, coffee, and tea. It was also the land of the eternal open mike. The only rule about playing there was that the music had to be acoustic.

Eventually we would be run out of the house where we had set up shop because the neighborhood association didn't like the "hippie" types hanging around. That was New Orleans in 1975; things got there a little late.

But when the coffeehouse was still thriving, Brooklyn Roberts used to sign up for the open mike now and then. He was thin, fine-boned, losing his dirty-blond hair too soon. I guessed that he was a little older than I was. He always came looking like a laborer from the early 1900s, dressed in old-fashioned, working-class Saturday-evening clothes. His performances on the guitar and piano were polished. He played rootsy blues, Robert Johnson tunes — that sort of thing. He'd finish his set, collect whatever tips he'd made, pack up his things, and leave. No, he'd disappear. Always.

I once asked him to play at a benefit for the

coffeehouse that was going to be held in a local park. He arrived, spiffily dressed as usual, carrying a little suitcase in addition to his guitar. The path to our tiny stage crossed an area where the children's railroad track ran. As he approached our gathering, he deliberately started walking between the rails of the miniature track. He looked up at me and smiled. He was in his persona, walking on a railroad track like a Depression-era wanderer.

He played a great set of old-time blues that day, interjecting an occasional sleight-of-hand trick. At one point, he flipped a silver dollar in the air and bounced it off the heel of his shoe and back up in the air into his hand. When he caught it, he appeared as amazed as the audience. He finished his set and disappeared. Lots of people wanted to talk to him, but he just vanished.

Later that year I attended an early incarnation of the New Orleans Jazz and Heritage Festival. I was waiting for Muddy Waters to play his set when I spied Brooklyn Roberts near the edge of the stage, talking to a stagehand or manager. I turned away to talk to some friends. Minutes later, when I looked back, Brooklyn Roberts was at the piano playing some wonderful ragtime and jellyroll blues. He played for about five minutes. I guessed that he had talked the stage manager into letting him play until Muddy was ready for his set. He'd had no introduction, nothing. Brooklyn Roberts just got up there and played, and then he disappeared.

The next year, I helped organize a benefit for New Orleans street musicians. My group performed at it, and so did Brooklyn Roberts. Again he played a terrific set of old-time blues on the piano; again he disappeared at the end of the set. He had come dressed in his usual period attire, but later, when I spotted him sitting in the audience a few rows away from me, he had changed into modern clothes and was wearing a floppy Gilligan-style rag hat. I called to him, wanting to congratulate him on his great set. He stayed where he was and smiled in acknowledgment. Then he just turned away and pulled down his hat a little farther.

Years later, after I'd left New Orleans, I asked a friend about him. She told me that he'd been shot and killed for his money and his jacket. My friend told me she'd heard that he'd said to his assailants, "You wouldn't shoot me for my jacket, would you?" And they did.

I made some other inquiries. All I ever found out was that he had been a well-liked coach — Coach Bob — at the local Jewish community center. I still have his business card. In the four corners are floral ironwork designs, and his name appears in capital letters in the center: BROOKLYN ROBERTS.

This is all I know about him.

ADOLPH LOPEZ
*New Orleans, Louisiana*

# $1,380 PER NIGHT, DOUBLE OCCUPANCY

A summer in a Manhattan hospital with ailments too boring to discuss. Eight roommates. One realization. The semiprivate room, the repository for all but the very rich or the very infectious, is the great leveler of society. It's where people who normally wouldn't mix suddenly find themselves sleeping together — and sharing a toilet.

"I'VE BEEN GOING TO THE BATHROOM FOUR TIMES A DAY FOR SIXTEEN DAYS AND HAVE HAD A PAIN IN MY ABDOMEN FOR FOURTEEN DAYS!" my first roommate cheerfully shouted at anyone who came near. But then he always shouted. Roommate Number One was an ex-Forty-second Street hustler, thirty years old, and looked forty-five. The fact that he hadn't used the john for thirty-six hours after his arrival didn't seem to lower the volume any. He just kept shouting about his supposed diarrhea, until finally he produced a turd the size of Kansas, which I know because he never flushed. His doctors said there was nothing wrong with him. He shouted louder. They tried to send him home. He responded by filing a grievance. Screaming and tantrums ensued, until a mysterious visit from a nurse and a man in a white coat.

"We're just teaching him how to give injections," the nurse assured him as the novice whipped out an enormous syringe.

"Oh my *God!*" shrieked Roommate One as the needle missed its mark.

On the third day he was still demanding to be allowed to stay when his friends with the bad haircuts arrived. They took Number One on furtive trips to the public bathroom for undefined illicit purposes, and it was after one of these excursions that he simply didn't come back. No one seemed surprised. They just got his bed ready for the next occupant.

Roommate Number Two was a retired and heavily sedated monsignor. He had been brought in from a nursing home and had no idea where he was. "Sometimes I think I like you, and sometimes I think I hate you," he droned groggily to a nurse's aide he had never seen before. Pausing to consider, he then delivered his verdict: "Today, I hate you."

A social worker came and shouted in his ear. "MONSIGNOR! I'M GOING TO GET SOME ICE CREAM! WOULD YOU LIKE SOME?" He perked up. "CHOCOLATE OR STRAW-BERRY?" The monsignor thought chocolate. "OKAY, I'LL BE BACK IN ABOUT TWENTY MINUTES!" and she scuffled from the room. About two seconds later, a nurse came in to administer some medication.

"Where's my ice cream?" demanded the priest.

"I don't have any ice cream. Just pills," she answered. There came a low growl from the monsignor's bed.

"Bitch," he hissed.

Roommate Number Three had recently been a homeless drug addict and was nothing but bones held together by a bag of skin. "Ninety-nine pounds!" chirped the nurse after she weighed the five-foot-eight man, who could have been any-where from twenty-seven to fifty years old — he was just too ragged to tell. He mostly slept, wak-ing only long enough to complain about the food or to spar with the technician trying to draw blood. "I know what you do with that blood," he told him ominously. "You sell it — five dollars a tube — you can't fool me."

With increasing urgency, Roommate Three's doctors implored him to give his formal assent for an HIV test, as they legally couldn't administer one without it. "If we had a diagnosis, we could prescribe medication that could really help you," they pleaded, but he was unmoved, seeming to think that HIV tests were part of some sort of evil conspiracy hatched by the medical establishment. Every day they begged some more. Every day he declined. I wanted to plead with him, too, but fig-ured that since I had overheard confidential infor-mation, it wasn't my place. Still, whenever he dragged himself out of bed to go to the bathroom, I'd watch him carefully, ready to call the nurse in case he toppled over. Somehow, he never did. Roommate Three was finally released to a shelter for homeless people with medical problems. I prayed that someone there would convince him to get the help he needed.

Roommate Number Four was pleasant, chatty, and covered in sores. He had a girlfriend who al-ways came at mealtimes. "I'll just taste this to see if you'll like it," she would tell him as she polished off his lunch. She talked nonstop while she ate, rattling off gossip about friends, about television, about nothing at all. Eventually she would whisper, "I've got the stuff," and the two of them would limp off to the public bathroom with the "stuff" concealed in her pocket.

Whatever his girlfriend's faults, Number Four was touchingly devoted to her. So much so that he carefully saved his nail clippings in a little bottle, just for her. "She likes to chew on fingernails but doesn't want to ruin her own," he explained, "so I give her mine."

"Oooh, these are *good* ones!" I heard her exclaim.

I always made sure the curtain between our beds was tightly closed.

Meanwhile, Miss Thomas had taken up residence in the room across the hall. Miss Thomas screamed. All night. Every night. And with her door directly opposite ours, it was like she was right in the room with us. "Evelyn!" she'd wail. "Evelyn! Evelyn! My butt hurts! Evelyn! Oh, the pain. The PAIN! Eve-LYYN! My BUTT hurts! EVE-L-Y-N-N!"

At first I felt sorry for this poor, deranged woman, obviously in agony. That is, until I heard her on the phone the next morning speaking in a normal, reasoned voice, "Oh, the service around here is horrible," she said. "Last night I had to scream. I just screamed and screamed until someone came in." That night, Miss Thomas was thirsty. "Evelyn! I need a glass of water! Evelyn! I'm THIRSTY! EVE-L-Y-Y-N-N!" I broke hospital regulations and shut my door.

Roommate Number Five was a soap star. Blond, chiseled, perfect teeth — the nurses were all over him for autographs. He had a cell phone, a personal assistant, and a hospital administration at his beck and call. "You can order out if you don't like the food," the beaming admissions-office staff said as they handed him a stack of restaurant menus.

*"I've* been here three weeks and nobody ever told that to *me!"* I called out, but they paid no attention.

The soap star had an infected testicle — a fact that he would happily share with anyone at any time without any provocation whatsoever. To a blood technician, "I knew they hung low, but not *that* low!" To me, "When I felt them brushing against my *knee,* I figured I should get them checked out!" On the phone, "The doctor said it's probably because I haven't been having enough sex, but I know *that's* wrong!" Everyone was dazzled. The only things missing were eight-by-ten glossies.

That night, Miss Thomas was cold. "Evelyn! I need a blanket! Evelyn! I'm so COLD! Get me a BLANKET! EVE-L-Y-Y-N-N!" Early the next morning, the obviously chagrined administration told the soap star that they were moving him to a distant, private room — at hospital expense — so he would "be more comfortable."

*"I've* been here three weeks . . ." I started, but they ignored me again.

That night, when Miss Thomas started screaming for Evelyn, a frustrated voice was raised in response. "Miss Thomas, you just have to stop all that screaming! We tell you to use your call button every night but you just keep on making all this noise! There are people trying to sleep, you know! Now if you don't be quiet, I'm just going to shut your door and NEVER come back to help you, and you know how much you'd hate that!" And then, as she turned to make her exit, one parting shot: "And another thing. My name's *Yvonne!*"

Roommate Number Six was moved up from intensive care. I think he had been in a coma. "Do you remember how you got hurt?" a social worker asked him. A long pause, and then a halting voice said, "Do I live in New York?" Later, he asked the overworked resident, newly assigned to him, "How long have I been here?" The resident didn't even look up when he gave the curt reply, "I don't know, a couple of days." Actually, I had heard someone say that Number Six had been there for weeks. "I began to remember something . . ." he started to say, but the doctor cut him off. "Listen, I can't talk now, I've got other patients to see." I never heard what Number Six began to remember.

One thing Number Six consistently forgot was that he was strapped into bed because he had a broken shoulder. Sometimes, on my trips to the bathroom, I would find him hanging off the side of his bed, tangled in his cloth restraints, looking mournful and confused. "Are you in trouble?" I'd ask, and he'd nod his head. "Do you want me to get your nurse?" and I'd trot off and find her. Finally they came and strapped him in so tight that he could barely move, and he, forgetting where he was, would crap all over the sheets. Eventually the nurse's aide would hustle in, spewing fury.

"What's the matter with you?" she'd shout. "Why do you make all this mess and make us come and clean you up? What are you, a baby?" After a couple of humiliations like this he got a little gun-shy. I'd pass by his bed and find him covered in shit, looking utterly miserable. "Are you in trouble? Do you want me to get your nurse?" and he'd nod, slowly, while trying to hold back the tears.

Roommate Number Seven was an older, working-class man from Queens. He had been undergoing chemotherapy for his cancer and spent the first couple of days throwing up. "I'm sick of this," he told his wife, miserably. "What's the point of going on if this is how I'm going to live?" And then he'd retch again. With me he was cordial and as pleasant as can be expected, but his poor wife received the brunt of his frustration. "What the hell is this?" he'd snap after she'd traveled for an hour to visit him. "I said *pitted* grapes! How can you be so stupid?"

But he started to get better, and for two days he was downright cheerful. That is, until the third morning, when his speech suddenly started slurring, he introduced me to a daughter who wasn't there, and then fell asleep while the doctor was talking to him. When he woke up, all he said was, "I miss Paris." I couldn't have agreed with him more. They whisked him off to another floor that afternoon.

Roommate Number Eight arrived late that night. He had a deep, kind-sounding voice with a lilting Latino accent. He also had long, painted nails, a bouffant hairdo, and preferred to be called Cynthia. He was just twenty years old and was running a high fever because one of his breast implants had become infected. He also had AIDS, was on welfare, and was estranged from his family. Yet through it all he remained remarkably calm and philosophical. When I finally went home the next day, he was patiently fielding phone calls for Roommate Seven, who had been moved so abruptly that no one, including his wife, knew where he was. "He's on another floor now, sweetheart," he said soothingly to some bewildered relative. "You just call the switchboard and they'll give you his number." I left him a couple of magazines that someone had brought me and all the juice I had been hoarding. "You're leaving, just as I was getting to know you," he said wistfully, but I was anxious to get home.

Besides, I knew he'd be having plenty of company soon.

BRUCE EDWARD HALL
*New York, New York*

315

# A SHOT IN THE LIGHT

Summer 1978: I was traveling through the Southwest as a jewelry and giftware salesman, selling a wide range of items from Austrian crystals to feather earrings. On the way to Los Angeles from Las Vegas, I stopped to help a motorist whose car had broken down in the Mojave Desert. He was down on his luck, had no plans and nowhere to go, so I let him travel with me.

His name was Ray, and he looked to be in his early twenties. He was small, muscular, wiry, and slightly gaunt, as if underfed. I felt sorry for him, and in the three days we were together, I grew to trust him. I even started sending him on errands while I visited stores to sell my wares. At one point, I gave him some of my clothes, and it pleased him to have something new to wear. He seemed calm and mostly satisfied.

The third night, we were camped out near Puddingstone Reservoir east of Claremont. I was sitting on the floor in the back of the large van, moving things around in the cupboards to make more room for the clothes, books, food, sample boxes, and my passenger's duffel bag and travel gear.

There was a loud explosion, and I felt a sharp, searing blow to the top of my head. Had the gas stove exploded? I looked up, but it was intact. Then I looked at Ray sitting in the driver's seat, and I saw the black gun in his hand. His arm was resting on the back of the seat, aiming the pistol at my face. A bullet had hit me! At first, I thought he was warning me — that he was going to rob me. That suddenly seemed fine. Take it all, I thought. Take it all. Just leave me outside and drive away.

Another explosion shook me, and my ears rang with a terrible, high-pitched whine. I felt blood dripping down my face, and the top of my head throbbed. He's not warning me, I realized. He's going to kill me. I am going to die.

There was no place to hide. I was stuck in an uncomfortable position surrounded by cabinets. There was nothing I could do. I heard myself whisper, "Relax. It's out of your control. Breathe. Stay awake." My thoughts turned to death, and to God. "Thy will, not my will, be done." I let my body go, and I started to relax, to slump back. I watched my breath, in and out, in and out, in and out. . . .

I began preparing for my death. I asked to be forgiven by anyone I had hurt and offered my forgiveness to everyone who had hurt me throughout my life. It was a full-color fast-reverse movie reel of my entire twenty-six years. I thought about my parents, my brothers and sisters, my lovers, my friends. I said good-bye. I said, "I love you."

Another explosion shook the van, and my body pulsed. I was not hit. The bullet missed me by a fraction of an inch, penetrating the cupboard I was leaning against. I relaxed back into my reverie. My luck could not hold out. Three bullets to go, if it was a revolver. I could only hope that the gun wasn't a semiautomatic.

Nothing mattered anymore but to be at peace. My van, my money, my business, my knowledge, my personal history, my freedom — all became worthless, meaningless, so much dust in the wind.

All I had of value was my body and my life, and that was soon to be gone. My attention was focused on the spark of light I called my Self, and my consciousness began to expand outward, extending my awareness in space and time. I heard my instructions clearly: STAY AWAKE AND KEEP BREATHING.

I prayed to my God, to the Great Spirit, to receive me with open arms. Love and light flowed through me, spreading out like a lighthouse beam, illuminating everything around me. The light grew inside me, and I expanded like a huge balloon until the van and its contents seemed small. A sense of peace and acceptance filled me. I knew I was close to leaving my body. I could sense the time line of my life, both backward and forward. I saw the next bullet, a short distance into the future, leave the gun, jet toward my left temple, and exit with brains and blood on the right side of my head. I was filled with awe. To see life from this expanded perspective was like looking down into a dollhouse, seeing all the rooms at once, all the detail, so real and so unreal at the same time. I looked into the warm and welcoming golden light with calm and acceptance.

The fourth explosion shattered the silence, and my head was pushed violently to the side. The ringing in my ears was deafening. Warm blood rushed down my head and onto my arms and thighs, dripping onto the floor. But strangely, I found myself back in my body, not out of it. Still surrounded by light, love, and peace, I began looking inside my skull, trying to find the holes. Perhaps I could see light through them? I did a quick check of my feelings, abilities, thoughts, and sensations, looking for what might be missing. Surely the bullet had affected me. My head was throbbing, but I felt strangely normal.

I decided to look at my assassin, to look death in the face. I picked up my head and turned my eyes toward him. He was shocked. Jumping up from his seat, he shouted, "Why aren't you dead, man? You're supposed to be dead!"

"Here I am," I said quietly.

"That's too weird! It's just like my dream this morning! I kept shooting at him, but he wouldn't die! But it wasn't you in the dream, it was somebody else!"

This was very strange. Who was writing the script? I wondered. I began to speak slowly and calmly, trying to settle him down. If I could get him talking, I thought, maybe he wouldn't shoot again. He kept yelling, "Shut up! Just shut up!" as he peered out the windows into the darkness. He nervously walked closer to me, gun in hand, examining my bloody head, trying to understand why the four bullets he had pumped into me hadn't finished me off.

I could still feel blood oozing down my face and could hear it dripping onto my shoulder. Ray said, "I don't know why you aren't dead, man. I shot you four times!"

"Maybe I'm not supposed to die," I said calmly.

"Yeah, but I shot you!" he said, with disappointment and confusion in his voice. "I don't know what to do."

"What do you want to do?" I asked.

"I wanted to kill you, man, to take this van and drive away. Now I don't know." He seemed worried, uncertain. He was beginning to slow down, to become less jumpy.

"Why did you want to kill me?"

"Because you had everything, and I had nothing. And I was tired of having nothing. This was my chance to have it all." He was still pacing back and forth in the van, looking out the windows at the black night outside.

"What do you want to do now?" I asked.

"I don't know, man," he complained. "Maybe I should take you to the hospital."

My heart leapt at this chance, this opportunity — a way out. "Okay," I said, not wanting to make him feel out of control. I wanted it to be his idea, not mine. I knew that his anger sprang from feeling out of control, and I didn't want to make him feel angry.

"Why were you so nice to me, man?"

"Because you're a person, Ray."

"But I wanted to kill you! I kept taking out my gun and pointing it at you, when you were asleep or not looking. But you were being so nice to me, I couldn't do it."

My time sense was altered. I realized that I had no idea how long it had been since the first bullet. After what felt like many minutes, Ray came up to me, still in my crouched, locked-in position, and said, "Okay, man, I'm going to take you to a hospital. But I don't want you to move, so I'm going

320

to put some stuff on you so you can't move, okay?"

Now he was asking my permission. "Okay," I said softly. He began taking various boxes filled with samples and stacked them around me. "Are you okay?" he asked.

"Yeah, I'm okay. A little uncomfortable, but it's all right."

"Okay, man. I'm going to take you to a hospital I know of. Now don't move. And don't die on me, okay?"

"Okay," I promised. I knew I wouldn't die. This light, this power inside me was so strong, so certain. Each breath felt like my first, not my last. I was going to survive. I knew it. Ray lowered the pop-top of the van, secured the straps, and started up the engine. I could feel the van backing up on the dirt road, finding the pavement, and moving forward to my freedom.

He drove on and on — to where, I had no idea. Were we bound for a hospital, as he said, or toward some horrible fate? If he was capable of killing me with a gun, he was capable of lying, or worse. How did he know where to go? We were in Claremont. Los Angeles was over an hour away. I used that hour to replay the scenes and analyze the past three days, trying to understand what had happened and why.

Eventually I felt the van slow, pull over, and stop. The engine was turned off. Silence filled the space. I waited. It was still dark outside. We had not pulled into a driveway. There were no lights. This was not a hospital.

Ray walked back toward me with his gun in his

hand. He pulled away one of the boxes and sat down on the foam bed, facing me. He looked distraught, head hanging down. His words cut deep through my cloud of hope. "I have to kill you, man," he said calmly.

"Why?" I asked quietly.

"If I take you to the hospital, they'll put me back in jail. I can't go back to jail, man. I can't."

"They wouldn't put you in jail if you take me to the hospital," I said slowly, still feigning injury, passivity. I knew that I might find an opening, a moment when I could surprise him, overpower him, take away his gun. As long as he didn't know I was okay, I had an advantage.

"Oh yes they would, man. They'd know I shot you, and they'd lock me up."

"We don't have to tell them. I won't tell them."

"I can't trust you, man. I wish I could, but I can't. I can't go back to jail, that's all. I have to kill you." He seemed forlorn. This was not where he wanted to be. He wasn't making any moves. His gun hung limply from his hand, pointed down toward the floor. The boxes were still stacked around me. I couldn't judge how much strength I had, whether it would be enough to push out and wrestle him down. He was small but strong. Was he still full of adrenaline? That would make him even stronger. My strength lay in words, in verbal swordplay. If I could keep him talking, he wouldn't take stronger action.

"Maybe I could go into the hospital alone, Ray. You wouldn't even have to be there. You could get away."

"No, man," he said, shaking his head. "As soon

322

as you told them, they'd come find me. They'd track me down."

I was silent. That didn't work, I thought.

He said, "Why aren't you dead, man? I shot you *four times* in the head. How come you're still alive and talking? You should be dead! I know I didn't miss." He looked again at my head, taking it in one hand and turning it to the left and right. "Does it hurt?" he asked. He seemed genuinely concerned.

"Yeah, it hurts," I lied. "But I think I'm going to be okay."

"Well, I don't know what to do. I can't take you to the hospital. I can't just let you go, because you'll go to the police. Why were you so damn nice to me, man? No one's ever been that nice to me before. It made it harder to kill you. You kept buying me stuff and giving me stuff. I just couldn't decide when to do it."

Not if, but when.

"What would you do with all this stuff if you had it, Ray?" I asked.

"I could go home and be somebody, I could do stuff. I'd have enough money to buy my way out of there, man." Ray began to talk. He talked about his home in East Los Angeles, the poverty around him, his anger, the schoolteachers who made him feel stupid, his father who drank too much and beat him, and being tough on the streets. He talked about joining the army, how that was supposed to make it work, but he couldn't stand being told what to do all the time, so he went AWOL. He talked about dealing drugs, and drug deals going bad, and how he ripped off his dealer

323

buddies. That's why he had to leave L.A., because they were looking for him. He talked about stealing his father's gun and money before he left, then he realized there was no place to hide, so he decided to turn back. Maybe he could do one more rip-off and get rich. He just needed one hit, one sucker. If his target was rich enough, he could pay off the dealers and start over. So he decided to kill whoever stopped. Whoever came by to help him. Me.

The night had turned to morning, the sky shifting slowly from indigo to blue. The sound of chirping birds made me grateful to be alive.

"I'm pretty stiff and sore, Ray. I'd feel better if I could get up and stretch." I was still in the same position I had been in for six hours. Dried blood was plastered to my hair and face, my shins hurt from being pushed against the edge of a cupboard door, and my back was stiff and throbbing.

"Okay, man, I'm going to let you up, but don't do anything stupid, okay?"

"Okay, Ray. You just tell me what to do and I'll do it."

Remind him that he is in control. Don't let him feel out of control. Look for an opening.

He moved the boxes from around me, stepped back with the gun in his hand, and opened the door. I crawled slowly out of the van, stretching upright for the first time. How beautiful the world was to my new eyes. Everything shone as if made of sparkling crystal.

We had stopped on a residential street near a small pond at the bottom of an embankment. He gestured down the dirt trail that led to the water.

324

As I walked down the steep incline I thought, "Is this death again, tapping on my shoulder? Will he shoot me in the back and push me into the water?" I felt weak and vulnerable, yet simultaneously immortal and impervious to his bullets. I walked erect and unafraid. He followed me to the water's edge and stood by as I squatted down and rinsed my bloodied hands and face, splashing cool, fresh water on myself. I stood up slowly and faced Ray. He looked at me curiously.

"What would you do if I handed you this gun right now?" he asked, holding the gun out to me.

My answer was my first thought: "I'd throw it out into the water," I said.

"Aren't you mad at me, man?" he asked. He seemed incredulous.

"No, why should I be mad?"

"I shot you, man, you ought to be angry! I'd be fucking furious! You wouldn't want to kill me if I gave you this gun?"

"No, Ray, I wouldn't. Why should I? I have my life and you have yours."

"I don't understand you, man. You are really weird, really different than anyone I've ever met before. And I don't know why you didn't die when I shot you." Silence. Better left unanswered. As we stood at the water's edge, I realized that Ray had undergone a transformation as deep as the one I had. We were no longer the same people we had been the day before.

"What should we do now, Ray?"

"I don't know, man. I can't take you to the hospital. I can't let you go. I don't know what to do."

So we continued our talk, seeking a solution to

his dilemma. We explored the possibilities — what could we agree to? I made suggestions, he told me why they wouldn't work. I made other suggestions. He listened, considered, rejected, and relented. We sought a compromise.

Ultimately, we found a bargain we could agree on: I would let him go, and he would let me go. I promised not to turn him in or report him to the police, but on one condition — he had to promise that he would *never* do anything like this again. He promised. What choice did he have?

As the sun was rising over the hills, we climbed back into the van. I sat in the passenger seat as he drove to a place that he knew. He parked, and I gave him all the cash I had, about two hundred dollars, and a couple of watches I thought he could pawn. We walked together across the street. The sun was shining. It was early in the day but already warm. He had his army jacket and sleeping bag under one arm, his duffel bag slung over his shoulder. Somewhere in the bundle there was a black gun.

We shook hands. I smiled at him, and he continued to look confused. Then I said good-bye and walked away.

In the emergency room of L.A. County Hospital, a doctor scraped away small bits of metal, skin, and hair, and sewed stitches into my scalp. He asked me how it had happened, and I told him, "I was shot, four times."

"You're a lucky man," he said. "The two bullets that hit you both glanced off your skull. You have to report this to the police, you know."

"Yes, I know," I said. I already knew that I was

lucky, but even more, I felt blessed. I didn't go to the police. I had made a promise and had received a promise in return. I kept my promise. I like to think that Ray kept his.

LION GOODMAN
*San Rafael, California*

# SNOW

I knew it was snowing before I opened my eyes. I could hear the sounds of shovels scraping against the sidewalks, and there was that special quiet in the air that comes when the city is heavily blanketed with snow. I ran to the windows in the front room to have a look at the block — my domain. It must have been very early. None of my friends had made it to the street; only janitors were moving about in the knee-deep snow. Relieved that I hadn't missed anything, I became aware that my sisters and brothers were now awake. I had no time to waste. If I hurried, I could be out there before any of my friends.

I dressed myself in an assortment of hand-me-down winter woolens, but there would be no mittens to keep my hands warm. I had lost them earlier in the season. I was in a real dither as to what to put on my feet; my shoes no longer fit into my rubber galoshes. I could wear shoes or galoshes, but not both. I decided to go with two pairs of socks and the galoshes.

As I was buckling them, I felt the presence of someone standing over me. It was my big brother, Lenny. He asked me if I wanted to go ice-skating at the indoor rink in Madison Square Garden. I immediately scrapped my other plans. My thirteen-year-old brother was actually asking me, his nine-year-old sister, to go ice-skating with him. Go? Of course I would go. But where would we get the money? Lenny said it would cost a dollar to get in and rent the skates. Only two obstacles stood between me and going skating with my brother — the blizzard of 1948 and one dollar. The blizzard I could handle — it was the dollar that presented the problem.

The quest began. We returned some milk bottles, asked our mother for a nickel, begged our father for a quarter apiece, collected a penny or two from coat pockets, discovered two coins that had rolled under the beds, and spotted a rare stray dime nestled in a corner of one of the six rooms in our cold-water railroad flat.

Eventually, fortified with a bowl of hot oatmeal and jamming the hard-earned coins into our pockets, we set out on the twenty-block journey — a city mile.

The wind-driven snow clung to every surface. Lenny and I pretended that we were in the Alps as we climbed over the three-foot mounds of snow that had been shoveled to the curbs. It was our world now — a myriad of tiny snowflakes had shut down the city and kept the adults indoors. The skyscrapers were invisible behind a white veil of snow, and we could almost imagine that New York had been scaled down for us. We could walk right down the middle of Third Avenue with no fear of being run over. It was hard to contain our joy, the incredible sense of freedom we felt out there in the snow.

The twelve blocks to Forty-ninth Street weren't difficult, but the long crosstown streets proved to be chilling. The harsh west winds blowing off the Hudson River made it almost impossible to push forward. I could no longer keep up with my brother. My playful imaginings were replaced by the gnawing cold of my feet. My head was uncovered, my mittenless hands were clenched in my pockets, and a few of the clasps on my galoshes had worked loose. I began to complain gently, not wanting to make a nuisance of myself because I was afraid that Lenny wouldn't ask me to go anywhere with him again.

Somewhere near Fifth Avenue, we stopped in a doorway to take refuge. I timidly told Lenny that my clasps were open. Lenny took his bare red hands out of his pockets and bent down to refasten the snow-crusted, icy metal clasps. Ashamed that Lenny had to take care of me, I stared straight ahead and saw the image of a man walking toward us through the chiffon curtain of snow.

I was unable to tell how old he was — all adults seemed the same age to me — but he was tall, thin, and had a gentle, handsome face. He wore no hat. There was a scarf around his neck, and his overcoat, like ours, was caked with snow.

I don't remember if he spoke to me or not. What I do recall is that he kneeled down before me, his face level with mine. I found myself gazing into soft brown eyes, feeling bewildered and mute. When he was gone, I felt his warmth in the soft, wine-colored scarf that he wrapped tightly around my head.

I don't remember ice-skating that day, or how we got home. All my memory holds is the snow, the kindness of a stranger, and my big brother, Lenny.

JULIANA C. NASH
*New York, New York*

# WAR

# THE FASTEST MAN IN
# THE UNION ARMY

My great-grandfather, John Jones, was a long-legged, blue-eyed farm boy from Green City, Missouri. When the Civil War began, he was just twenty years old. He went to his mother and said that he was against slavery and did not want to see the Union break apart. She gave him permission to join the Eighteenth Missouri Volunteers. His unit was at the center of some of the most horrific battles of the war.

At one point the regiment was ordered to guard a railroad line. They dug some earthworks surrounding the railroad, and in the early morning hours a battalion of Confederate cavalry charged their position. They held their ground until their ammunition ran out. John Jones could see the enemy advancing over the embankment, and as the Union soldiers in the forward positions crawled out of their earthen bunkers and stood up, their heads were chopped off by the saber-wielding Confederate horsemen. He jumped to his feet and started to run. He heard several Southern soldiers yell, "That Yankee is mine." He looked over his shoulder, and sure enough, several cavalrymen were galloping after him at full speed. He said to himself, "If God ever gave me long legs, it was for this moment." He knew that he was running for his life and somehow managed to stay ahead of the pursuing cavalrymen. He saw a thicket, plunged straight into it, and came out running on the other side. The horses had to slow down when they came to the bushes, and John Jones got away.

The men who survived the battle said that it was the first time they had ever seen a man outrun a horse.

MICHAEL KURETICH
*Glendale, California*

# CHRISTMAS, 1862

*From the memoirs of James McClure Scott, CSA — my
great-great-uncle — while under command of Jeb Stuart.*

DECEMBER, 1862.
I went with my company on Stuart's celebrated
"Christmas Raid"; its line of march being around
the west flank of the Yankee army, then facing Lee
at Fredericksburg, came by Lignum, crossing at
Kelly's Ford, on to Dumfries and Buckland near
Leesburg, and to Aldies and Middleburg where a
party of young people had a Christmas frolic burning President Lincoln in effigy.

Just after the battle of Dumfries in which this
Confederate cavalry was repulsed by Federal infantry, the Confederate troops were stationary till
dark, then moved towards Buckram. I was in the
advance column and had missed the captured
stores, being on duty elsewhere, and was famished
from a thirty-six-hour fast, besides worn with the
fatigue of hours spent in the saddle, sleeping in the
saddle also at night as we marched night and day.
I had no time to forage for myself or my horse.
The weather was bitter and between hunger and
fatigue I was desperate.

On Christmas night as I was marching in front
of the column I saw a light across the field at a
house. I left ranks, knowing I could regain the col-

umn before it passed. Accompanied by another man, we made our way across the fields towards the light. Having reached the house I dismounted, and knocked at the door. Within were all the sounds of a jovial party at supper. At length the owner of the house appeared. I asked if two men could get supper. The man replied with a question, "Who are you?" I answered, "Jeb Stuart's men." The man exclaimed, "Well, you are in the wrong place for these are Yankee officers and their wives in the house," to which I replied, "Unless they hold a mighty good hand, it will be the worse for them." The man still demurred, saying he did not want any trouble, for the Union troops would visit it on him and burn his house. I answered, "I want supper, not prisoners or trouble." The man then turned to go to the dining room saying he would ask his wife. I realized this would be a notification of my presence to the Yankees within, and walking in the door followed him, keeping just behind him.

The supper party were amazed to see their host appear in the door followed by a fully armed Confederate soldier, evidently fresh from "the war path." I stood with an easy touch on my pistol while the host explained my demand.

One of the officers sitting near a back door started to rise. I told him, "Just keep your seat, I only want my supper." One of the women implored me not to take her husband prisoner. My reply was, "I want my supper, and will not take prisoners or make trouble, but if trouble is raised, they would get the worst of it."

A place was quickly set for me at the end of the

table nearest the door by which I had entered. Two of the women waited on me, plying me with REAL coffee, oysters, turkey and all accessories to complete a Christmas meal. With my pistol beside me and the officers seated at the same table, I bolted my supper, but did precious little chewing.

Meantime the sound of the Confederate column could be heard as it marched by. When full to repletion, I rose and offered Confederate money as pay for my supper which, being declined, I slid unmolested out the door, back to my horse, with a feeling of intense relief that the adventure was safely over. Utter silence reigned in the house as I rode off and quickly regained the line of march of my column. My companion had disappeared at the first intimation that Yankees were in the house.

GRACE SALE WILSON
*Millwood, Virginia*

# MOUNT GRAPPA

In June 1917 my father left the Grinnell College campus before graduation ceremonies to join the Red Cross Ambulance Corps in Chicago. Most available ambulances had already been shipped overseas. The men drilled like army recruits, and then, without a single day of training behind the wheel of an ambulance, they were sent off to the battlefields of Europe.

My father wound up in northern Italy, at the foot of Mount Grappa. He and the other drivers were given a few primitive ambulances. After a couple of turns around the camp grounds, they headed up the mountain to a pass where Italian soldiers were engaged in heavy combat with Austro-Hungarian forces. The road was little more than a goat path. They often had to travel in the dark, knowing that the descending drivers were barely in control of their vehicles.

The attack waxed and waned in November. Finally reinforcements arrived from France and England, and the enemy was driven back as the Alpine winter gripped the region.

The enemy retrenched, and a fresh attack was mounted in the spring. Current records estimate the casualties of the two Italian campaigns as more than 150,000 men.

The number of the wounded was so great that the medical facilities at the base of the mountain were overwhelmed. Orders went out from the Italian military command that medical corpsmen were to ignore the enemy wounded and bring down only wounded Italian soldiers. This change of policy did not sit well with the ambulance drivers, least of all with my father. He had come there to save lives.

Not long after the order was given, my father picked up an Austrian soldier and started carrying him to the ambulance. An Italian soldier ordered him to halt and drop the man. "I won't do that," my father said, and the Italian said, "Then I'll have to shoot you." So the soldier lifted his rifle and took aim, and the American ambulance driver with the wounded man in his arms just stood there. They looked at each other for what must have felt like an eternity. They were both in their early twenties; neither one had ever expected to be involved in a war.

After who knows how long, they started to laugh, and the soldier waved him on. Still laughing, my father carried the Austrian down the mountain.

MARY PARSONS BURKETT
*Paw Paw, Michigan*

# SAVENAY

During the First World War, my father was stationed with the American army at Savenay, a small town in west central France. When I visited Savenay a few years ago, I carried along a few of the photographs he had taken there. One of them showed my father standing on a country road with two girls. There was a small house in the background. Alongside the road not far from Savenay, I found that house — a small brick cottage surrounded by a low stone wall. I went through the gate and knocked on the door. An old woman poked her head out of an upstairs window and asked me what I wanted. I handed up the photograph and asked in my best French if she recognized it. She disappeared into the house. After a long discussion with another woman inside, she opened the door. The old woman asked me where the photograph had come from. I told her that it was my father's and that I thought it had been taken on the road in front of her house. Yes, indeed, she said, the photograph had been taken on the road, and she and her older sister — the other woman inside the house — were the two girls in the picture. Her sister remembered the day the picture was taken, the old woman said. Two soldiers were walking on the road and had stopped to ask for water. I told her that one of those soldiers was my father — or became my father much later. Unfortunately, the old woman said, their mother had not allowed the girls to give water to the soldiers. This had distressed her sister very much, she said. I thanked her for her time and turned to leave. A moment later, the woman called me back and said, "My sister wants to know if you'd like some water."

HAROLD TAPPER<br>
*Key Colony Beach, Florida*

# FIFTY YEARS LATER

As a German pilot in World War I, my father was flying a reconnaissance mission over eastern France when he was attacked by French fighters, whose machine guns disabled his plane. Without engine power, he managed to make it across the Swiss border and crash-landed in a field among startled haymakers. At war's end he returned to Germany from internment in neutral Switzerland, continued his studies, graduated as a geologist, and eventually immigrated to the United States.

Half a century after this wartime incident and near the end of his career as a geology professor at a leading American university, he had partially related the experience to a group of students gathered around a campfire at the end of a day's geological fieldwork, when one of the students interrupted him, saying, "Let me finish the story." Whereupon, to the amazement of all, the student provided the correct details of how the farmworkers had found the observer/photographer seated behind my father dead, had extricated my dazed but uninjured father from the plane, and had provided him with food and water until the Swiss police arrived and interned him. In his youth, the student had heard the story many times from his mother, who had been one of the girls among the haymakers in that Swiss field.

GISELA CLOOS EVITT
*Stanford, California*

# HE WAS THE SAME AGE
## AS MY SISTER

I'm nearly sixty-seven years old, but every October when the weather turns, I am eleven again.

In the last year of the war, fall in Holland was cold and wet. No lighted stoves, no coal. No lamps to make the room seem warm, no electricity. No supper worth the name. The soup from the central kitchen, a mixture of potato peels and cabbage leaves in water without salt, was cold by the time we got it home.

That day in October, just when it began to get dark, army trucks closed off our street, as they had done many times before, and a platoon of German soldiers started a house-to-house search for men.

"Raus! Raus!" The loudspeaker drove us outside to stand on the sidewalk while soldiers ran through our houses, poking in attics and closets. "Raus! Raus!" My little brothers forgot to grab their coats. Jacob's little body warmed me.

Our street filled up with women and children. We could talk freely, since the soldiers didn't understand Dutch, but we kept our voices low. Jokes flew around. Why are there so few men here? Haven't you heard of the virgin birth? I didn't understand what they were talking about, but I liked the laughter. Then news was exchanged. They're in Maastricht! Why won't they come north?

It got colder. The soldiers had nearly come to

the end of the street, and no men had been found. We became quiet. And then we heard someone crying. All the mothers turned. It was the sound of a crying child. On the stoop of Mr. van Campen's house sat a soldier, his rifle propped up next to him, his face hidden in his coat. He tried to swallow his sobs, but then he gave up.

A mother walked over and talked to him softly in German. "What's wrong?" she asked. She bent over him as he spoke, and when he was finished, she stood straight up and announced to us, "This war must nearly be over. He's sixteen years old and hasn't had anything to eat today." Two or three mothers slipped away from the group and went into their houses. A German officer came walking down the street half a block away. I was scared — and very cold. The mothers managed to get back in time. A cold cooked potato, a piece of bread, a wrinkled apple were passed through the group to the boy. The officer came closer. The boy turned into a soldier again. "Danke," he said, and then climbed to his feet and grabbed his rifle.

The truck engines started up. We could go inside. For the rest of the war, for the rest of my life, I have remembered that soldier who cried. He was the same age as my sister.

MIEKE C. MALANDRA
*Lebanon, Pennsylvania*

# BETTING ON UNCLE LOUIE

Gamblers in Amsterdam, New York, talked a lot about my Uncle Louie that year.

In the spring of 1942, Uncle Louie — five-two, 160 pounds, flat feet, bad eyes, and nearly thirty-five years old — had received a letter to appear at the military medical examining board in Albany. Along with selling cigarettes and newspapers part-time at the city bus station on Main Street, my Uncle Louie was a gambler. He had taken me to my first "day at the races" at Saratoga the previous season, about the time I started first grade and several months before Pearl Harbor. When his gambling buddies learned about the letter, they laughed — and then they started placing bets. Was Louie up to the challenge of defending America? The odds were overwhelming: the only one who bet he'd be drafted was Uncle Louie himself. That's how he was able to deposit $350 into the Amsterdam Savings Bank shortly before he shipped out, first to Camp Upton in New York, and ultimately to Europe.

The first gift he sent me was a big red cross outlined in white on a blue field, a rayon flag of Iceland. Sometimes a postcard would arrive with the picture of a black volcano trailing white smoke like a halo. Sometimes there would be a letter with no news but a lot about the weather: "Iceland," he'd write, "is as cold as Amsterdam in the winter,

345

but with less snow." My mother would knit khaki sweaters by the dozen, I would roll foil from gum wrappers into huge balls, and my father, 4-F because of his cataracts and his family status, would give blood every month. We kept writing Uncle Louie about what we were doing and sending messages from his cronies at the newsstand. "Ask him," Goody might say, "what he's runnin' over there in Iceland." For emphasis, he'd tap a long gray ash from his cigar. "Dice? Craps? Poker? Ha ha ha!"

Every evening, after radio programs like *Captain Midnight* and *Portia Faces Life*, I'd set the table and my mother would put out bowls of cool salad or steaming soup. Then we'd listen to the six o'clock news. My father would write down the countries or cities mentioned, and after supper we'd move the red and blue pins around the world map tacked to the kitchen wall. After D-day, I began to notice guarded glances between my parents during the news, and short comments in Yiddish, which I couldn't understand. I overheard a phone call about one of my mother's cousins; he hadn't been heard from for over a year and was now a POW somewhere in Germany. I saw two people on our block wearing black armbands. After the postcards stopped arriving in the fall of 1943, we completely lost track of Uncle Louie.

It wasn't until fifty years later that I found out where my Uncle Louie had spent the war. Oh yes, he'd sent me a small bottle of Chanel No. 5 from Paris — and my mother a big bottle of cologne, which she immediately traded for my perfume. And we did get that handsome sepia army photo, which still stands in my bookcase. He's seated at an angle, so his corporal's stripe would show on his left sleeve; his body is trim, his face smiling, his dark hair cut short. And I did buy a roll of white shelving paper in the summer of 1945; on the wooden picnic table in our backyard, with my jumbo box of Crayola crayons softening in the sun, I drew a rainbow-colored sign and stretched it across the front porch: Welcome Home Uncle Louie!

But it was not until half a century later, while driving him to the Jewish cemetery just outside Amsterdam to visit the rest of our family, that I asked him what he had done during World War II. About the Normandy invasion: "This Chinese guy and I were just too short to hold our guns over our heads and run through the water — we'd have drowned. So the sergeant yells, 'Hey, idiots! Drop the guns! Run or swim to shore! Pick up something when you get there!' " About the Battle of the Bulge: "Liège was bad, the worst time of my life. I was working in the radio room. No signals, only bombs. And when I walked out —" he wouldn't continue, except to indicate that he was one of the few men in his unit who'd survived. And about the march into Paris: "Flowers, music, cheers, hugs, more music! Nothing in my life ever compared, not even my big win at Saratoga after I got home — when I bet all that money I'd won for getting drafted on one winning horse! But nothing ever felt like Paris."

When I asked him why he'd never left Amsterdam after the war, never took advantage of the GI Bill or other opportunities, he only said, "I left once, honey, in 1942, and that was enough to last me a lifetime."

JEANNE W. HALPERN  
*San Francisco, California*

# THE TEN-GOAL PLAYER

It was midyear, 1942. My squadron was in New York, slated for duty overseas. Nazi U-boats were sinking thousands of tons of Allied shipping every month. The convoy system hadn't been perfected, and air cover was good for only about 10 percent of the voyage. Being shipped out was not a trip to look forward to.

Two of my best friends in the squadron were "Doc" Saunders, the flight surgeon, and John Milburn. We were all hoping for a nice, quiet time together on our last night in America. We wanted to collect our thoughts, to be with friends, and to remember home. Somehow, Doc fixed it so we could be out until 10 P.M. — a small concession on the night before our own personal D-day. With the extra hours in hand, John invited Doc and me to his parents' home on Long Island for a going-away dinner.

Doc and I knew that John Milburn's family was wealthy. In the '30s, in North Dakota, being wealthy meant that you had enough to share with neighbors. But John had attended private academies, driven fast cars, and taken a degree at Oxford. During the dark days after war broke out in Europe, John sailed home in a first-class cabin on the *Athenia*. But Doc and I didn't really understand how wealthy John was until we reached his place. We drove through the grounds of a manicured estate. Servants took our flight jackets at the door.

The dinner was grand. This American aristocratic family welcomed us as if Doc and I were their own. I was wondering if I would ever see America again after tomorrow. But John's parents did their best to make it seem like we would be back with them soon, enjoying food, wine, and learning about new ways — like polo.

As men of wealth often are, we learned, John's father was an ardent polo player. On the wall of the second-floor hallway of their palatial home was a life-sized painting of John's father dressed in full polo regalia. "My dad's a ten-goal player," said John when we passed that painting. To a boy from the Midwest this didn't mean much, but I soon learned that being a ten-goal player meant something like hitting fifty home runs in a season or winning the Masters. "There are only a few ten-goal players in the world," we were told.

A year passed. The war had not gone particularly well for the Allies, but there were hopeful signs. The Afrika Corp had been stopped. Göring had almost run out of planes. Doc and I were still together, but our friend, John Milburn, had been transferred out. We lost touch, as too often happened when wartime mail was the only hope of keeping connected.

Then the squadron moved to a base deep in the English countryside. On our first day at the new field, a distinguished-looking man called to Doc and me from the perimeter fence. "Yanks," he said, "join me for a cup of tea?"

His house was old English. It had a tall,

thatched roof covering its oldest part, while a large, new addition in the back showed that this was a man of means. The gentleman gave us a tour. Passing a large office and den, which was fitted out in the way one would expect of a British sporting man, I stopped in my tracks. There, in the middle of a wall, was a painting of a polo player. It was a companion piece to the picture of John's father we had seen on Long Island. "That's John Milburn's dad," I said in amazement. "I say, do you know him?" our new English friend asked. "He is my best friend. He was on my polo team for years. He's a ten-goal player, you know."

Doc and I had tea at our new friend's house many times in the room dominated by the picture of an American polo player. It was in that room that our new friend received a letter telling him that John Milburn had been killed in action. We read the letter from the ten-goal player while he watched, silently, over our shoulders from the wall.

PAUL EBELTOFT
*Dickinson, North Dakota*

# THE LAST HAND

The damnedest poker game I ever played in was held in my office on an island near the equator in the western Pacific during World War II. Japanese bombers interrupted play twice during the first hour of the game. Each time, we had to run outside in the rain to a crude bomb shelter, where we sat in the dripping darkness and waited for the all clear.

As bad as the conditions were, the most frustrating thing was that nobody was getting a decent hand. There hadn't been a ten-dollar pot in the half-dozen hands we had played. Each participant was playing on money he had won during the month, so there were several thousand dollars available for betting.

Finally, as host and dealer, I suggested we play one last hand in which each player would ante five dollars. That way, somebody would win a few bucks, and then we could go back to our tents and lie down on our wet cots for a nervous night's sleep.

But that wasn't the way it happened. The player to my immediate left opened for the amount in the pot — thirty-five dollars. The next man raised seventy dollars. Each player in turn either called or raised. Nobody folded. By the time the betting got around to Lieutenant Smith, who was sitting on my right, he made the bet an even thousand. Smitty was a good friend and a very good poker player; I knew he had won a lot of money in the last few weeks.

I "sweated" my cards again: three, four, five, six of diamonds and a nine of clubs — possible straight, possible flush, and possible *straight flush*. I had to stay and draw a card even though it would cost at least a thousand bucks. I called, and so did two other players. I calculated that there were five thousand dollars in the pot. I was having a hard time breathing as I dealt the players their draw cards.

The man who had opened stayed pat, as did Smitty. I took one card. I "sweated" my cards again, trying to muster the courage to look at the hand. As I peeked at the new card and saw that it was a two of diamonds, I thought I was going to die. A straight flush! I had never held a natural one in my life. I hoped that the other players couldn't see my "poker face."

The first two bettors checked to Smitty, the raiser, and Smitty looked me up and down. "Cap'n," he said with a wry smile, "you look like you just swallowed a canary. I'm going to let you name your poison. But I don't want anybody to look at my hand for nothing, so I bet two hundred dollars."

I counted my money on the table — seven hundred dollars. Most of it represented previous winnings, but about two hundred of it was my own hard-earned dough. With a deep sigh I pushed it all into the pot and squeezed out the words, "I raise five hundred dollars." This was like the movies — I was sweating through my pants.

Only Smitty called. I laid down my cards and

announced triumphantly, "Straight flush!"

Smitty gulped and said, "How high?"

My heart fell. I knew he had won. My two to six was about as low as you can get. He beat me with a seven-high club straight flush.

He scooped up the armload of money into his shirt and thanked us for our contributions.

Half an hour later, a lone Japanese bomber dropped his load on Smitty's lighted tent. We picked up more than eight thousand dollars strewn around the area and sent it back home to his widow. At his funeral the next afternoon, we got word that Smitty was on the promotion list and was about to be made captain. We changed the rank on the white burial marker. It was truly the last hand.

BILL HELMANTOLER
*Springfield, Virginia*

# AUGUST 1945

We were being briefed by the colonel for another mission. It would be our seventh since arriving in the Pacific theater six months ago. Intelligence described it as extremely risky, involving invasion of mainland Japan, and reports suggested that the Japanese had advance knowledge of our plans and were preparing a massive resistance. Stunning as this information was, we took in the details as though it were a routine briefing. We figured we'd gambled our last survival chips months before anyway.

"This is a volunteer mission," barked the colonel. "Any man who doesn't want to undertake this mission just needs to report to my quarters, stand at attention, look me in the eye, and say, 'Colonel, I'm yeller, sir!' And you'll be shipped out, back to base at Oahu on the next ship. Is that clear? Dismissed!"

After dozens of missions, we were exhausted. Although none of us said it out loud, each knew what the other was thinking. It was what I was thinking, too. I wished I had the guts to go in there and tell the colonel I was yellow. We were too tired to admit fear, too proud. We were seasoned soldiers, veterans of the many battles that would eventually end up as battle stars on our uniforms and hang in our closets until the moths ate holes in our lapels or until some kid took the jacket off the hanger for Halloween. And we knew enough of battle to have real fear. But I feared something more than looking into the colonel's eyes and telling him I was afraid. I feared looking into my own eyes, even though in the middle of the Pacific we didn't have mirrors, and I knew that, battle-fatigued and frightened as I was, I could never bring myself to walk into the colonel's tent.

But one man, Symes, did go in to the colonel. The colonel was true to his word and transferred Symes out of the unit. His orders were to board the *Jasper*, a supply ship returning to Oahu to restock.

I resented Symes. I hated him. We all did. We knew that Symes had fought next to us throughout our tour, facing fire as well as any of us had, no better, no worse. But he was the only one who had the guts to say that he was a coward, and now he was going to get out of this hellhole. He was going to be shipped out, to eat at a table, to sleep in a bed with sheets, to smell fresh sea air instead of the constant stink of gunpowder and dead bodies, to hear the soothing rhythm of the ocean instead of the whistle of bullets and the gut-thumping blow of heavy artillery. And maybe he'd spend the rest of the war behind a desk or on the receiving end of a radio on a base. (And he'd still have the battle stars; who would know what he'd said to the colonel but us? And in a week we might all be dead anyway.)

We all made sure we had other things to do while Symes packed his duffel and marched down to board the *Jasper*. Then we began to pack up for the next battle. We all wrote letters to our families, to our wives, to our girls, trying to tell them good-bye without letting them know where we were going and what we were thinking.

Then, on the morning we were preparing to board the transports, one of the Filipino truck drivers came running toward us, gesturing excitedly "Never mind. No bother. Big bomb dropped. War over!" We turned on the radio and listened to the news of the bomb that had been dropped on Hiroshima.

As we all stood around soaking up the meaning of this news, we received a second message: the *Jasper* had been torpedoed at sea, all aboard lost.

ROBERT C. NORTH
AS TOLD TO DOROTHY NORTH
*Woodside, California*

# ONE AUTUMN AFTERNOON

*My brother was a member of the Eighty-second Air-borne Division, which had trained near Columbus, Georgia. We knew that he had been in North Africa, but when we received the news of his death, we were told that he had been killed in France on August 21, 1944. He was nineteen years old.*

*This is how I remember that afternoon when I learned of the terrible thing that had happened.*

I could never say that I had any intuition or fore-boding about how that day would turn out. I walked into our house after the school bus had let me off at the end of our road, and I had no idea what was waiting for me. I remember that it was the best time of the year, one of those golden days, summer almost gone, fall coming on fast. The leaves on the trees were just beginning to turn color, getting ready for their vivid swan song before we moved on to the somber season ahead.

It was 1944, and I was just beginning my sopho-more year in high school. My mother and I were alone most of the time out in the country in the old house that had been left to our family by my father's parents. Our few acres were in the midst of dairy farms in upstate New York. My father worked on the Barge Canal and could get home only on weekends, partly because of the distance involved but also because of the strict gas rationing that was in effect. My brother, who had signed up to become a paratrooper immediately after graduating from high school, had been shipped overseas in March of that year. His letters to us were from North Africa, but they hinted that he would be moving on soon.

As I walked into the house through the kitchen, there were signs of activity that had been interrupted. Wisps of steam rose from a big kettle on the cook stove, and a dish towel laid out on the table held empty canning jars lined up and waiting to be filled. Other tools of the trade, knives and ladles and funnels, were strewn about the kitchen. A box that held the red rubber rings used to seal the jars had been opened. Some of the rings had spilled out onto the table. It was as if all action in the room had been halted just an instant before. Why was everything so quiet? Where was my mother? She always met me in the kitchen when I came home. As I started through the house to look for her, I remember noticing a shaft of brilliant afternoon sun striking a basket of tomatoes. They glowed red.

Our dining room was on the north side of the house and was always dark. In the gloom I saw a creased yellow paper lying on the table, and in one terrible moment everything became clear to me. Written on the paper were the most dreaded words of those wartime years. "We regret to inform you . . ."

WILLA PARKS WARD
*Jacksonville, Florida*

# I Thought My Father Was God

These things happened in Oakland, California, at the end of World War II. I was six years old. I didn't know what war was then, but I was aware of some of its consequences. Rationing, for one thing, since I had a ration book with my name on it. My mother kept it for me, along with the ration books that belonged to my brothers. I remember the blackout, the air-raid warnings, and the sight of warplanes flying overhead. My father was a tugboat captain, and I remember talk about troopships, submarines, and destroyers.

I also remember my grandmother taking fat to the butcher shop to be reclaimed and going downtown to the federal building to toss aluminum scrap into the window wells on the sidewalk side of the building.

But what I remember most is Mr. Bernhauser. He was our backyard neighbor. He was especially mean and unfriendly to kids, but he was also rude to adults. He had an Italian plum tree that hung over the back fence. If the plums were on our side of the fence, we could pick them, but God help us if we got over the fence line. All hell would break loose. He would scream and yell at us until one of our parents came out to see what the fuss was about. Usually it was my mother, but this time it

360

was my father. No one liked Mr. Bernhauser very much, but my father was particularly against him because he kept all the toys and balls that had ever landed in his yard. So there was Mr. Bernhauser yelling at us to get the hell out of his tree, and my father asked him what the problem was. Mr. Bernhauser took a deep breath and launched into a diatribe about thieving kids, breakers of rules, takers of fruit, and monsters in general. I guess my father had had enough, for the next thing he did was shout at Mr. Bernhauser and tell him to drop dead. Mr. Bernhauser stopped screaming, looked at my father, turned bright red, then purple, grabbed his chest, turned gray, and slowly folded to the ground. I thought my father was God. That he could yell at a miserable old man and make him die on command was beyond my comprehension.

I remember that Ray Hink lived across the street. We were in the same grade, and his grandmother lived upstairs. She was a tiny old woman who always wore a high-collar dress. She sat in the window with a pair of opera glasses and kept watch on the neighborhood. If we were good, she would let us look through the glasses and smell the rose petals she kept in an alabaster jar on her table. She said that the rose petals were from Germany and the jar was from Greece. One afternoon, I was allowed to handle the precious glasses and was looking out at the street. A cab pulled up, and a tall, skinny sailor got out. He shook hands with the cabby, who took a seabag from the trunk, and I knew that it was my Uncle Bill, home from the war. My grandmother came running down the steps into his arms. She was crying. I remember

361

the stars that hung in the windows of some of our neighbors' houses. My grandmother told me it was because someone had lost a son in the war. I was glad that we didn't have any stars in our window. That night we had a huge celebration for Uncle Bill. I went to sleep feeling glad that my uncle was home safe. I didn't think about Mr. Bernhauser anymore.

ROBERT WINNIE
*Bonners Ferry, Idaho*

# THE CELEBRATION

August 14, 1945 — VJ-day, the day Japan surrendered, ending World War II. I was stationed at an
airbase on the outskirts of Sioux Falls, South Dakota. We received word of the surrender late that
afternoon, and immediately just about everyone on
the airbase headed into town to celebrate. There
weren't nearly enough jeeps and trucks, so most of
us hitchhiked in. How peaceful it was as we passed
through the gently rolling farmland, with a few
cows munching away under a sky that was bluer
and brighter than ever, with a few puffy white
clouds that were whiter and brighter than ever.

What a wonderful state of affairs. I had flown
and survived seventy-nine combat missions over
Europe without a scratch, would not have to fight
in the Pacific, and would soon be going back to
college at Columbia after four years of military
service. The world was at peace, and I was headed
into town to celebrate.

When I got there, the celebration was well under way. Thousands of soldiers had gathered in
the center of town, along with hundreds of civilians. Liquor was flowing freely. As the celebration
progressed, I bought a bottle of beer and made my
way up to the roof of a one-story building, joining
the group that was observing the wild, noisy scene
below. Grateful civilians were hugging and kissing
the soldiers and thanking us for winning the war.

363

A farmer arrived in a battered old pickup truck and immediately and unwillingly sold the truck to an intimidating group of drunken soldiers who had passed the hat for donations to pay for it. Promptly upon taking possession of the truck, they set it afire. The fire department arrived quickly with sirens shrieking, hooked up their hoses, and were promptly overpowered by the mob that grabbed the fire axes and severed the fire hoses. As the fire consumed the truck, the crowd, including soldiers, civilians, and even firemen, roared their approval.

As the center of action shifted down the block, I came down from the roof and followed. The drunks got drunker and noisier, and what had started out as a joyous celebration of the end of the bloodiest and most terrible war in the history of mankind became a wild, chaotic, violent scene. Store windows were smashed and fights broke out. The few policemen on hand were powerless to bring order to the situation. It didn't even appear that they wanted to.

A scuffle broke out involving six or eight white soldiers pummeling a black soldier. There were shouts of "Kill that nigger" and "Kill that black bastard." He managed to break free and run up a side street with a look of stark terror on his face, a look that I'll never forget as long as I live. The mob pursued him, brandishing empty whiskey bottles. To the black soldier's surprise, he found that the side street was a dead-end alley, and there was no way out. I felt that I should go to his rescue, but I was afraid of the mob.

As soon as he reached the end of the alley, he

turned, faced his pursuers, and stood waiting for their next move. He was dripping with sweat. The look of terror on his face became a look of steely determination. His pursuers all came to an abrupt halt, except for one soldier who advanced toward him, took a swing at him, and got the surprise of his life when he was knocked out flat with one punch. Stepping over the unconscious body of his assailant, the black man clenched his fists and said, "I'm leaving now." There was total silence. Everyone stepped aside, and they let him go. I was tempted to congratulate him, but I was afraid that he would say, "Where were you when I needed you?" After that, I lost interest in the celebration and hitchhiked back to the airbase.

Thinking about that ugly incident, I felt guilty that I had not gone to the man's defense. That guilt reminded me of something I had once read in a short story. A man watches in silence as another man is lynched in the Deep South. He is at once shocked and fascinated by what he has witnessed.

The mob disperses, leaving the corpse dangling from a tree limb, and the man walks home ashamed of himself for having been too afraid to intervene. When he walks in the door, his wife, noticing the look of guilt and shame on his face, blurts out, "You've been with a woman, haven't you?"

REGINALD THAYER
*Palisades, New York*

# CHRISTMAS, 1945

The war had ended a few months ago, and our unit was stationed in Kyoto, Japan. Our Christmas promised to be as bleak as the compound in which we lived. Emperor Hirohito meant *us* when he said, "We must bear the unbearable." On December 22, we dispatched a truck to pick up a Christmas tree and a bundle of ornaments at corps headquarters.

The five meanest men in the 569th were assigned to decorate the tree. We hoped for a mutiny so we could pack the whole lot of them off to a stockade. No such thing happened. In fact, they did a good job of it. But at no time has a Christmas tree been decorated under a spell of worse language. Merton Mull, a star among the "Impossible Five," gave up that day his hopes for a medical discharge. He could barely walk. His spine, he said, was a garland of slipped discs. From a wee crack in the mess-hall door, I observed Merton hanging by one arm from the heights of a crossbeam as he attached a silver star to the top of the tree.

It was sad. The company, long proud of its unity and of its Sixth Army citation, had by Christmas developed a rift. Many who had been with the unit through its New Guinea and Luzon campaigns had gone home, replaced by recruits from the States. The old guard found the bravado

366

of these nineteen-year-old hotshots intolerable. Even their hates ran shallow.

A public-relations stunt was needed to make things whole. Buzz and stir moved through the ranks when we posted the duty rosters for Christmas Day. All the low-level chores had been given to the noncoms, seasoned old-timers every last one. The higher the rank, the more menial the task. The first sergeant, after first waiting on tables, would do pots and pans, the most despised of all kitchen duties. The supply sergeant, a four-striper, would spend much of his Christmas Day cleaning toilets. The platoon sergeants were assigned general KP, and the corporals would man tedious guard posts. "The brats don't deserve it," said many. The first sergeant broke character during dinner, but only briefly. He "decorated" the five "meanies" who had decorated the tree. The citation spoke of "service beyond the call of duty."

Healing took place that day — a lot of it — but due largely to some unexpected visitors we received on Christmas Eve. In mysterious ways they infused our public-relations hypocrisy with a more genuine spirit of Christmas. I hurry to tell you about it.

I was in the orderly room writing a letter home when Corporal Duncan, our company clerk, rushed in with unbelievable news. A group of Japanese with a flatbed truck equipped with a foot-pedal organ stood at our gate and requested entry. They wore white choir robes and claimed to be Christians. According to Duncan, two of the women were unquestionably angels.

Granting permission meant a violation of our strictest security regulation. After some hesitation, the truck, running on inferior fuel, coughed its way into the compound. The organist began to play, and a youthful chorus, seven women and three men, sang familiar Christmas songs in Japanese. The driver and the organist, both men, may have made for a symbolic twelve. With the gracious movements of a tea ceremony, the carolers lit candles, which they handed out to the soldiers who had crowded around. During their finale, they passed out gifts — silk kerchiefs.

We could do no less. With the help of one of his cooks, our Jewish mess sergeant scoured his kitchen for surplus. They laid cartons of groceries on the truck. The motor-pool corporal slipped the truck driver five gallons of gasoline. Others raced to find things. Chewing gum, candy bars, toothpaste, shaving cream, razor blades, toilet paper, endless bars of soap in various stages of use, along with some scattered yen, were all tossed into a wastepaper basket that I rightly suspected to be my own, stolen from the orderly room by that rascal Duncan. One crime more or less hardly mattered. The entire affair, from start to finish, had been illegal. As enemies, the Japanese gave us unity. When we were about to lose it, a small band of Japanese Christians helped to bring us together again.

The Good Book says that rain falls on both the just and the unjust. There can be no other explanation. A month or so after this remarkable Christmas, Merton Mull did get his medical discharge. I vaguely remember reading words about as follows: "Pvt. Mull suffers from a chronic aberration of mind that leads him to believe that he has a bad back."

LLOYD HUSTVEDT
*Northfield, Minnesota*

# A Trunk Full of Memories

When I first read about the plan to establish a Holocaust museum in Washington, my mind went directly to a large blue trunk in the basement of my Greenwich Village apartment house, filled with memorabilia from the war. I hadn't looked inside the trunk for forty-five years, and it occurred to me that perhaps finally I had found a use for its contents. I wrote a note to the director of the museum, and two days later one of the curators telephoned to say that she would like to come to New York to see the material. Steeling my nerves, I brought the trunk up from the basement and opened it. The first thing I saw was my old duffel bag. From it I extracted two heavy Nazi army helmets, with the names of their owners on the linings, and an enormous red banner emblazoned by a black-and-white swastika. I remembered that as my infantry division pushed into Germany, we were ordered to confiscate all weapons, and when we "liberated" a German officers' weapons room attached to a barracks, we had to dismantle the racks and cases and take the contents away. We were told that we could keep all the ceremonial side arms as souvenirs, and I helped myself to one sword and one dagger with Nazi insignias on the handles.

Besides the duffel bag, I found two brown boxes tied with string. They contained about two hundred photos I had taken, my own personal record of our advance through France and Germany. Apart from the usual groupings of my buddies and the rubble and debris of the war, there were pictures that I took when my division captured Franz von Papen, Hitler's vice-chancellor, the first top-flight Nazi to be captured by the Allies. As I flicked further through the packet, I came to the photos I dreaded to see.

Just before the end of the war, somewhere in the Ruhr, in a town called Warstein, we came upon a camp surrounded by a wall and barbed wire. It was one of the lesser-known but equally horrible death camps, where captured Russians were kept alive as slave laborers. Not one of them survived. As food grew scarce, the German SS forced the Russians to dig their own graves and then shot them dead. Our men found the gaping graves with the uncovered bodies in and near them. Our officers quite rightly required every citizen in that town to be led on a tour of the camp.

The last object I came to in the trunk was not German at all. It was something I acquired just after the armistice. My company was located in a town called Ludinghausen. One day a colonel from headquarters summoned me to accompany him as interpreter — I had studied French and German in high school — to a conference with his British and French counterparts for a purpose not revealed to me.

We left early one morning and drove north and west across a devastated countryside. At about three in the afternoon, we arrived at the appointed meeting place, an inn, and the colonel went in to announce himself. Soon he emerged to say that the meeting was to be conducted in English and I would not be needed.

I sat in the jeep, and for the next hour or so read a paperback novel that I had brought with me. Suddenly, the stillness was broken by a horse's galloping hooves. I got out of the jeep and held firm to the strap that secured the carbine over my shoulder. The horse advanced rapidly, a huge animal, bearing a rider in uniform. I swung my carbine to the ready and flipped the safety catch.

When the rider saw me, he brought the horse to a halt. They were both huge. Silhouetted against the setting sun, they looked like an equestrian statue. I stood with the weapon in hand as the rider dismounted.

I now saw that he was not wearing a German uniform: he was dressed in wool khaki, wore high leather riding boots, and his cap and jacket neck band were decorated with red insignias. What could he be? I wondered. He was much taller than I was, much larger and much stronger. But he made no menacing gestures, and his face broke into a broad smile as he walked toward me, revealing a mouthful of gold teeth.

He said something to me that sounded like a question: Was I French? English? I replied with a single word: "American."

"American?" He couldn't believe it. "American. American," he repeated. And then he pointed to himself. "Russki," he said, or something like that.

I knew it was hopeless to try to find out what a solitary Russian cavalryman was doing on this road. "American. American," he said again, his blue eyes flashing. Then he started to undo the broad belt he was wearing around his waist.

A moment later, he slipped out the enormous saber that was attached to the belt, took it in both hands, and ceremoniously held it out to me. I stepped back, but he pressed it on me. I took it and swished the air with it a couple of times, to the Russian's great delight. He gestured to make it perfectly clear that he intended it as a gift.

I realized that I had to do something for him. But what could I give him? Ah, I had my watch. I took it off and handed it to him. He beamed and put it on his hairy wrist. Then he removed his cap, bowed his head, remounted his steed, and with a wave and a gallop was off down the road.

MORTON N. COHEN
*New York, New York*

# A WALK IN THE SUN

We medics of the Third Battalion Medical Detachment, 351st Infantry Regiment, stationed at the San Giovanni barracks on the northern outskirts of Trieste, had a rather relaxed existence for troops on alert against the postwar menace of Marshal Tito. Contrary to normal army procedure, we held sick call at 1600 hours, or four in the afternoon, instead of in the morning. Not surprisingly, we had very few soldiers turning up for medical attention after the day's duties were over and the men could go out on pass for the evening. Our aid station was at all times staffed by at least one medic, the CQ, or charge of quarters, so we were always prepared to care for any man who needed us. Still, except for an occasional serious illness or injury, we had virtually nothing to do most of the day. We never stood reveille with the rest of the battalion but would roll out just in time for breakfast. At times we even slept through breakfast, and when we woke up we'd send someone out to the local Italian deli for sandwiches and slaw.

Another privilege we granted ourselves was to ride in the ambulance whenever the battalion went on an all-day route march with full field gear. Our battalion surgeon, Lieutenant William A. Reilly, never questioned this practice.

The inevitable happened. Toward the end of one route march, our battalion commander, Lieu-

374

tenant Colonel Dured E. Townsend, stood along the road observing his troops as they marched by. He saw our ambulance pass, but he noticed that there were no medics in sight. He stopped the ambulance, had the driver open the back doors, and stuck his head in. There we were, comfortably arranged on the stretchers, showing no signs of fatigue whatsoever. His sudden appearance sent us into speechless shock, and we fully expected to be reamed up and down right then and there. But no. In measured tones, all he said was, "Sergeant, I want you and these men to report to me tomorrow morning, 0700 hours, at the main gate, with full field equipment."

We appeared at the appointed place at the appointed time, just as the colonel himself was arriving. "Now," he said, "you men are to hike the same route as the battalion did yesterday, plus another five miles, as per this map." So saying, he handed the map to our sergeant, Joe Grano, who saluted and replied, "Yes, sir." With that, the nine of us marched smartly out the gate in a column of twos, executed a column right, and headed up the hill toward the high back country of Venezia Giulia.

Once over the crest of the first hill, we descended into a small valley. Led by our resourceful Sergeant Grano, we turned left off the road. Forming a single file, we followed a path that emerged through some brush into a flat open area with steep slopes on either side that formed a rather secluded hollow. There our leader called us to a halt, and we easily threw off our backpacks. I say easily because, while they appeared to be ex-

375

pertly filled according to regulations, they were actually shaped by empty cardboard boxes which enabled us to bring along our sporting gear: softball, gloves, a bat, and also a football. Forsaking GI rations, we had purchased our real lunch the night before from our deli. That, too, came out of our fake backpack loads.

Our first hour was spent in idle talk, and also in resting from our twenty-minute hike up the hill. Next we stripped to our skivvies, laid out a ball field, and chose up sides for a rather exciting softball game. We were all ballplayers from our regimental league team, the "Blue Medics." We rationalized that our game would help develop our character, competitiveness, and sportsmanship. We played until we got hungry, and then enjoyed our deli lunches, which we washed down with the wine that some of us had brought in our canteens. After that, to use an army phrase, we crapped out for a nap under the sunny Italian sky.

We calculated that we should probably reappear at the barracks at around 1600 hours. So, midafternoon, we got back into our battle fatigues, chose up sides again, and began a brutal game of tackle football. We played hard, getting our uniforms all sweaty and grimy and our combat boots all scuffed up, not to mention acquiring some minor bruises and abrasions of our own.

When the game was over, we polished off what was left of the wine, reassembled our dummy backpacks, and pulled them on again for our return hike. There was Colonel Townsend, evidently anticipating our arrival, watching from the main gate as one sweaty, smelly, dirty detachment trudged wearily down the hill and executed a sloppy column left, coming to a halt right in front of him. As he looked us over, his immense satisfaction was all too apparent. He didn't have to say it, but he did. "I guess I've taught you medics a lesson you won't soon forget, haven't I?"

No one answered him aloud, of course. But we all agreed that he had.

DONALD ZUCKER
*Schwenksville, Pennsylvania*

# A SHOT IN THE DARK

I was a young marine in Vietnam, stationed only fourteen miles from Da Nang, but it was so far from civilization that it felt like the end of the world. We lived in large fourteen-man tents with dirt floors and used candles for light in the evening. The whole base of operations was contained within an abandoned Vietnamese village, which was surrounded by dense trees and overgrown foliage. That shielded us from the intense heat of the sun, but it also protected us from sniper fire.

Days and nights were spent going out on patrols, encountering snipers, and keeping up regular contact with the local population. After two or three days in the field, we were allowed to go back to the base for a day and a night. When we were in our "secure" area, we didn't do much more than try to stay cool, write letters home, and watch an occasional movie.

The movies were shown in a makeshift theater with a metal roof supported by large wooden poles. It was open on all sides, and the benches had no backrests. At the front there was a plywood movie screen that had been painted white. It was supported by two sturdy wooden poles, and at the base of the screen there was an elevated stage.

It is a rule of war, a scientifically proven fact, an empirical law, that men in combat must never stand, sit, or lie down in close proximity to one another, for then they become an inviting target to the enemy. If there is a special situation, and if a man should happen to find himself in a group of two or more closely assembled people, then at least he should be quiet.

It was getting dark, and the theater was nearly full. The movie started, but after a few seconds the film slipped the sprockets, and the projectionist shut off the projector. A few minutes later, the movie started again. And again the film slipped the sprockets. The projectionist again shut off the projector to fix the problem. The theater was pitch-black. We all had flashlights with us because we had to find our way back to our tents after the movie. Electricity was scarce on the base, and it was used only for refrigeration and other critical functions. We were lucky to have some power available for the luxury of an occasional movie.

Over the next forty minutes, there were a number of failed attempts to start the film. The crowd was becoming loud and impatient. When some people began to call out and whistle, others of us grew nervous because of the noise. Finally, some of the men left the theater. Another contingent began shining their flashlights at the screen, making designs and pointing their lights around at the remaining group.

In the Marine Corps, when someone calls out the word "corpsman" during combat, we all know that someone has been shot, hurt, or killed. It stops us in our tracks, stuns us into an immediate awareness that something tragic may have happened.

At first we barely heard it. Then, as always happens in the urgency of combat, the word spread. It was a strange and surreal moment. First one, then ten, then forty flashlights were shining toward the front of the theater. That was where the call had come from. It was clear that someone had been hurt. Just below the screen, in the middle of a darkened area on the stage, a marine was cradling another marine in his arms. The second marine was limp. He had been shot in the head.

Later on, after we had returned to our respective unit areas, we found out that just one bullet had been fired. A lone sniper, tempted by the lights and the noise, had fired a single bullet into the crowd. In spite of the dense foliage that surrounded us, we knew that light could be seen from a great distance. We hadn't even heard the shot because of all the noise we were making. We had been careless. We had suffered for it.

Some went to help, and then someone else took charge and declared in an authoritative voice that the movie had been canceled. We were all told to disperse. Cautiously, I decided to wait until most of the others had left before going back to my tent.

As I went to the back of the theater, I saw the projectionist standing beside the projector. I asked him the title of the movie we were supposed to have seen. It was with Peter Sellers and Elke Sommer, he said, a movie called *A Shot in the Dark.*

Chills ran through me in the damp and sweltering blackness of that tragic night. It was 1966. Thirty-four years later, that night stands out in my memory as no other ever will.

DAVID AYRES
*Las Vegas, Nevada*

# CONFESSIONS OF
# A MOUSEKETEER

When I was twelve, I became one of the original Mouseketeers. Walt Disney said to me, "Doreen, being a Mouseketeer is probably the greatest thing you will ever do with your life."

Years later, during the Vietnam War, I worked as a USO entertainer at American military installations around the world. Eventually, I wound up "in-country," arriving in Saigon during the Tet Offensive of 1968. I performed with a band of Filipino musicians called The Invaders, and by the time we were flown in to play for the Seventh Army Cavalry, Black Horse, we had been doing shows every day for a month and were exhausted.

As the chopper makes its landing, a field of army green can be observed in front of a flatbed truck that resembles a stage. Before the blades stop twirling, we are unloading the instruments. I'm escorted by a nurse to her barracks, where I can change into my costume and repair my makeup. A few minutes later, I reappear — dressed in miniskirt, clinging T-shirt, and knee-high white boots, with platinum hair hanging long and loose.

Each step I take plunges the white go-go boots into the red mud. As I ascend the steps of the flatbed, globs of mud are left behind. The crowd goes wild. I grab the mike from its stand and swing it high in the air, catching the cord in time to retrieve the mike and belt out "Hold On, I'm Coming." Again the audience goes crazy with excitement. Some of the soldiers in the front row start dancing with several of the nurses. As long as the music goes on, the reality of the war is forgotten.

After a while, some of the fellows are getting pretty drunk. They open beer cans with their teeth, laughing hysterically between each gulp. One guy's lip is cut on an open beer can. Blood spurts out as he tries to stop the bleeding with several slugs of beer. He smiles up at the makeshift stage, showing me his bloody teeth.

Our last number, "We Got to Get Out of This Place," drives the audience into a frenzy. As the band and I take our bows, the applause becomes deafening. Then, out of the corner of my eye, I see a pair of Mouseketeer ears being passed down the aisles. A good-looking guy in the middle row puts the Mickey Mouse ears on his head. Then, "magic time" begins. It happens when an audience becomes connected. Call it electrical energy — or the excitement of the moment. The mouse-eared soldier stands up and starts singing the Mickey Mouse Club theme song. One by one throughout the audience, men start standing — until the whole audience is standing at attention. "Now it's time to say good-bye to all our company, M-I-C, see you real soon, K-E-Y, why, because we love you, M-O-U-S-E." I cry as I watch these grown men singing with such reverence. I had traveled halfway around the world, and still, I couldn't escape the past.

Mickey Mouse was everywhere.

DOREEN TRACEY<br>
Burbank, California

# FOREVER

My brother, Ralph, died in Vietnam in June of 1969. He was twenty-one years old. I was nineteen. We were the only two children in the family, and we were the best of friends.

Losing him has been one of the most important events in my life. He was at the center of my world, and everything I am is bound up in who he was. Only now, as a woman of fifty, do I understand what a profound impact he had on me and how my life has changed because of what happened to him.

When he was inducted into the army, I never once said to him, "Don't go. You could get killed, or you could wind up killing others. Run for your life. Go to Canada or become a conscientious objector."

If I could turn back the clock, that's what I would say to him now.

My brother was pulled out of the pool of working-class people who did what they were told to do. I belonged to that pool of unquestioning passivity as well. I was young back then, and I hadn't yet begun to think for myself.

It was only many years later that I tried to understand what had happened in Vietnam and to learn about the national tragedy that still haunts us today.

I was in my midthirties when I went to the library to read about the war. I checked out a book called *Fire in the Lake*. It was beyond my scope at the time, and I had read only a few pages of it when one day I went for a hike on a nearby mountain trail. By chance, I met a man at the base of the trail who was quite talkative and friendly. He told me that his ambition was to become a war correspondent. The conversation then turned to Vietnam and my brother's death.

We struck up a friendship, and a few days later he presented me with a couple of books about Vietnam. They were written for and by the grunt American soldier, which was what my brother had become. They were written from the heart and gut. And so I went into the hearts and guts of these young men who had found themselves confronted by unspeakably cruel deeds, and who had committed such deeds themselves. And who had experienced profound love and caring as well.

One book, *Everything We Had*, was especially riveting to me. For a brief moment, Ralph seemed to be alive again in one of the soldier's accounts. It was in a section of the book called "The Black GI." Each statement was preceded by the soldier's name, rank, division, time of service, and the battles he fought in. The black GI spoke of the deep bonds of friendship that develop between men in combat. The color of your skin, he said, loses significance when you're out in the trenches together. He then told of a friendship he had formed with a white soldier whom he referred to as the Sicilian. He said that this soldier wanted to take him home to meet his family when they got out of Nam. He said they were so close that they each knew when the other had to relieve himself. He abruptly ends by saying, "Then he died." He said that after this happened, he never allowed himself to become close to anyone in Vietnam again.

I could hear my heart beating while I read this passage. I was quite certain that the Sicilian could have been my brother. I contacted the author of the book, who gave me the address of the black GI. I wrote him a letter asking him to confirm my heartfelt belief that the friend he had spoken of was my brother, Ralph.

A short time later, I was in an airport passing time between flights at a newsstand/bookstore. By chance, I found yet another book about the American GI grunt. There were photos in it, and in one of the photos there stood my brother. He was with a group of soldiers, standing in the last row with only his head showing.

All these events occurred within a span of three or four weeks. I never heard from the black GI, nor was my letter ever returned. Therefore, I will never know for sure. It would have been so nice. I had so longed to talk to that person.

Perhaps the ultimate importance of this experience was to discover what my brother had lived through, and for that I am grateful. I no longer feel passive. I feel awake, sober, and alive, even though I still cry for my brother today. I still miss him, and I will go on missing him forever.

MARIA BARCELONA
*Santa Fe, New Mexico*

386

# UTAH, 1975

My friend D. reports that when the Vietnam War was winding down, his young son told him that he wanted to celebrate on the day the war ended. "How?" D. asked. And his son said, "I want to blow the horn in your car."

When the war ended, Americans made little of it. No parades. No band music, few outward shows of excitement. Except in a suburban area of Salt Lake City, when a nine-year-old boy got permission and pressed on the horn button of his father's car until the battery died.

STEVE HALE
*Salt Lake City, Utah*

# LOVE

# WHAT IF?

I received my discharge papers on April 25, 1946. I had survived three years of army service in World War II, and now I was heading home on a train to Newark, New Jersey. The last thing I'd done at the base in Fort Dix was to buy a white shirt at the post exchange — a symbol of my return to civilian life.

I was eager to put my grand plan for the future into action. I would return to college, launch my career, and look for the girl of my dreams. And I knew exactly who that girl would be. I'd had a crush on her ever since high school. The question was: How could I find her? We hadn't been in contact for four years. Well, it might take some time, I thought, but find her I would.

When the train pulled into the station, I gathered up my bags, tucked my new shirt under my arm, and headed down to the bus platform — the last leg of my journey home. And then, miracle of miracles, there she was, just as I had remembered her: a short, slim, dark-haired winsome beauty. I walked up to her and said hello, hoping she hadn't forgotten me. She hadn't. She threw her arms around my neck and kissed me on the cheek, telling me how glad she was to see me. Fortune was truly smiling on me, I thought.

It turned out that she had been on the same train, coming home for the weekend from Rutgers University, where she was studying to be a teacher. The bus she was waiting for wasn't mine, but that didn't matter. I wasn't about to let my opportunity slip away. We got on the same bus — hers — and sat together reminiscing about the past and talking about the future. I told her of my plans and showed her the shirt I had bought — my first step toward making my dream come true. I didn't tell her that she was supposed to be step two.

She told me how lucky I was to have found that shirt, since men's civilian clothing was in such short supply. And then she said, "I hope my husband will be as lucky as you when he gets out of the navy next month." I got off at the next stop and never looked back. Alas, my future was not on that bus.

Thirty-one years later, in 1977, I met her again at a high-school reunion — not quite so dark-haired, not quite so slim, but still winsome. I told her that my career was going well, that I was married to a wonderful woman, and that I had three teenaged children. She told me that she was a grandmother several times over. I thought enough time had passed for me to mention that meeting three decades before — what it had meant to me, and how every detail of it was etched in my memory.

She looked at me blankly. Then, putting a coda to half a lifetime of "what ifs," she said, "I'm sorry, but I don't remember that at all."

THEODORE LUSTIG
*Morgantown, West Virginia*

# THE MYSTERIES OF TORTELLINI

Brian and I were a few months into our relationship, and I still hadn't cooked for him. He was a classically trained professional chef, and that intimidated the hell out of me. I was an appreciative audience, though, and would try anything he prepared for me when he came to my house with his wok and knives and sauté pans to seduce me with his cooking. But the thought of cooking for a chef terrified me. Mostly because the foods I knew how to make involved cans and jars and a pound of meat, your choice, which you threw into one pot and called a meal. Casserole. Lasagna. Or my roommate's specialty: pork chops smothered in cream-of-mushroom soup. Standard fare from our southern Ohio upbringing. But definitely not something to serve a California chef.

But I was beginning to feel guilty. So one Wednesday, after he had cooked one of his meals for me, I announced that I would make dinner for him Saturday night. He looked impressed and said that he would be over at seven o'clock.

I bought an Italian cookbook at the drugstore and found a recipe that looked doable: tortellini. From scratch.

Saturday afternoon, I made the filling. No problem. I made the dough, starting with the egg in the well of flour, which magically transformed into a mound of dough. I began to feel pretty confident. Even cocky, if the truth be told.

"Keryn, where's that rolling pin?" I called out to my roommate, who had promised to disappear for the evening.

"What rolling pin?" she yelled from the living room.

"You know," I said, "the wooden one."

"We don't have a rolling pin," she called out.

Stopping to close my eyes, I remembered where that pin was. In my mother's kitchen. Two thousand miles away. And it was 6:30 P.M.

I glanced around the kitchen, swearing under my breath. My eyes lit on a bottle of wine I had bought to go with dinner. Not as good as my mother's rolling pin, since it had only one handle, but it would have to do. I rolled as best I could, breaking into a sweat even though the air conditioner was going. I then cut the dough with a water glass, and from there I seemed to be back on track. I covered a baking sheet with tortellini, properly filled and twisted into shape.

Just as I was finishing, the doorbell rang. I slammed the tray of pasta into the fridge and greeted my dinner guest, flour dusting my clothes, my face shiny and flushed. He had brought along a bottle of sparkling wine and a rose to celebrate the occasion.

A glass of champagne later, I was collected enough to begin cooking the tortellini. The pot of water began to boil. He watched with interest as I pulled the baking sheet out of the refrigerator, and his eyes popped when he saw the rows of tiny twisted shapes. "You made that? By hand? I don't even make that, and I have a pasta machine."

I dropped the pasta into the boiling water, then served them. They looked beautiful. We sat down, and I watched as he put one in his mouth and chewed. And chewed. And chewed. I tried one. They were as dense as a pencil eraser.

It was over. I knew it. I had had a good thing going, and now he'd survive the meal, then beg off early with a headache and disappear into the summer evening, his box of knives and pans never to spend the night in my apartment again.

But he ate them. Every last one of them, admitting only that, yes, they were a little thick, but really not bad. So I confessed the story of the rolling pin. He didn't laugh. His look told me that this guy was the one.

When people ask us when we knew it was the real thing, Brian says, "The first time she cooked for me. She made me tortellini — from scratch." And I say, "The first time I cooked for him — he ate my tortellini."

KRISTINA STREETER
*Napa, California*

# An Involuntary Assistant

He called her "Bumps." It was a term of endearment — she had big cheekbones. When she smiled, her cheeks grew even larger, turning pink, almost glowing. She would tilt her head downward, blushing, not from embarrassment but because she had the natural shyness of a farm girl. She smiled a lot with Kevin.

Kevin was my college roommate, and Bumps was his girlfriend. Kevin thought of himself as urbane, sophisticated, witty — destined for some lofty, genteel existence. Marriage to a shy, apple-cheeked farm girl didn't fit into his image of the future. He decided to end their relationship before it got too serious.

Months later I ran into Bumps one afternoon. We sat and talked about the obvious: How was Kevin; was he seeing anyone? I told her he was doing okay and hadn't seen anyone more than once or twice. (Although I knew he missed her, he wasn't yet willing to admit that to himself or anyone else.)

Suddenly, and I have a difficult time explaining this, a thought or scene came into my mind. For a few moments I was somewhere else. I suppose you could call it a vision, but that sounds too dramatic, too much like a saint's epiphany. From somewhere high in the air, I watched Kevin and Bumps getting married next to a lake I'd never seen before. There was an incredible sense of peace as I watched.

Slowly, I became aware that Bumps was talking. I didn't know what to make of what had just happened. I was confused, yet relaxed in an odd way. I said nothing about it to her. If she and Kevin were going to get back together, it wasn't going to be because I told them I'd had a "vision" of them getting married. I told myself not to say anything about it to anyone.

Later, when I arrived home, I stood on the doorstep for a moment, repeating my resolve not to mention what had happened. Inside, unknown to me at the time, Kevin had just asked his friend Jerry, "Do you think I should start seeing Bumps again?" Before Jerry could answer, I opened the door between them and said, "I think you should start seeing Bumps again." It was as if I couldn't control my mouth, as if someone else was speaking. I was a spectator watching an actor in a play delivering a line. Kevin was as surprised as I was. Laughing it off, we agreed that it was weird and left it at that. Years later, I still wonder about it.

I never told them anything about what I had seen. I never mentioned the lake or the marriage scene to anyone. The next summer, Kevin and Bumps got married next to that lake.

C. W. SCHMITT
*Phoenix, Arizona*

# THE PLOT

When I was twenty years old, I fell in love with a man who was forty-three. It was 1959, and the news came as a shock to everyone in my family. I was a student nurse, and John had been a patient on our unit. My parents threatened to cut off the funding for my education if I didn't stop seeing *that man.*

He had been married and divorced and had no kids. To me, John was the essence of manhood: Gary Cooper and Randolph Scott rolled into one. We lived in Colorado, and everything about him seemed to belong to the West: the way he looked and talked, his love of the land. He had the confident stride of someone who knows who he is and offers no apologies. I loved his jutting jaw, and I loved his small, swaggering hips. No man ever looked more seductive in blue jeans.

Whenever he smiled at me, and whenever he started pouring out his thoughts in that western drawl of his, I thought I would melt.

One day, as we were driving down the road that runs parallel to the local cemetery, he said, "Oh, by the way, I bought a burial plot today. You might as well know where it is."

"You what?" I said.

"Well," he drawled, "some guy came to the door today and was selling plots in this new area. There's this place right near the statue of Jesus and Mary. I kinda like the idea of being buried there, since I was so close to my mother."

I was stunned that he was thinking about death at his age. As far as I knew, he was in excellent health. It didn't make any sense to me.

"Now, honey," he said, "don't you go gettin' all excited. There's nothing wrong with me. I just figured it was a good price, the guy was there, I liked the location, so why not?"

We had been dating for a year by then, and I knew that once his mind was made up, that was it. There wouldn't be any going back on the decision. That was just the way it was.

Another year passed, and the pressure kept mounting on me from all sides. My parents enlisted my girlfriends at school, my pastor, my favorite aunt, and my sisters to help convince me that I should date guys my own age. I knew that John really loved me. He could see all the turmoil this was causing for me and my family, so one day he said that maybe we should have a brief separation. I cried for days, but in the end I agreed. After a while, I started dating a fellow hospital worker who was close to my age. My mother and father were overjoyed.

We had agreed not to see each other for three months. We weren't supposed to have any contact, but John, my true love, called every now and then, and we still talked on the phone.

Before the three months were up, I discovered that I was pregnant — and not with John's baby. It was 1960. The only choices were to get married or to give up the baby for adoption. I decided to get married. I wrote to John, but he didn't answer my letter.

The baby was due in September. On August twenty-fifth, I picked up a newspaper and read that John had been killed in a car accident on I-25. He had been buried the previous day.

I knew where the plot was, and so I went directly to the cemetery.

That was forty years ago. Twenty years after that, my father died, and my mother chose a plot for him that was just around the corner from John's. She had no idea that John was buried nearby, nor that I had known about the location since a year before his death.

Every Memorial Day, I place a single rose on his grave.

BEV FORD
*Aurora, Colorado*

# MATHEMATICAL APHRODISIAC

In the days when John and I used to break up all the time, we made a decision to see each other only casually. Dates were okay, but no more than once a week. We were going to lead separate lives, getting together occasionally when the spirit moved us, but without worrying about commitment.

One day at the beginning of this period, we were sitting together on the floor of John's one-room apartment. He was knitting himself a sweater and I was reading *Fermat's Last Theorem*. Every now and then, I'd interrupt his knitting to read him passages from my book.

"Did you ever hear of amicable numbers? They're like perfect numbers, but instead of being the sum of their own divisors, they're the sum of each other's divisors. In the Middle Ages, people used to carve amicable numbers onto pieces of fruit. They'd eat the first piece themselves — and then feed the other one to their lover. It was a mathematical aphrodisiac. I love that — a mathematical aphrodisiac."

John showed little interest. He doesn't like math much. Not like I do. It was one more reason for us to be casual.

Christmas fell during this period, and since I hate to shop, I was glad to be able to cross John off my list. We were too casual for presents. While I was shopping for my grandmother, however, I saw a cryptic crossword puzzle book and bought it for John. We had always worked on the cryptic crossword puzzles at the back of *The Nation*, and for five bucks I figured I could give it to him.

When Christmas rolled around, I handed John the book — unwrapped, very casual. He didn't give me anything at all. I wasn't surprised, but my feelings were a little hurt, even though I wasn't supposed to care.

The next day, John invited me over to his apartment. "I have your Christmas present," he said. "Sorry it's late."

He handed me an awkwardly wrapped bundle. When I pulled it open, a rectangle of hand-knit fabric fell onto my lap. I picked it up and looked at it, completely confused. One side had the number 124,155 knitted into it; the other side had 100,485. When I looked up at John again, he was barely able to contain his excitement anymore.

"They're amicable numbers," he said. "I wrote a computer program and let it run for twelve hours. These were the biggest ones I found, and then I double-knit them in. It's a pot holder. I couldn't give it to you last night because I still hadn't figured out how to cast off. It's kind of geeky, but I thought you might like it."

After that Christmas, we were a lot of things, but we weren't casual anymore. The ancient mathematical aphrodisiac had worked again.

ALEX GALT
*Portland, Oregon*

402

# TABLE FOR TWO

In 1947 my mother, Deborah, was a twenty-one-year-old student at New York University, majoring in English literature. She was beautiful — fiery yet introspective — with a great passion for books and ideas. She read voraciously and hoped one day to become a writer.

My father, Joseph, was an aspiring painter who supported himself by teaching art at a junior high school on the West Side. On Saturdays he would paint all day, either at home or in Central Park, and treat himself to a meal out. On the Saturday night in question, he chose a neighborhood restaurant called the Milky Way.

The Milky Way happened to be my mother's favorite restaurant, and that Saturday, after studying throughout the morning and early afternoon, she went there for dinner, carrying along a used copy of Dickens's *Great Expectations*. The restaurant was crowded, and she was given the last table. She settled in for an evening of goulash, red wine, and Dickens — and quickly lost touch of what was going on around her.

Within half an hour, the restaurant was standing-room-only. The frazzled hostess came over and asked my mother if she would be willing to share her table with someone else. Barely glancing up from her book, my mother agreed.

"A tragic life for poor dear Pip," my father said

when he saw the tattered cover of *Great Expectations*. My mother looked up at him, and at that moment, she recalls, she saw something strangely familiar in his eyes. Years later, when I begged her to tell me the story one more time, she sighed sweetly and said, "I saw myself in his eyes."

My father, entirely captivated by the presence before him, swears to this day that he heard a voice inside his head. "She is your destiny," the voice said, and immediately after that he felt a tingling sensation that ran from the tips of his toes to the crown of his head. Whatever it was that my parents saw or heard or felt that night, they both understood that something miraculous had happened.

Like two old friends catching up after a long absence from one another, they talked for hours. Later on, when the evening was over, my mother wrote her telephone number on the inside cover of *Great Expectations* and gave the book to my father. He said good-bye to her, gently kissing her on the forehead, and then they walked off in opposite directions into the night.

Neither one of them was able to sleep. Even after she closed her eyes, my mother could see only one thing: my father's face. And my father, who could not stop thinking about her, stayed up all night painting my mother's portrait.

The next day, Sunday, he traveled out to Brooklyn to visit his parents. He brought along the book to read on the subway, but he was exhausted after his sleepless night and started feeling drowsy after just a few paragraphs. So he slipped the book into the pocket of his coat —

which he had put on the seat next to him — and closed his eyes. He didn't wake until the train stopped at Brighton Beach, at the far edge of Brooklyn.

The train was deserted by then, and when he opened his eyes and reached for his things, the coat was no longer there. Someone had stolen it, and because the book was in the pocket, the book was gone, too. Which meant that my mother's telephone number was also gone. In desperation, he began to search the train, looking under every seat, not only in his car but in the cars on either side of him. In his excitement over meeting Deborah, Joseph had foolishly neglected to find out her last name. The telephone number was his only link to her.

The call that my mother was expecting never came. My father went looking for her several times at the NYU English Department, but he could never find her. Destiny had betrayed them both. What had seemed inevitable that first night in the restaurant was apparently not meant to be.

That summer, they both headed for Europe. My mother went to England to take literature courses at Oxford, and my father went to Paris to paint. In late July, with a three-day break in her studies, my mother flew to Paris, determined to absorb as much culture as she possibly could in seventy-two hours. She carried along a new copy of *Great Expectations* on the trip. After the sad business with my father, she hadn't had the heart to read it, but now, as she sat down in a crowded restaurant after a long day of sight-seeing, she opened it to the first page and started thinking about him again.

After reading a few sentences, she was interrupted by a maître d' who asked her, first in French, then in broken English, if she wouldn't mind sharing her table. She agreed and then returned to her reading. A moment later, she heard a familiar voice.

"A tragic life for poor dear Pip," the voice said, and then she looked up, and there he was again.

LORI PEIKOFF
*Los Angeles, California*

# SUZY'S CHOOSY

My first real job after college was as an advertising copywriter for a textbook publisher in Boston. The office was at the corner of Mt. Vernon and Joy Streets on Beacon Hill. My boss was a man in his midfifties, I was twenty-two. I was attracted to him immediately and took every available opportunity to get close to him at work.

One evening I made an excuse to come back to the office and collect a book after everyone else had left. He was still there, and we left together and walked down Beacon Hill to the common. As we were about to go our separate ways, he asked if I wanted to have a drink with him. By that time, I knew that his wife was spending the summer in Belgium with her mother. We stayed on for dinner, and by the time he walked me home, I had given him my heart completely.

After that he began to hand me notes, and we would meet for lunch once or twice a week. Soon the company moved to new offices on Tremont Street, farther downtown. My cubicle was next to his. I found an ad for typewriter ribbons in a magazine, and I cut it out to hang over my desk. It was a cartoon of a young woman in an office, and the caption read, "Suzy's Choosy."

Our regular lunch place was now a little Italian restaurant less than a five-minute walk from Tremont Street. I'd leave first, always taking the sam

407

route, past Jordan Marsh and Filene's, then a quick left up a side street and I was there. I always hurried to make the most of our precious time together.

I'll never know why, but one day as I turned the corner onto Washington Street, I darted into the entryway of a store to look at a pair of shoes that had caught my eye. As I glanced up through the showcase, I caught sight of a woman walking quickly past. I recognized his wife from a picture. She was going to the restaurant to confront us.

After a few minutes, I recovered my senses enough to pick up a sandwich somewhere and go back to the office. When I entered my cubicle, I saw at once that "Suzy's Choosy" was gone.

SUZANNE DRUEHL
*Fort Wayne, Indiana*

# TOP BUTTON

My parents had strict ideas about collar buttons. They were of the school that believed that whether one wore a tie or not, the collar of a boy's shirt ought to be closed. Around the house or at other informal times, it didn't matter. But for school and dress occasions, the collar was to be done. This wasn't simply a matter of style. It had to do with propriety, and it carried all the weight of a moral imperative.

Tenth grade was the first year of high school. Being a dutiful son, I still followed the rules and showed up every morning with my collar buttoned. But the rules hadn't figured on Miss Scot. My math teacher was a tall, long-haired young woman who often crossed her legs and half-sat on the front of her desk as she spoke. I hasten to add that she wore above-the-knee skirts — not far above, but above nevertheless. The shoe on the foot of her top leg would hang down from her toes but never quite fall.

As luck would have it, my seat was in the first row, just in front of her desk. I was very backward for my age. I knew about the differences between boys and girls (my mother was a nurse and had explained the plumbing to me), but everything else was a mystery. Indeed, among the potential recruits for the sexual revolution of that decade, I was definitely 4-F. Still, by whatever alchemical force at work inside our brains, I knew that there was something special about Miss Scot.

One morning, not long after the school year began, Miss Scot bent forward from her perch and, to my amazement, reached out with her right hand and unbuttoned my collar. A bolt of electricity shot through my body and burned its way into my soul. My mother had touched me many times, of course, but it had never felt like that. Miss Scot cast a fleeting glance in my direction, but she went on talking to the class without missing a beat.

Knowing that my mother wanted the collar closed, I redid the button. This woman might have been my teacher, but she did not have the right to overturn a maternal directive. But Miss Scot was not to be denied. Once again, she reached over and undid the button — and then straightened out my collar with both hands. "You look better that way," she said. If she had kissed me on the lips, I don't think I could have felt more exhilarated than I did at that moment.

The collar stayed open that day, but this was not the sort of thing that one told one's mother. From then on I buttoned the collar before I left the house, but once I had walked down the street a little ways, it would always pop open.

EARL ROBERTS
*Oneonta, New York*

# LACE GLOVES

My father, Joseph Cycon, joined the army in 1943 and was assigned to Company F of the 262nd Regiment of the Sixty-sixth Infantry Division, which was activated in April 1943. By December 1944, he had attained the rank of staff sergeant.

In late November 1944, the division went to England to prepare for combat in Europe. When the Battle of the Bulge took everyone by surprise in December of that year, my father's regiment was quickly mobilized to be sent as reinforcements. So it was that they were in the English Channel on December 24, 1944, on the Belgian troop carrier *Leopoldville*, which was torpedoed by a German submarine that evening; 802 lives were lost. There were 197 men assigned to Company F, and only nineteen of them survived. My father was one of the five men from the Second Platoon who lived.

My mother, Margaret Gill Cycon, was at home in Sidney, New York, at the time, living with her parents and expecting a child the following June. She received a letter from my father written on January 11, but the censors kept him from saying anything substantial to her about what had happened. In the meantime, my mother was receiving many phone calls and letters from anxious relatives of men in my father's company, asking her if she could obtain information from him about

411

their sons and husbands, whom they had not heard from since Christmas. She was very depressed and worried herself and so did not do much more than open a package she had received from my father. It contained a pair of blue French lace gloves. A few weeks went by before she finally tried them on, at the urging of a friend. When she attempted to put the gloves on, one finger refused to go all the way in. Something was stuck inside it. Wedged into the glove was a small rolled-up newspaper item. It was a short article concerning the troopship *Leopoldville*, which had been sunk on Christmas Eve. In this way my father was able to outwit the censors and inform my mother that he had survived the sinking while so many of his good friends had been lost.

KAREN CYCON DERMODY
*Hamilton, New Jersey*

# SUSAN'S GREETINGS

As a single woman in my twenties, I used to send out photo greeting cards for Christmas. I had snapshots taken of myself throughout the year in various poses and then would pick the best one to use on the card.

In these pictures I was always nude.

I gained many fans. Men would stop when they saw me and say, "Susan's Greetings?" I sent out these Christmas cards for six years, and by the last year my list had grown to 250 names.

One subscriber was the man who took care of my car, Ted. He was thirty years older than I was and a heavy drinker, but he was a great mechanic. He also had a heart of gold. I knew that he had girlfriends, but I never met them.

I needed Ted, so every year I sent him a card. He started sending photo greetings to me, too, but in his pictures he was always holding up a huge fish.

After I moved out of town, I seldom saw Ted anymore, but we kept exchanging cards until I stopped the practice.

Fast forward twenty-three years. I'm back in my old neighborhood, having a radio put in my car. While I'm in the waiting room, a man comes up to me and says, "Susan? I'm Paul, Ted's son."

"Oh, sure," I say, "how you doin'?"

Paul told me that Ted had died in the fall. He

413

and his sister had to pick out a suit for their father to be buried in.

The sister opens a sock drawer and sees my Christmas picture in there. "Hey," she says to Paul, "Dad's gotta keep this," and so she slips the picture into his breast pocket. Which means that Ted is buried with me naked at his breast. He would like that.

A week later, I find one of Ted's cards in my house. It's the photo of him holding the fish and smiling at me. The corners of the card have been chewed away by mice.

I turn it over, and there, in Ted's writing, I read, "Susie, you've been on my thoughts and in my heart for seventeen years. I hope you're well and wish you the best. Love, Ted."

SUSAN SPRAGUE
*Willamina, Oregon*

414

# EDITH

Her name was Edith, but no one ever called her that. Behind her back everyone called her "Edie," though to her face she was always addressed as "Miss Burgoyne." She lived alone with her mother and father just west of town. Later on, I learned that they weren't really her mother and father. They were her maternal aunt and uncle, and she was the illegitimate child of her aunt's sister. The aunt and her husband had never had any children of their own, so they took in this baby girl shortly after she was born in 1906 and raised her as their own.

That would have made her about forty-six years old when I was a boy of ten. She was already a legend in the community. Perhaps it was her noble-sounding name — Burgoyne — which resonated in a village of Norwegian surnames that all seemed to end in "son." More likely, it was the social distance she kept from the other people of the town. A spinster in a world of married women, she did not belong to any of the church congregations or women's social clubs. And she was college-educated. She had graduated from the University of South Dakota in 1928 with a B.A. in music. For her graduation, her father had bought her a new Buick, and all during the summer she would drive around town in it, going from house to house to give music lessons for fifty cents an hour. I was one of the kids who studied with her. We all wanted to play the piano, but we hated the discipline of practice, the humiliation of lessons, and the misery of having her call us "Dear." Her dowdy clothes were so out of fashion, they seemed to have been the same ones she had worn in college. That was enough to brand her as an eccentric, but there was also the business of the adhesive tape she put over the odometer of her car. After my lesson one day, I ran outdoors while she was still visiting with my grandmother, crawled into the car, and peeled away the tape. The odometer on her 1928 Buick showed that she had driven just over 5,200 miles — 5,200 miles in twenty-four years!

One summer day, as I was passing the time sitting around the gas station, Miss Burgoyne drove by on her way to the post office and her afternoon schedule of music lessons. Uncle Pete, my grandfather's brother, happened to be in charge that day.

"I wonder what happened to Edie's railroad man," he said, almost as if he were talking to himself.

"What railroad man?" I asked.

And that's when I heard the story that everyone else in town had known for years.

The town of Naples was just a little spot in the road. We used to say, "Don't blink or you'll miss it!" It was located about five miles north and a shade west of Vienna. A branch line of the Milwaukee Railroad ran from Sioux Falls through Vienna and Naples and on up to Bristol, where it turned around and headed back to Sioux Falls the next day. By the time Miss Burgoyne began riding that train in the summer of 1935, the Milwaukee had been a familiar part of the prairie landscape for half a century.

"Yup," Pete said, "she got on that passenger train toward evening one day that summer and rode it to Naples three times a week every week for the next year. There she'd get off and walk home."

"What did she do that for?"

"Nobody knows for sure. The depot agent says she fell in love with a conductor on the train, named Bill, but that Bill had a family. Nobody really knows for sure. But she did it for about a year and then quit as sudden as she had started. Even on the coldest winter evenings, she would walk those four miles from Naples back home three times a week."

"How did she meet this Bill, the conductor?"

"Nobody knows for sure," Pete said. "I don't think there ever was a love affair between them. I think she was just a lonely thirty-year-old woman who rode the train and wished that conductor was her boyfriend. But I don't know. Nobody knows for sure."

The train is gone now. So is the depot. The railroad tracks were removed and salvaged years ago, and the right-of-way was abandoned. Miss Burgoyne's father died in the early 1950s, and her mother died a few years later. Miss Burgoyne continued living in the bungalow on the homestead and giving music lessons to the children in the area. A spinster in her sixties then, one day she left for some vague place in Iowa where her folks were supposed to have originally come from and where they were now buried, and she never returned.

Sometime in the mid-'70s, town folks heard that she had died. Gossip was that she had been living with a man, but nobody knew for sure. Today even the homestead where she lived has been razed and the land reclaimed for farming.

Now I am forty-six, about the age she was when I stole that look at the odometer of her 1928 Buick, covered with the small, neatly cut piece of adhesive tape.

When the restlessness and indecision of middle age settle upon me, I sometimes picture in my mind's eye that college-educated teacher of music with her noble-sounding name, her regal bearing, her civil sophistication, and her citified air.

I picture her at the depot, near evening, waiting alone for the Milwaukee. It arrives in a cloud of steam and fury from the south. She gets on, and ten minutes later, in Naples, she gets off and walks home alone in the early evening along the gravel road — home to where her aunt-mother and uncle-father wait by the light of lanterns for her. For the ten minutes between stops I imagine her intently watching the conductor, the railroad man, all decked out in his blue uniform with the red accenting and the quasi-military MILWAUKEE ROAD insignia, as he travels from the city of Sioux Falls to Bristol and back three times a week.

As I sit at my piano in my basement study and play a few nearly forgotten chords, I remember Miss Burgoyne and, like all the other folks in that village, I imagine.

But nobody knows for sure.

BILL FROKE
*Columbia, Missouri*

418

# SOULS FLY AWAY

I was putting away the laundry when this feeling came over me that my husband was dead. He was on a business trip, and although I had heard from him just two days earlier, I was sure at that moment that he was no longer with us.

We had been married for ten years. Our three children were playing out in the backyard at that moment, unaware that their mother was upstairs losing her mind. I was dizzy and disoriented. I put down the basket of shorts and T-shirts he hadn't packed for the trip and sat on the edge of our bed. The feeling had come out of nowhere, a huge wave of everything we'd shared since we were both in our early twenties. It came crashing down on me and I was suffocating, unable to get air. My chest was tight and my mouth was dry. All the laughter, all the joy of having children together, all the peace and security of our life together was compressed into milliseconds.

It was the same feeling I'd had when my neighbor's wife, Michele, died. We were at her son's wedding and she was at home, dying of cancer. The family decided to go ahead with the wedding, leaving Michele at home with her mother and her pain medication. The minister got to the part of the ceremony where he asked Darin, "Who gives this man?" and Darin's dad, Hugh, stood up from his place in the front pew and said, "His mother

419

and I do." And at that moment there was an impossibly bright light that broke through from between the dark clouds of that February afternoon, through stained-glass panels of Jesus and his sheep, and I remember squeezing my husband's hand so hard he almost cried out, right in the middle of the ceremony. A few hours later, after we arrived at the reception, we learned that Michele had died at the same moment Darin was given to Ellen. The daffodils in Michele's front yard bloom that same day every year.

It was also the same feeling I had when my grandmother died. I was camping out in the woods with my husband and kids, not far from where my mother lived. We'd had enough of bathing the kids in the cold river, so we piled into the jeep and drove to my mother's to take hot showers. My grandmother had been ill for some time but had recently been moved from her home to the Penticton hospital. I asked my mother how she was doing, and she said she'd talked with Grandpa that morning and that Grandma was hanging on. At that moment, I remember feeling that I was going to faint. I burst into tears and hugged my mother, and she held me until the feeling passed. We found out later that day that Grandma had died right at that moment.

So now you can understand my confusion and panic. I was quite certain that this was the same feeling, but I was also fairly certain that my husband was alive, even though I could "see" him in a crumpled pile on the floor next to our bed. I could feel myself thrown down across his still-warm but lifeless body and every fiber in my

420

body knew that feeling of finality.

I was able to reach him at his hotel that evening. Too embarrassed to share my fears, I made conversation about what the kids had done that day and asked him about the weather in Lima. Our fourth child, Claire, was born six months later.

He remained in Peru for four months, completing his engineering project after a brief two-week trip home, during which things seemed normal between us. After he returned home the second time, he explained that he had met a woman in Peru near the end of that trip. He told me that she was a former Miss Peru and had been his wife in another lifetime. He confessed that he had made a terrible mistake marrying me instead of waiting for her. He said he was sorry and excused himself to serve me with divorce papers. He married the Peruvian beauty queen, who likes the United States very much. They have a beautiful little girl with black-brown ringlets that resemble her half-sister Claire's. But he doesn't see his other four children or me very much, even though he lives just fifteen miles away.

It would be several more months before I realized what I had felt that day while I was doing our laundry. I had felt some part of him die. His soul sneaked out of our family nest and flew away to her nest, and it happened so quickly that he didn't have time to consider staying.

LAURA MCHUGH
*Castro Valley, California*

# AWAITING DELIVERY

I work as a postal letter carrier in Charlotte, North Carolina. One day a couple of years ago, I drove up to a mailbox. Christy, the young divorcée who lived there, was waiting by the side of the road. She said that she had a story to tell me.

About six months earlier, it seems that I had delivered a letter to her which had her street number on it but was addressed to another house with the same number on a different street in the neighborhood. She had to run some errands, so she decided to drop off the letter at the correct house.

It turned out that the letter had been intended for Stan, who happened to be single. They talked for a little while, and later on he called. They started dating and had been going out together ever since.

I was embarrassed about delivering the letter wrong, but I was pleased that I had brought these nice people together.

A few months later, a For Sale sign went up in Christy's yard, and then the wedding invitations were sent out. In short order the house was sold, the wedding happened, and Christy and her kids moved into Stan's house.

A few months later, I saw a For Sale sign in *their* yard. I feared the marriage might be in trouble, so I made up an excuse to go to their door and check on them.

Christy opened the door, smiled broadly, and pointed to her huge stomach. "We're having twins!" she said. "This house won't be big enough, so we have to move."

As I walked back to my truck, I was suddenly overwhelmed by the thought that my one mis-delivered letter was now giving two little yet-to-be-born people a shot at life. Awesome.

JOHN WILEY
*Charlotte, North Carolina*

# THE DAY PAUL AND I
# FLEW THE KITE

It was a hot Florida day twenty years ago, and the wind was blowing out of the west. Paul and I were trying to get sober. We had gotten drunk together, watched each other wreak havoc on our lives, held each other up, let each other down, and loved each other. Paul was my friend, my spiritual brother. Now we were trying to make normal lives out of what was, for a very long time, abnormal behavior.

Paul was six-foot-six, with a huge laugh and a great big smile. He was a surfer back then, with the blond hair and brown muscles they all seem to have. And, of course, he was a newly sober infant, just like me.

I was a short, blond schoolteacher in a teeny little bikini. But the truth was that I still had alcohol behind my ears and not a clue about how to get through the day without a beer.

We headed for the beach. What else was there to do on a hot summer weekend in Florida in 1980? We packed our little cooler with soda water, grabbed a couple of towels, and went. Paul had a kite. I remember thinking . . . why would he bring a kite to the beach? Why would anyone want to fly a kite anyway? What is the point of flying a kite? Paul was always a little quirky.

He had a monofilament line. It was clear and

tough and there was a lot of it.

We settled down in the shade of a clump of palm trees on the dunes and Paul started hooking up the kite. I don't remember what he used for the tail, but I do remember that the kite was red and not very big . . . just an ordinary little red kite. He tied the monofilament line to the kite, attached the tail, and let it go. The wind was blowing from behind us, strongly out of the west — out over the ocean. We didn't have to run with the kite to get it up. We didn't have to do anything at all. Paul just let the kite go and it flew. It really flew. Paul's smile was huge.

We had so much monofilament line, there must have been a mile of it. Paul let the kite out and pulled the line until the kite dipped and danced, bobbed and whirled — out farther and farther over the ocean. Finally, the little red kite got lost in the glare of the blue sky. The only way we could tell that it was still there was the strong pull on the fishing line we were both holding. We stared out into the sky, tried to find the kite, laughed at how it had disappeared, and then Paul grabbed a couple of cans that had been tied together with a string. He looped them over the monofilament line, which was stretched over the beach and pointing toward the sky.

The cans bobbed in what looked like thin air. In the bright light it was impossible to see the kite line that held them up — they just bobbed and swung in the breeze as if they weren't held up by anything. Then someone walked under the floating cans and noticed them tacked up there in the sky. He looked, looked again, walked back and forth, looked around, and finally spotted us and knew something was up — but wasn't sure what. We were young and we laughed.

One beautiful young woman in a slinky black bathing suit saw the cans and stared at them for a long time. She wasn't ashamed to let us see that she was completely confused as to how they'd gotten up there. She finally walked over to Paul and asked him what the trick was. He wouldn't tell her, and she couldn't figure it out. She finally left, walking down the beach still wondering. We should have told her — or maybe not. The cans looked like magic.

We spent a day with each other and with that kite, watching the cans hanging in thin air, watching people walk back and forth underneath them. In fact, we never saw the kite again, just knew it was there by the pull on the line. When it was time to go home, neither one of us could bear to bring in the kite . . . so we left it there, far out to sea with the cans bobbing merrily on the monofilament line just above everyone's reach.

Later that evening, Paul went back to tie the kite more strongly and lost it. It blew away, even farther out to sea — probably all the way to the Canary Islands. The wind almost never blows out of the west on the beach. It may never have done so since that day. I don't really care, because it did that day.

Paul was my friend then, and he is now. We are in our fifties and live thousands of miles apart. He is in frozen upstate New York, an odd place for a tall, blond surfer. I still live in Florida. We fall in love with other people, but we never completely lose each other. We will be sober twenty years this July. I believe that even today we are still at that beach, still hanging our cans on a strong line that no one can see, and still knowing the little red kite is out there by the strong pull we both feel.

ANN DAVIS
*Melbourne, Florida*

# A Lesson in Love

My first girl was Doris Sherman. She was a real beauty, with dark curly hair and flashing black eyes. Her long tresses would flow and dance in the wind whenever I chased her on the playground during recess at the country school we attended. We were seven years old and supervised by Miss Bridges, who would slap our faces for the slightest infraction.

To my eyes, Doris was the most attractive girl in my class of combined first- and second-graders, and I set about winning her heart in the feverish manner of a smitten seven-year-old. The competition for Doris's affection was strong. But I was undaunted, and finally I was rewarded for my persistence.

One balmy spring day, I discovered a tin badge on the playground. It must have been an election badge (perhaps for FDR). The front was still bright and glossy, but rust was beginning to show on the obverse side. With little hesitation I decided to offer this newfound treasure to Doris as a token of my love. As I proffered the badge (bright side up) on my outstretched palm, I could see that she was impressed. Her dark eyes sparkled, and she quickly took it from my hand. Then came these memorable words. Looking me straight in the eye and whispering in solemn tones, she said, "Alvin, if you want me to be your girl, from now on you must give everything you find to me."

I remember thinking it over. In 1935 a single penny was a small fortune to a boy of my age and circumstance. What if I found something really important — like a nickel? Could I hide it from Doris, or would I tell her I'd found a penny and keep a four-cent profit for myself? Had Doris made this same arrangement with my many rivals? She could become the richest girl in the school.

Faced with all these questions, my regard for Doris suffered a slow decline. If she had asked for 50 percent, we might still be an item. But her imperious demand for *everything* so early in our relationship nipped it in the bud.

So, Doris, wherever you are and whatever you may be, I would like to thank you for my early lesson in love — and, more important, that tricky balance of the love-economics equation. I also want you to know that from time to time, when dozing off, I am once again chasing you in that school yard, grasping for your dark and dancing curls.

ALVIN ROSSER
*Sparta, New Jersey*

# BALLERINA

Everyone says that I drive them crazy — especially my wife. I never tell her she's beautiful or cute, even when I think so. Instead, I say she looks nice. She says her mother looks nice. I say nice is good, real good. Nice is good to me. What if she looks beautiful one day, then the next day she looks even better? I won't have anything left in reserve. You've always got to have something in reserve.

I see people with no reserve all day. That's why I got interested in becoming a pain expert to begin with. What's great about pain is that there's no bullshit. There's no need to spend a lot of time talking. By the time I see them, the patients have been given up on by everyone else. There's no meat left on the bone. I admire pain. It demands to be honored. There is no more basic fear than the fear of constant, unending pain.

L. came to my office complaining of pain in the left leg. She is all smiles. I think, this lady is goofy. When I examine her, I see that not only does she have pain but also can't walk very well because her leg has become so stiff. Both she and her husband are smiling like loons. I suspect a spinal-cord tumor and get proven right. I ask the neurosurgeon to biopsy her spinal cord and he does. After the biopsy, her spinal cord has even less reserve and so she learns how to catheterize herself, starts a bowel program and can't use her other leg so well. The biopsy comes back inconclusive. I can't believe it. I spend a lot of time calling the world-renowned pathologist and ask if he can't take another look at it for me. I call the neurosurgeon who says, "I think I got a good piece of it."

"Well, sometimes that happens," she smiles.

I put on a full-court press. I present her to my colleagues, take her spinal fluid, look at her skin, her lungs, her brain, and her blood. Except for an unexplained spinal-cord tumor and pissing and crapping in her bed, she is perfectly healthy. Over the next few months her tumor doesn't get any larger, and I throw some drugs her way. Some pills to make her bladder and legs spasm less and some steroids to make myself feel better.

Her husband smiles excitedly and tells me he is so happy to have me. I have the urge to lock the door and keep them shut up forever so they don't get out on the streets. That's all I need, him beaming and her thin as a skeleton in her wheelchair with her tumor announcing to anyone within earshot, "See, look what a great doctor we have. We're so glad to have him!"

There isn't much more to do. Nothing has changed in months. I figure that she'll have a kind of life, but at least it will be hers. I hear from them every now and then. Prescription refills, requests for more physical therapy. They live about a hundred miles away and sometimes come for a fifteen-minute visit. We talk for thirteen of it and then I examine her. I try to schedule them when no one else is around. I'm still their favorite doctor.

One Friday her husband calls up. These symptoms sound different. I tell them to drive the hundred miles to the clinic. A scan shows a two-inch-wide tumor in the back of her brain where three months before the scan showed only brain. She is minutes away from dying from the pressure. Her husband runs up to me and pumps my hand a couple of thousand times and says, "I'm so glad you're here." Her eyes are jiggling around from the tumor and she has a headache, but she's happy to see me too. That night the neurosurgeon unroofs her skull. She starts to feel better pretty quickly. Several pathologists and oncologists from around the city decide that this is an uncommon, but not rare, tumor.

She has started her treatments and comes back today to see me. They are both beaming. Her legs are thin and blotchy red. There is no hair or flesh on them. Her toenails are a fright. She says, "Oh look, look!" She kicks both feet back and forth in her wheelchair to show me. Then she says, "Look at this." She pushes herself up hard, with her hands. Her feet and toes are pointed down because after the spinal-cord damage, her Achilles tendons have shortened and pull her heels up tight. Her face is big and round, a moon face because of the steroids. A layer of fine hair covers it. Her eyebrows are arched and her forehead is maximally wrinkled. She is all smiles and her still-jiggling eyes are pointing down to show me she is standing on the balls and toes of her feet. She looks like a kid. A ballerina. Her husband is proud and looks at her feet, too. Then she sits back down and complains, "Oh, if I could

432

just get rid of this big face."

"No," I tell her. "You are beautiful." And she is.

NICOLAS WIEDER
*Los Angeles, California*

# THE FORTUNE COOKIE

For many years, my parents had a fortune from a fortune cookie that read, "You and your wife will be happy in your life together." They kept it in a framed picture of themselves smiling near a beach in Cuba. I always enjoyed seeing the picture and the fortune; it gave me a sense of stability. It felt like they were saying to anyone who cared to look that they were happy and that they were actively planning to stay happy. I would say that they had a wonderful twenty-six-year marriage. There were, of course, good times and bad times, but they were able to work together to make the life they wanted. In my opinion, there is not much more that one can ask for.

When my mother was fifty-one, she was diagnosed with an aggressive form of cancer on her tongue. Operating would have rendered her mute, and she would have been required to use a feeding tube for the rest of her life. She chose radiation treatment, but the cancer moved to her lymph nodes. She had an operation on her neck to remove them. Within a year of the diagnosis, the tumor returned on her tongue. She was so weak and thin that she no longer had the choice of an operation. Weeks later she was forced to have a tracheotomy, which meant that she lost her voice and had to start using a feeding tube. She decided with my father not to undergo any more treatments and to stay at home. During this extremely difficult time, I married my husband. We moved in with my parents to help my father and to be with my mother. Five weeks after my wedding, my mother died at home with the whole family present. (I am crying as I write this.)

The day after her death, my family went out to eat — we really weren't up to cooking a big family meal. My father chose a Vietnamese restaurant. We ate our dinner, talking about my mother and sharing memories. It was a bittersweet moment. We had all loved her so much, but at the same time we were glad that her suffering was over. After dinner, we opened our fortune cookies. My husband's fortune read, "You and your wife will be happy in your life together." We keep it in a framed picture of us smiling on our wedding day.

SHARLI LAND-POLANCO
*Providence, Rhode Island*

# DEATH

# ASHES

My mother died on August 18, 1989. A charming and magnetic woman, but not always the easiest person to get along with, she had "lived more lives than one." She was born in Sweden, but the Gypsy blood that ran through her veins kept her moving around the world through four marriages and four children. Her first husband was a Swedish town planner. The next was a Russian artist, the one after that a Cape Cod carpenter, and the last one an Irish Communist. I was the product of her third and shortest marriage.

After she died, I had her cremated. My cousin made a handsome wooden box to hold the ashes. I hadn't decided what to do with her, so for the time being I kept her in a chest of drawers. There were several possible plans. One was to send her to Sweden. Another was to throw her into the waters of the Rio Grande — or else to scatter her from a windy hill in San Francisco, where she had lived the longest.

While I was still contemplating what to do, burglars broke into my house one night and the box was stolen. The police told me that local fences had become so efficient that there was a good chance my mother would wind up in an Arizona flea market within a couple of days. Still, I thought that once the thief realized his mistake, he might come back and leave the box on my doorstep. After all, there were no jewels inside it — just a heap of ashes. But this never happened, and little by little I was forced to conclude that my dead mother was still roaming around the world, just as she had done in life. It was a strangely poetic twist.

Five years later there was a message on my answering machine from a Father Jack Clark Robinson of the Holy Family Catholic Church. There was another Sara Wilson who lived in the area, and I often received calls that were meant for her. As I had found out from listening to those misguided messages, she was active in a church and coached soccer. Naturally, I thought that the good father had the wrong number. I returned his call and tried to explain to the receptionist that he had the wrong Sara Wilson, but she transferred my call and I had to repeat my explanation. The father then asked me if I was the daughter of Kerstin Lucid. "Yes," I said slowly. They had found a box containing ashes in the church vault, he said, and inside the ashes they had found an identification tag from the Vista Verde Mortuary, which they had in turn traced to me. Father Jack had been at the church for only two years and did not know how or when the box had arrived. He had talked to the priest who had worked at the church before him, but that man didn't know anything about the box, either.

Later that day I drove out to the south valley of Albuquerque to pick up my mother. She had been such a pagan all her life, it was ironic to find her in a Catholic church. Father Jack, dressed in the brown robes of St. Francis, took me to his office. The reappearance of my mother was quite unnerving, and I think he read this on my face. As he gently gave her back to me, I decided to keep her. My family and I now decorate her box for holidays and parties, and we always make sure that she is on the piano when we dance.

SARA WILSON
*Corrales, New Mexico*

# HARRISBURG

On August 27, 1996, my mother woke me in the middle of the night and asked me to call 911. An ambulance arrived at the house and took my father to the local hospital in South Jersey. The following evening, he went into a coma, and the doctors decided to medevac him to a hospital in Philadelphia. By the time my mother and I reached the hospital, he was already in surgery.

Twelve hours later the doctors called the waiting room and said, "An aneurysm erupted in his brain. We don't think he'll ever wake up."

Soon after he was brought to his room in NICU, we went in to see him. While we were talking to him, I said, "Hi, Daddy," and at that moment, he opened his eyes.

The doctors came into the room and asked him several questions. "How old are you? What year is it? Who is the president?" He answered the first three questions correctly. When they asked him the last question, however — "Where are you?" — he answered, "Harrisburg."

Over the next couple of days, he seemed to be making progress. Then, on September 4, the first day of my senior year of high school, I was picked up early. When I reached the hospital, my mother was waiting for me. "He had a relapse," she said. "The doctors have pronounced him brain dead."

A few minutes later, a nurse approached and

asked us to sit down. She wanted to know if we had any questions. Words came out of our mouths, words that no one in our family had ever spoken before. Those words were "organ donation." We knew that it could give others a chance to live, and we wanted to help.

About a week after the funeral, we received a letter from the Gift of Life donor program telling us where the recipients were from and how their recoveries were going.

The list started with the liver and the kidneys. The next sentence read, "A fifty-three-year-old man with three kids received Raymond's heart. He lives in Harrisburg, Pennsylvania." Chills rushed through me, and I dropped the paper.

I believe my father knew that he was going to die, and I also believe he knew that his heart would not die with him. Did he somehow know that it would go on living in Harrisburg?

RANDEE ROSENFELD
*Egg Harbor Township, New Jersey*

# Something to Think About

For my birthday in 1970, my father gave me a birthstone ring. It had a dark-blue sapphire with small diamonds on each side set in a white-gold band. The word "FAITH" was inscribed inside the band. I treasured this ring and wore it often.

In November 1991 I visited a physician's office and accidentally left the ring in his examining room. I called fifteen minutes after leaving his office to notify the staff to search for the ring. The room could not be searched immediately because a patient was being examined there. When the patient left and the room was cleaned, the ring was gone. I reported it missing to the local police and gave them a detailed description. I posted notices in the elevator of the building. I advertised in the local paper, offering a reward for its return. Over the years, I searched in many different jewelry stores, pawnshops, and antique shops to see if I could find a similar ring, but I never could. My father died in 1978.

My mother had a ring with an aquamarine stone, which had been given to her by her grandfather. She wore it always and told me that when she was gone she wanted me to "put it on and never take it off." In October 1991 she came down with an acute illness and had to enter a nursing home.

In early March 1995 an official from the nursing

home told the family that my mother had only a few more days to live. On March 5, I was wearing her ring on a necklace. I was afraid that if I wore it on my finger, I might lose it as I had lost the ring my father had given me. Sitting in her room that afternoon as she lay in a coma, I said to her silently, "Well, Mom, when you get to the 'other side,' maybe you could help me find my ring, so I won't be afraid to wear yours." My mother died on March 7.

On Thursday, March 30, one of the nurses in the clinic where I am employed was doing some paperwork. I entered her office to speak with her, and as her hand moved under the table lamp, a ring she was wearing gave off a great flash of blue light. I said, "Oh, Gloria, what a beautiful ring!" In looking more closely, I immediately realized that it was identical to the ring I had lost in 1991. I asked if I could see it up close. There, inside the band, worn but still visible, was the word "FAITH." Gloria said her boyfriend had found the ring in a used car he was cleaning out for a car dealership. She had had it for some time and had worn it previously. I worked with her often, but I had never noticed. I told her my story and she returned the ring without question. We have since become close friends. I might mention that the ring is also her birthstone. Her birthday is in September, two days before mine.

Needless to say, I have puzzled long and hard over the meaning of this incident. Did my mother somehow "hear" my thoughts through her coma? Was finding the ring a coincidence? Did my mother reach "the other side" and somehow know to look for the ring? Did my own desire to find it activate the chain of events that brought the ring back to me? I cannot solve this puzzle. Perhaps it was a message to me from both my parents. My only certainty is that this event tells me to "have faith."

P. ROHMANN
*Charlottesville, Virginia*

# Good Night

It was that perfect kind of summer evening when children beg to stay outside just a little longer, and parents, remembering their own childhoods, give in. But even such idyllic times must end, and the little ones were finally put to bed.

We sat on the tiny patio just outside our bedroom, enjoying the stillness and lingering warmth. Then came the music. Unprecedented, tentative at first, exploratory notes of a trumpet. Then, gaining confidence, the sound blossomed into a sweet and sentimental melody, an outpouring at once heartfelt and skilled.

Our house sat on a half acre back from the street, which was really just a short, narrow lane. There were two as-yet empty lots in front, parallel to our neighbor's larger property, and groves of walnut trees. We looked up toward the house just above us on the hill, clearly the source of the music, and wondered.

It was an old frame house, maybe the first in the area, two stories, hidden among mature trees. We had never been inside, but our children had, just as the children who lived there, all five of them, had often been in our house. Their ages bracketed those of our three. The oldest, a boy of about twelve, was the senior member of the community of children that lived and played in that sheltered neighborhood defined by the road and the oak-covered hills close by to the west. Their only daughter, leader of the neighborhood girls, both feminine and bold, was always full of ideas. All their children were polite, well-disciplined, and possessed of high spirits.

We did not know the parents well. The father was a sales representative and was often away; the few times we had contact he seemed quietly amiable but remote. The mother, whose soft, southern accent belied their family origins, was a friendly woman, always gracious but reserved.

At the first tentative notes, we speculated that one of the children had taken up the instrument, but almost at once it became evident that this was an older, more practiced performer. It was music of the past, poignant and soulful, the product of a talent and passion we had never suspected. Beautiful but short-lived, the music soon ended. Not long after, we turned out our lights and went to bed. In the silence of the peaceful night we fell asleep.

But the silence did not last. Some time before dawn, we were awakened — sirens, quite close, then lights flashing in through the patio door, pulsing red and white against the leaf patterns on the wall. Muffled sounds, more sirens. Then stillness once again.

In the morning we were told. The children heard first. The father of the family next door, the source of that unexpected serenade, had suffered a heart attack in the night and had not survived.

ELLISE ROSSEN
*Mt. Shasta, California*

# CHARLIE THE TREE KILLER

This is a story that my friend Bruce told me about his great-uncle Charlie. We call him Charlie the tree killer. When Bruce was a boy, he spent many holidays with Uncle Charlie, a successful farmer, and his wife. Together they had raised a fine family in a happy home.

As a young man Charlie planted a wall of saplings around his property, hand-watering them through several dry summers and carefully mowing around their torsos in spring and fall to discourage field mice from devouring their tender bark. By the time Bruce knew him, they had grown straight and tall, raucously sporting leafy festoons in summer; conservatively attired, dignified companions in winter.

But something happened to Charlie as he grew into old age. The trees that had once been his pride and joy became a source of irritation. He would rant that they were going to outlive him and that he would not stand for that, by God. When Bruce recounted these scenes, his face was a flood of emotion, and I could see Uncle Charlie sharpening his axe and plodding into the frozen morning.

Within weeks, many of the trees had been felled. The corpses lay in ghastly formation, with their heads and shoulders turned away from the house. Charlie's wife became frantic and spent her days at a neighbor's farm. She could not bear to see Charlie so distressed or to hear the reports of the axe or the moaning of the trees as they swayed with each blow before losing their balance and crashing to the earth.

One evening Charlie's wife returned home to a dark house. Charlie was not in his chair. She found him outside lying on the ground, his skull crushed in by the weight of a tree that had fallen on top of him.

Friends from miles around came to the wake. Soon Charlie's wife moved into town. Neighbors hauled the best of the logs to the sawmill and cut the tops into cordwood. The farm was sold. Nothing remains of Charlie but the stumps cut close to the earth, now grown over, and the dozen or so surviving trees whose branches have long since spread — so that the house stays cool all summer.

FRANK YOUNG
*Staten Island, New York*

# DEAD MAN'S BLUFF

When I was growing up, we lived in a tiny apartment in Queens. It was in a new building surrounded by vacant lots. My father had brought us to this barren land to escape the Lower East Side of New York, now the hippest part of Gotham. My birth had been the impetus to get us near the suburbs.

Every Friday night my father's friends would come over to play cards. The living room would be transformed into a busy street corner. In a two-bedroom apartment with two sisters, I always slept in the living room. On Fridays, when pinochle was played into the early morning hours, I stayed up pretty late for a ten-year-old. My father would set up a temporary bar in the kitchen: seltzer, soda, scotch, and rye. A tray of ice cubes alongside the bottles. You'd take a coaster and mix yourself a drink. My mother would cut up a pineapple and decorate the plate, surrounding the yellow slices with red cherries. She'd make it look like a boat ready to sail away.

I would hang around the men, a student ready to soak up everything the professors could teach him. Smoke hovered over the card table in big clouds. Leo Gold always blew these serene, slow-moving smoke rings. When the rings broke up and drifted away, the game would begin. Once the cards were dealt, everyone would dig in. It became so silent, you could hear the ice melting in the glasses.

I loved to watch my father work the cards. They became alive in his hands, his dexterous fingers shuffling and dealing with perfect precision. The sounds and rhythms hypnotized me every time. The man who blew smoke rings, Leo Gold, was my father's favorite pinochle partner. My father played cards with Leo for more than twenty years.

I grew up, got married, and raised a family, and my father became a frail old man. Eventually he was admitted to a nursing home. When I went to visit him, if he wasn't too tired, we played cards. It pained me to see my father wither away, but cards remained a lifeline for him.

One Saturday, after an afternoon of poker, my father seemed happy. I kissed him and said good-bye. He died the next day.

The burial was a long distance away, out on Long Island. We followed my father's hearse in a limousine. Such a strange time to sit in luxury. It was a warm and beautiful summer day.

Friends and relatives gathered at my father's grave site. His pine box was lowered into the ground. I put the first shovelful of dirt onto his coffin. When I looked up from the grave, sunlight streamed into my eyes.

I blinked. Then I noticed that the stone next to my father's grave bore the name Leo Gold. Could this be the Leo from the card game? I took a step back to where my mother was standing and leaned toward her. "Leo Gold is here," I whispered.

With tears in her eyes, she scanned the crowd. "Where's Leo?" she asked. "I don't see him."

"No, Mom," I said, "he's lying next to Dad."

Leo Gold, carved in granite, just a few feet away from my father — the two of them lying side by side, in a cemetery in the middle of nowhere.

My mother cried, "If this is our Leo, then Daddy won't be too lonely out here. At least they can play cards."

I smiled, thinking about life's tricks. Or was it death's tricks?

That evening, my mother called Leo Gold's number. We learned from his wife that Leo had died about six months earlier, and that he was in fact buried in the same cemetery.

JOEL EINSCHLAG
*Queens, New York*

# MY BEST FRIEND

Although she wasn't a blood relative, I considered Patty Minehart my sister. We first met in 1943 when we were both sophomores at Victory High School. From the very beginning, we were soul mates. There was always something between us that let one friend know when the other was in need. When she had a stroke in 1996, I was devastated. When they discovered a terminal malignancy three days later, I thought my own life was ending.

During her hospital stay, her family members and I would take turns sitting at her bedside. One Monday I promised I would get there at two o'clock the next day to relieve her daughter Barbara. But on Tuesday morning, after I had taken a shower and dressed, I started to feel extremely uneasy. I walked aimlessly around my house and couldn't seem to focus on doing any one thing. Then, at eleven, I suddenly got a strong urge to leave for the hospital.

When I got to the oncology floor, Patty's older sister, Thurza, was sitting in the waiting room. When she saw me, she jumped up and said, "Oh, they called you!"

I replied, "No, they didn't. She did."

"But she's too weak to dial your number," Thurza said.

"Oh, she didn't call on the telephone," I told her.

Thurza looked puzzled. Together we walked down to Patty's room.

Later that afternoon, Becky, Patty's youngest sister, said to me, "I was trying to leave her bedside all morning to call you, but at around eleven o'clock, Patty said, 'Never mind. I've taken care of it.' "

As always, I had gotten Patty's message.

OLGA HARDMAN
*Clarksburg, West Virginia*

# I Didn't Know

My husband died suddenly at the age of thirty-four. The next year was filled with sadness. Being alone frightened me, and I felt hopelessly insecure about my ability to raise my eight-year-old son without a father.

It was also the year of "I didn't know." The bank levied a service charge on checking accounts that went below five hundred dollars — I didn't know. My life insurance was term and not an annuity — I didn't know. Groceries were expensive — I didn't know. I had always been protected, and now I seemed completely unprepared to handle life alone. I felt threatened on all levels by the things I didn't know.

In response to the high cost of groceries, I planted a garden in the spring. Then, in July, I bought a small chest freezer, hoping it would help to keep the household food budget down. When the freezer arrived, I was given a warning. "Don't plug it in for a few hours," the deliveryman said. "The oil needs time to settle. If you plug it in too soon, you could blow a fuse or burn up the motor."

I hadn't known about oil and freezers, but I did know about blowing fuses. Our little house, wired by a demented electrician, blew lots of fuses.

Later that evening I went out to the garage to start up the freezer. I plugged it in. I stood back and waited. It hummed to life with no blown fuses and no overheated motor. I left the garage and walked down the drive to soak in the soft, warm air. It was less than a year since my husband had died. I stood there in the glow of my neighborhood, watching the lights of the city twinkling in the distance.

Suddenly — darkness, everywhere darkness. No lights burned in my house. There were no neighborhood lights, there were no city lights. As I turned around and looked into the garage, where I had just plugged in my little freezer, I heard myself say out loud, "Oh my God, I didn't know . . ." and an audible bubble of giddiness escaped. Had I blown the fuses of a whole city by plugging in my freezer too soon? Was it possible? Had I done this?

I ran back to the house and turned on my battery-powered police-band radio. I heard sirens in the distance and feared they were coming to get me, "the widow lady with the freezer." Then I heard over the radio that a drunk driver had taken out the breaker pole on the main road.

I was overwhelmed by both relief and embarrassment — relief because I hadn't caused the blackout, and embarrassment because I'd thought that I could. Standing there in the darkness, I also felt something replace the fear that I had been living with since my husband's death. The feeling was somewhere between lightness and joy. I had giggled at my misplaced power, and at that moment I knew I had my humor back. I had lived a sorrowful and frightened year of "I didn't know." The sadness wasn't gone, but deep within myself, I could still laugh. The laughter made me feel powerful. After all, hadn't I just blacked out a whole city?

LINDA MARINE
*Middleton, Wisconsin*

# CARDIAC ARRESTS

He arrived at the emergency department in full cardiac arrest. Paramedics were performing CPR. He had received two rounds of drugs — epinephrine, atropine, and sodium bicarb. His airway was intubated in the field. On arrival, he was found to be in ventricular fibrillation. More epinephrine and electrical shock produced no response, and he was pronounced dead: a seventy-one-year-old man who had lived alone in a local trailer park, presumed to have succumbed to a massive heart attack.

She arrived at the emergency department in full cardiac arrest. Paramedics were performing CPR. She had received two rounds of drugs — epinephrine, atropine, and sodium bicarb. Her airway was intubated in the field. On arrival, she was found to be in ventricular fibrillation. More epinephrine and electrical shock produced no response, and she was pronounced dead: a forty-two-year-old woman from out of town here to bury her father. She was staying at his place in a local trailer park. Tasteless, odorless — carbon monoxide had also poisoned her.

SHERWIN WALDMAN, M.D.
*Highland Park, Illinois*

# GRANDMOTHER'S FUNERAL

After my grandfather died, my grandmother lost whatever interest she still had in life. Though she lived on for another ten years, well into her eighties, she spent most of her time in worry and fear, anticipating her own death. Two terrors preoccupied her: that she might die alone and that she might, in spite of her fervent prayer and determined avoidance of sin, be consumed in the hellfire of her religious belief. She planned her own funeral.

She lived with her son and daughter-in-law in a ranch-style house in Indianapolis. Her sister's religious paintings, including a wall-sized oil of the Palm Sunday Jesus, surrounded her. Less to her liking, but company nonetheless, were several cats and a couple of dogs. My uncle and aunt ran a men's hairpiece business at the back of the house. Since they worked at home, they almost never left my grandmother alone.

One Sunday afternoon a friend who lived just around the corner called and invited my aunt and uncle to visit her husband, who had just come home from the hospital. My grandmother was napping. They were going to be gone for only half an hour, so they went.

Whether it was true or not, the firemen assured my uncle and aunt that my grandmother had probably never woken up. She died in her sleep of smoke inhalation. The cause of the fire was faulty wiring that must have been smoldering deep inside the insulation for a long time and chose to ignite on that particular Sunday. The animals didn't survive. The paintings were destroyed.

On the day of the funeral, everyone in the family was still in shock. I tried to think of something to say to my older sister, who was walking beside me through the cemetery. Finally I commented that the snow-white dress she and my mother had chosen for my grandmother's burial was particularly lovely.

"We didn't choose it," she said. "You didn't hear?"

"Hear what?" I asked.

"It was very strange. It gives me the chills even now."

I waited for her to explain.

"That was the dress that Grandmother was saving to be buried in," she said.

"So?"

"It was in the house, in the closet in the back hall. Everything in the closet was destroyed by smoke, flame, or water — everything except that one dress."

MARTHA DUNCAN
*Surry, Maine*

# HIGH STREET

After remarrying fifteen years ago, I moved from Massachusetts to Hall Avenue in Henniker, New Hampshire, where my new husband had (and still has) a dental practice. At that time, my parents lived in Florida, and I would frequently receive mail from them. When the letter was from my father, our mailing address usually had a "cross-out" in front of the "Hall Ave." part of our address. I finally remembered to ask my father why there was almost always this cross-out. He replied that he had a mental block on our street address: he wanted to write "High Street" instead of Hall Avenue.

A few years after I moved here, I was doing some historical research in the library. It was then that I discovered that Hall Avenue had been named High Street until after World War II, when it was renamed for a local boy named Hall who had been killed in the war.

JUDITH ENGLANDER
*Henniker, New Hampshire*

# A FAILED EXECUTION

Tomas is a renowned photojournalist. He is talking about his experiences amidst tragedy. Without braggadocio, he talks of war zones, political events, lost friends, and anonymous passings. His clipped words are accentuated by his Swiss accent. Though fluent, he struggles when he believes his vocabulary is keeping him from communicating the power of a situation. He shouldn't worry. The events are simple; the implications clear.

From a time in Sarajevo he talks of having to drop his camera to help deliver a newborn only to see the baby lose its hospital bed to a dying child whose head had been blown apart by shelling. From a time in America he talks of being blindfolded and having his fingertips taped by lepers intent on illustrating their plight. The evening wears on; our discussion turns to the suicide of a fellow photographer.

"Photographers are haunted," says Tomas. "You witness all these things, but the images will not leave your mind. They are like nightmares."

"Do you have nightmares?" I ask. He nods silently and begins his tale.

It is 1994 and Tomas travels to South Africa to cover the election of Nelson Mandela. Upheaval reigns throughout the country; he and several other journalists drive to a poverty-stricken region where white supremacist rebels are preparing to

463

confront the black population, which is agitating to gain voting rights.

As Tomas and his colleagues enter the region, they inadvertently drive into a convoy of white rebels. Bullets fly past their vehicle, but no one is injured. Suddenly the motorcade jerks to a stop. Black soldiers are attacking white rebels. A gunfight ensues. The terrified photographers scramble out and hide behind the car.

Slowly the soldiers gain a bloody upper hand. Most of the rebels have now fled or been killed. Those that have survived lie injured and indignant, cursing and insulting those they had come to kill.

Tomas emerges from the powdery dirt of his hiding place. He hurriedly snaps photos of the eerie surrender that has unfolded. Nobody knows what will happen next.

A black soldier, rifle aloft, approaches the rebels.

A shot rings out and a listless white body drops to the dry ground. With another shot, the soldier kills a second rebel. Tomas, in a daze, can only observe and record the horrifying scene. There can be no intervention. The executions continue; the chaos deepens. The photographers eventually flee, terrified of what might occur next.

Several days later, the photographers receive a call from a news cameraman who had been at the scene of the executions.

"Come over here," they are told, "there's something you should see."

As Tomas enters the editing room, the tape rolls. The battle scene slowly replays. He sees the rebels and the soldiers. But then he sees someone else — himself.

He and a fellow photographer can be seen to one side as they capture image after image of the bloody executions. Then a figure appears above them, a black soldier. His weapon is pointing not at the rebels but at the oblivious photographers. He shakily raises his weapon, squeezes the trigger and . . . click. Nothing happens. The soldier hesitates and examines his weapon. It has jammed. A sharp whack ejects the bullet. The soldier reloads. Click. Again nothing. Another whack, another ejected bullet, and another reload. Click. Nothing again. Then, outside the field of vision, a distraction occurs. The soldier flees the scene, leaving the photographers to complete their work.

Tomas slumps in the edit booth. He has just seen his own death.

DAVID ANDERSON
*New York, New York*

# THE GHOST

When I was fifteen I became involved with a civic organization whose membership consisted of Mexicans and Mexican Americans. My father, who was Mexican, was a member, and I participated in folk dances during the festivities that were held for Cinco de Mayo and Mexican Independence Day on September 16.

The young woman who taught us the dances decided to teach me one that involved only two people. More than likely, it was because I didn't have much skill at dancing, but she wanted us all to do our best. At any rate, the dance I learned was a play about a boy trying to pull a young girl out onto the dance floor and her refusal, up to a point, to dance with him. Over the next couple of years, this particular dance became my own, and I always performed it at the holiday programs. The one thing that changed over time was my partner, and I eventually had three different ones. They were all a few years older than I was, and because they knew my father, they were much too respectful, as far as I was concerned. Eventually, as my teenage life became full of high-school activities and friends, my participation in the holiday programs lessened. By the time I was eighteen, my dancing days were far behind me, but my father would give me news of one kind or another about the young men who had been my partners.

466

I came home from school one evening and started to go into my room to change out of my school clothes. I'm old enough to have been one of those girls for whom wearing pants to school was a fantasy. I opened the door to my room, and as I started to step in, I froze in my tracks. The room was small, and on an early spring evening it was already dark in there at six o'clock. Before I could reach in to turn on the light, I had seen a figure sitting on my bed, but the figure was in my mind's eye. I quickly pulled back and closed the door. My heart was pounding, and I was truly frightened. I had sensed someone in that room, and to make it even stranger, the image I saw was of a young Mexican man dressed in the traditional *charro* outfit, which consisted of tight black pants, a bolero jacket, and a large black felt sombrero. Needless to say, I was startled at my thoughts and felt somewhat disconcerted at not being able to go into my own room. I simply could not walk into it.

At the time, my household consisted of my parents, myself, and my maternal grandmother, who spoke only Spanish. Although she had been living in the United States for about forty years, she was still culturally a product of Mexico. She would tell me stories about her home and her family, all of whom had died long before I was born. Unfortunately, her dead relations seemed to have this terrible habit of coming to visit her, or so she said. "Your father," she would say to my mother, "came to see me last night. He stood right in this doorway and he said . . . ." I would stare at the doorway, not quite believing her but feeling scared just the same to think that a ghost had been in my house while I was sleeping. I mention this in order to explain how an average American girl could have accepted the idea of an unseen presence so readily. For me, that presence was as real as the door I couldn't open.

I spent that whole evening attempting to go into my room, and every time I tried there would be that same image of the young Mexican man sitting and waiting. I didn't know exactly what he was waiting for, and I was too frightened to find out. I spent an uncomfortable and frankly bizarre evening avoiding my room, but finally at around ten o'clock I decided that I absolutely had to go in. I walked to my door and, holding my breath, pushed it open and immediately reached for the light switch. As soon as the room was lit, the image vanished, and so did my fear. I went to bed, and by the next day I had put the entire experience out of my mind.

The next evening, I came home at the usual time and went straight to my room to change. I did have a moment's hesitation just before opening the door, but there was nothing wrong, and I went in without a problem. A little while later, I went into the kitchen to see my parents, who were preparing dinner. When my mother saw me come in, she told me that she had some bad news for me. It seemed that one of my old dance partners, José, a young man of about twenty-five who was from Mexico, had died. I had known he was in the hospital because my father had gone to see him, but I had been told he was being treated and was expecting to be released. My mother then told me

he had died at about five o'clock the previous afternoon.

G. A. GONZALEZ
*Salt Lake City, Utah*

# HEART SURGERY

I am a practicing cardiac surgeon in a western state. Several years ago, I performed high-risk coronary-bypass surgery on an elderly gentleman. I believe he was in his midseventies. The operation appeared to be a success, but three days later the patient developed an arrhythmia, and his heart stopped beating. I performed CPR on him for three hours and, amazingly, we were able to resuscitate him. In the process, however, the man suffered a brain injury. The symptoms were altogether unusual. He now thought he was fifty years old. During the three hours when I was performing CPR on him, he had lost more than twenty years of his life.

I followed the patient for a couple of months, and during that time he seemed to regain about ten of those years. When I lost track of him, he was convinced that he was sixty years old. He had the strength and energy of a man twenty years younger than his chronological age.

About a year and a half later, I was playing golf with a good friend of mine. He had brought along a friend of his, and that man happened to be the patient's son-in-law. He pulled me aside and told me that his father-in-law had died earlier that month. I expressed my sympathy. At that point, the man proceeded to tell me a story that I will never forget.

Prior to his heart surgery, my patient had been

an alcoholic, a wife-abuser, and impotent for about twenty years. After his cardiac arrest and re-suscitation — and the loss of twenty years of memory — he had forgotten all these things about himself. He stopped drinking. He began sleeping with his wife again and became a loving husband. This lasted for more than a year. And then, one night, he died in his sleep.

DR. G.
*place withheld*

# THE CRYING PLACE

In the early '60s, when I was fourteen years old and living in a small town in southern Indiana, my father died. While my mother and I were out of town visiting relatives, an unexpected and very sudden heart attack took him. We returned home to find that he was gone. No chance to say "I love you" or even "Good-bye." He was just gone, forever. With my older sister going away to college, our home went from a bustling, happy family of four to a house where two stunned people lived in quiet grief.

I struggled terribly with the pain and loneliness of my loss, but I was also very worried about my mother. I feared that if she saw me crying for my father, her pain would be even more intense. And, as the new "man" of the house, I felt a responsibility to protect her from greater hurt. So I devised a plan that would allow me to grieve without causing more pain for my mother. In our town, people took the trash from their houses out to large barrels in the alleys behind their backyards. There, it would be burned or picked up by the trashmen once a week. Every evening after dinner, I would volunteer to take out the trash. I would rush around the house with a bag, collecting scraps of paper or whatever else I could find, and then go out to the alley and put it in the trash barrel. Then I'd hide in the shadows of the dark bushes, and that's where I would stay until I had cried myself out. After recovering enough to be certain that my mother couldn't tell what I'd been doing, I would return to the house and get ready for bed.

This subterfuge went on for weeks. One evening after dinner, when it was time for chores, I collected the trash and went out to my usual hiding place in the bushes. I didn't stay very long. When I returned to the house, I went to find my mother to ask if she needed me to do anything else. After searching through the entire house, I finally found her. She was in the darkened basement, behind the washer and dryer, crying by herself. She was hiding her pain, to protect me.

I'm not sure which is greater: the pain you suffer openly or the pain you endure alone to protect someone you love. I do know that on that night, in the basement, we held each other and poured out the misery that had driven us both to our separate, lonely, crying places. And we never felt the need to cry alone again.

TIM GIBSON
*Cincinnati, Ohio*

# LEE

In February 1994 my twelve-year-old nephew, Lee, died suddenly and unexpectedly after playing in a hockey game. It was the single most horrible thing that had ever happened to our family. When my mother called to give me the news, I immediately got a mental picture of my sister down in a deep pit. I had never experienced that level of grief before. It was devastating.

My sister and I had been pregnant together with our first children, and they were born just four months apart — my daughter first, then her son. We were "older moms" (twenty-eight and thirty-one), and we both quit our jobs to stay at home with our babies. We breast-fed the children, and once, when I was taking care of him and he wouldn't accept a bottle, I even nursed my nephew. Lee took the breast, looked up at me with an expression of relief, and allowed me to take his mother's place. That was a very intimate thing. I mention it now to stress how strong the bond was between us and how traumatic his death was for me.

He died on a Saturday, and the funeral (with his whole hockey team there in uniform) was on Wednesday. Friday morning I cried hard again and asked God to help me. Help me to understand, I prayed, help me to accept — give me a sign that you hear me, that you exist, that everything will be all right some day. It was freezing out that morning and I was emotionally exhausted, but I took my dog for a walk. I was oblivious to my surroundings, lost in my own thoughts. I had barely left my yard when a young man came up to me on the street. It felt as though he had appeared out of nowhere. He was very friendly and talkative and asked me a lot of questions about my dog. I had never seen him before, so I asked if he had just moved into the neighborhood. No, he said, he'd been living there for sixteen years, in a house just down the block. I was barely paying attention. I was in a fog, and I didn't respond much to his steady stream of conversation. When we arrived in front of his house, we said good-bye, and I turned to continue on my way. Suddenly, I heard him yell out behind me, "By the way, I'm Lee."

He couldn't imagine the effect this had on me. I had just asked for a sign, and now I had been given one. I had asked for help, and I had been heard. I continued around the block, tears falling down my face. He hadn't said, "Oh, by the way, my name is Lee." He had said, "I'm Lee." What were the chances that he would be out there in the street with me on that freezing cold Friday morning when no one else was around? He had been living down the block from me for the entire eleven years I had been there, and I had never seen him before.

"I'm Lee." Those words were a great comfort to me, and my faith was deepened because of them. Whenever I have doubts about myself and the world, I remember what happened that day, and it helps. It also helped my sister.

JODIE WALTERS
*Minneapolis, Minnesota*

475

# SOUTH DAKOTA

In the 1970s I was a teenager living with my soon-to-be-divorced parents in the suburbs of Atlanta. My mother had grown up on the South Dakota plains, the daughter of a farmer and a farmer's wife. She came from sturdy German and Danish stock, people who had come to this country with a few humble possessions, received great expanses of flat land, and then had set about to make a life farming. Not an easy living, even in the best of times. Weather reigned supreme in these flat lands, and life revolved around it. Nearly every Sunday, the pastor in church made a reference to the weather, usually asking for it to change: an end to the drought so the crops could grow, an end to the rain so the harvest could begin, an end to the snows so the cattle could be saved. Eventually my grandfather tired of praying to God over the weather and got a job on the highway patrol. Which didn't keep him from regularly tying one on at the Mansfield Supper Club and then hitting the road in his patrol car. Gregarious by nature, he loved practical jokes, dancing, parties, and women. My grandmother, by contrast, was shy, demure, and hardworking. She kept the farm going when my grandfather was away, which was often, and didn't shrink from any difficult task that presented itself. Once, she found that the sheep had gotten into a grain bin and gorged themselves. They were swollen up like balloons, bawling in agony. Knowing that they would die unless she did what had to be done, she set about expertly deflating each sheep with a sharp kitchen knife to the flank. I could picture it — her topknot of soft brown hair, in a plain dress and sturdy boots, puncturing sheep, the awful odor of fermenting grain and sheep bowels hissing into the air.

My mother was the last of three daughters. Her oldest sister had been a navy wave and married a boy handpicked by my grandfather. In fact, she had been in love with another boy, who happened to be a Catholic. He may as well have been a tribesman with a bone in his nose, so impossible was the idea to my grandfather that any daughter of his could marry a Catholic. As a member of the local police force, my grandfather was able to make life unbearable for him and ran him out of town in short order. My mother's other sister had dutifully married a farmer and stayed in South Dakota, where they had four boys and carried on farming the land.

The three sisters kept in close touch. One day my mother was talking with her sister in South Dakota. These phone calls often detailed some tragic event, such as, cousin Bernice slipped trying to get her door prize from the church supper out of the backseat of the car, hit her head, and lapsed into a coma; or a cow panicked when calving and ran all over the pasture with her uterus hanging out and bled to death. My mother seemed to relish retelling these tales of woe. On this particular day, however, she had listened quietly, spoken little, and when she hung up the phone, she was visibly shaken. My aunt told her that they had found Diane Wellington.

Diane Wellington had been a high-school classmate of my mother's. She was the local rich girl, and the other girls, mostly farmers' daughters who rode plow horses to school, often borrowed her clothes and jewelry for special events. My mother said that Diane was quiet and mostly kept to herself. Although the girls borrowed her fine clothes, they weren't really her friends. Her family took vacations in airplanes to places with beaches and sit-down restaurants. Farm families never took vacations. My mother and most of her friends had never even been out of the county and had never been in a plane, except for the crop dusters. Although they admired her, Diane didn't fit in. One day Diane didn't come to school. Later that same day, her parents called the school to say that she was missing. Teachers questioned the students for details about where Diane might be. But no one knew her that well. No one knew where she might have gone.

Diane's desk stayed empty for days, then weeks. Eventually, her locker was cleaned out and the contents sent home to her parents. The possibility of foul play was dismissed. Except for the occasional outburst of domestic violence — which wasn't considered to be a police matter at that time, anyway — crime was nonexistent in their small community. The police labeled Diane a runaway and filed the case. My mother and her classmates invented exciting stories about how Diane had run off to the city. They imagined her as an actress or a model with a new life in her beautiful clothes. They imagined that she had created a new identity and was living in a penthouse apartment far away from the smells of tractor diesel and manure. Or maybe she had become a wealthy man's wife. The only boys they had known her to date were prep-school boys from out of town. Maybe there was some scandalous reason why she had disappeared. Maybe she had run off with an older man or, even better, a married man. They imagined her on the arm of a handsome Ivy League collegian or a smartly dressed businessman, conspicuously older than she was. But eventually, as the separate events of their own lives unfolded, they all forgot about her and her mysterious disappearance. They did think it strange that she never called or wrote her parents, but no one ever said so aloud. My mother said she hadn't thought of Diane for over twenty years. Now, my aunt told her that she had been there all along.

It was common farming practice to allow fields to lay fallow from time to time. Stripped of nutrients after years of planting and harvesting, fields were left unplanted to allow them to become rich again. After years of absorbing rain and snow and sun, nature changed them back to fertile land. It was just such a field that a farmer eventually turned over. And in breaking up the long-undisturbed black crust, the discs of the plow churned up bones. Not those of a coyote or a calf, but unmistakably human bones. The bones, they discovered, were those of Diane Wellington. What chilled my blood, however, was the thing my mother told me in a whisper, her voice weighted with the shame of the past: along with the bones of the teenage girl in her shallow grave were a handful of tiny, birdlike bones — the bones of a fetus.

Abortion had become legal and safe only a few years before her bones surfaced. I tried not to think about it: a girl of about my age in a dark, dirty room with the abortionist and his tools; her terror and pain as the car bounced over rutted fields while she was dying in the backseat, her young life ebbing out of her. Or had she died in that horrible room? Had the boy been with her? Or was it a man, someone they knew? Did anyone hold her hand? Or had she lain there in the dirt and weeds alone and watched the red taillights grow smaller and bounce out of sight? Had she lain there alone in the deep darkness looking up at the vast South Dakota sky? I hoped that if she had, the stars' light had been there for her. That it had been some comfort to her, that the heavens had reached down and stayed with her until the end.

NANCY PEAVY
*Augusta, Maine*

# CONNECTING WITH PHIL

It happened in 1991, but sometimes it seems like part of the distant past. On the other hand, I can remember the ride home after my wife picked me up from the hospital as if it were yesterday.

I was emotionally and physically exhausted from my bizarre afternoon, which had culminated in two anxiety-filled hours in the emergency room. When the paramedics had arrived, there had been no color in my face. My hands had been cold and clammy, and perspiration had been pouring down my sides and back. I had been afraid that I was going to die. The paramedics had measured my pulse and blood pressure, and although they found nothing wrong with me, they had decided to take me to the hospital. A few minutes later, I was inside a speeding ambulance, an oxygen mask over my nose and mouth.

Later, when she was driving me home, my wife asked me if I was all right. Of course I said no, and then I attempted to describe exactly what had happened, even though I wasn't sure myself. As to why it had happened, I had no idea. I told her how it had all started with a vague feeling of unease, which had sent me pacing around the house like a nervous cat. For no particular reason, I'd believed I was coming down with a cold, and I'd started taking my temperature every five or ten minutes. To say the least, my behavior had been odd.

481

Then came the pain, first in my abdomen, then in my lower back. That's when I had become frightened — with the pain in my lower back. My brother Phil had lost the use of his kidneys and had been on dialysis for several years. I had tried to remember how Phil had become ill, but my mind wouldn't cooperate — it was racing from thought to thought, and I couldn't control it. I'd felt as if I was on a speeding roller coaster. Then I'd started feeling dizzy and decided to sit down. Somehow, I'd landed on a chair next to the phone. My hand had been shaking as I dialed 911.

I stared out the car window, my mind drifting into a fog. When we were about halfway home, my wife turned to me and told me that Phil had died.

Phil dead? How could that be? I had just spoken to him on the phone the night before.

Phil had moved to Florida eleven years earlier, and since then we had visited each other only a handful of times. But when his health took a turn for the worse, I had found myself calling him every couple of weeks. Recently, there had been something in his voice that had told me he was more aware of his mortality and was becoming more afraid of death.

However, when we'd spoken the night before, Phil had sounded like his old self: relaxed, cheerful, more alive than he'd been in years. I'd hung up the phone feeling close to him again, as if we weren't separated by fifteen hundred miles.

The next day, when the paramedics were placing the oxygen mask on my face, my brother was breathing his final breaths.

Ever since I realized that he wouldn't live a long

life, I had promised myself that I would be there for my brother in the end. But the possibility of his dying a sudden death had never crossed my mind. Maybe it was a mere coincidence, but what are the chances that I would have a panic attack during the same hour that Phil was found dead in his bathroom? I prefer to believe that he sent me his pain and fear when I couldn't fulfill my promise.

TOM SELLEW
*Wadsworth, Ohio*

# THE LETTER

I was third officer on an American supertanker that loaded crude oil in the Persian Gulf and discharged it alternately between ports in South Korea and Bonaire, Netherlands Antilles. It was 1980. The vessel was returning to the Persian Gulf after stopping in Bonaire. We were crossing the South Atlantic Ocean, and in six days we would be passing Cape Town, South Africa. I was at the end of my work period and would fly home from Cape Town to Massachusetts.

One day, leaving the galley after lunch, I picked up a six-month-old copy of a newspaper called the Singapore *Straits Times*. I was planning to work overtime in the afternoon, and I headed to my cabin to get a little rest before taking to the deck. All the cabins were furnished with lounge chairs, which we referred to as "overtime eaters" because they had a way of preventing us from going back on deck.

Willing to risk the powers of the chair, I settled in with my newspaper full of out-of-date news. One article in particular caught my eye. It was an interview with the director of an American funeral home, talking about his job. He said that the hardest part of what he did was helping people deal with grief. One of the most common and painful aspects of grief, he said, was the feeling of not having told the deceased everything that needed telling. He had found that writing a letter to the person who had died and placing it in the coffin could alleviate much of this torment.

When I had finished reading the article, I put the paper aside and leaned back, closing my eyes. That was when the picture of my mother lying in a casket came to me. I tried to dismiss it, but it was strong and vivid, and I was suddenly filled with grief. Inside the vision, I wrote her a letter.

I forget most of the words I used, but I can still feel the letter's meaning. I remember expressing an overwhelming love for her, something I had never allowed myself to do before. In this vision, I realized that never having told her I loved her would be a source of anguish for me when she died. I spent some time getting this down in my letter, and all the while, the image of my mother in her casket remained fresh. I saw myself folding the letter and placing it in her coffin, and finally the feeling of grief subsided. I started thinking about what I'd be working on when I went back out on deck.

Later that evening I woke up and prepared for my evening bridge watch. There was a knock at the door. When I opened it, the captain, an imposing man, stood there filling my doorway. He came into the room and asked me to sit down. Then he said that this was the hardest part of his job. I was only half-listening to what he said next as I started to review everything I had done on the voyage. What mistake could I have made in the past three months that would cause him to fire me? Forcing myself to pay attention, I looked up to see him with tears in his eyes, reading the telegram that brought me the news of my mother's death.

BRIAN F. MCGEE
*Pensacola, Florida*

# DRESS REHEARSAL

My eighty-nine-year-old mother had been diagnosed with congestive heart failure. The doctors said that she was too old and too sick to save and that they would "make her as comfortable as possible." No one knew how much time she had left: it could be days, weeks, or months.

We'd had a rocky time together. She had never been easy to get along with, especially when I was a child. Maybe I wasn't easy, either. Finally, when I was forty-two years old, I gave up hoping she'd turn into the kind of mother I'd always wanted. On Christmas Eve, while visiting her and my father, I cut the umbilical cord at the top of my lungs. I stopped talking to her for a year and a half. Then, when we were back on speaking terms, I stuck to only the most superficial subjects. This sat very well with her; in fact, at one point she sent me a letter saying how glad she was that we had become so close.

The retirement community she lived in was four hours away. When I got word that she was dying, I started to spend a lot of time visiting her. The first month after she received her prognosis, she was very depressed and distant. She either slept or stared at the wall, silent, her face a mask of misery. She'd insisted on being catheterized so she'd never have to get out of bed again, and then she'd settled down to the business of dying. One day during that month, I was sitting in the chair next to her bed. The sun had set and her room was almost completely dark. I shifted my chair closer and rested my elbows on the edge of her bed. She reached out her hand to touch my face and stroked it very gently. It was a wonderful thing.

During another visit a couple of weeks later, my mother experienced the first of the six little deaths that preceded her real death. When I arrived, my father went out to do some errands. I was playing a game of rummy with my mother, and she was cheating like crazy, when she announced that she had to go to the bathroom. I helped her out of bed and "spotted" her as she made her slow way to the toilet with her walker. When we got into the tiny bathroom, she let out a long breath and collapsed. I caught her and lowered her to the floor. She was breathing the agonized breaths of the dying and was unconscious, her eyes open but blank. I was paralyzed. She eventually let out a long final breath and didn't take another one in. I watched her face turn blue and her lips turn purple. Then I looked at the pulse on her neck, which was easy to do because she was so heartbreakingly skinny. As I watched, the pulse stopped. She was completely still. I held her there for a moment, frozen. I asked her out loud if she was dead; of course she didn't answer. I thought about what an honor it was that she had chosen me to die with, and then — oh no, oh no, oh no! I gently lowered her head to the floor and told her that I had to make a call and that I would be right back. I went to the phone and called the main desk. Then I went back into the bathroom and looked down at her. She seemed small and forlorn. I sat on the floor behind her head, hauled her into a half-sitting position, and held her in my arms for a few minutes, wondering how long it would take before someone got there.

All of a sudden, her body jerked. I almost jumped out of my skin. Then I thought: it's just her nervous system settling. A couple of minutes later, there was another big body jerk. Then the agonized breathing started up again.

I couldn't believe it: she was alive. I struggled to adjust to this new reality while she began huffing and puffing, flailing around, smashing her arms against the sink and wall. She was weeping and moaning. I tried to quiet her, telling her where she was. Finally, she came back to consciousness, the blankness left her eyes, and she saw that she was on the bathroom floor. I had pushed her walker into the corner, and she reached for it, saying, "Get me up! I have to get up!"

I said, "I can't get you up alone, Mom. People are on their way to help. Just stay still with me until they get here."

She eventually gave in and collapsed against me, breathing hard. The doorbell rang, and then the resident nurse and the attendant from the front desk let themselves in, rushing to the bathroom, fully expecting to find my mother dead. But there we were on the floor, two living people, one holding the other. The three of us got my mother onto the toilet, cleaned her up, and put her back in bed. Ten minutes later, my mother was beating me in a game of rummy, cheating like mad.

Later that day I was sitting on the edge of my mother's bed. I can only imagine how stunned and exhausted I must have looked, because she said to me, "Now, dear, when I'm really dying — not one of these dress rehearsals I seem to be having — but when I'm really going, I want you to know that I'll be kissing you all over!" Then she fluttered her hands around my head. With love pouring from her eyes, she said, "Kiss! Kiss! Kiss! Kiss!"

I'd never seen her so full of joy.

The next day, I had to leave, even though I didn't want to. Just as I was walking out the door, the phone rang. It was Sister Pat, a nun who worked with the hospice organization that was caring for my mother. She said that the nurse had told her what had happened to my mother and asked if I thought it would be a good idea for her to pay a visit. Since both my parents shunned any open talk of God or spirituality, I said I didn't think so. I said I'd like to chat with her on the phone, however.

I told Sister Pat that my mother had made a complete turnaround in the past twenty-four hours. I told her how she had been completely and inconsolably miserable, and that now, after what had happened, she seemed happy and content. It was like night and day, I said.

There was a long pause. Then Sister Pat said, "Your mother is a very fortunate woman."

"Huh?" I said, thinking, She's dying — that's fortunate?

Sister Pat continued. In her twenty-odd years of working with dying people, she said, she had observed that the ones who had "little deaths" were very peaceful for the rest of their lives. She said it was as if they got to take a little look-see and real-ized that there was nothing to be afraid of on the other side.

My mother and I had six more months after that. She had five more dress rehearsals and was proud of them all. One time, I called her up, and when she got on the phone she said, "Guess what I did today?"

"What, Mom?" I asked.

"I died again!"

We never talked about much — just the weather, bits of news — but it didn't matter any-more. We lived in a little blue egg of light, and the love poured back and forth between us inside the egg. I finally got the mother I'd been waiting for.

ELLEN POWELL
*South Burlington, Vermont*

# The Anonymous Deciding Factor

I come from a family of morticians. My grandfather, my uncle, and my father were all in the business, and I grew up in a household where normal topics of conversation included cremation, the rising cost of caskets, and the sudden jerk of a dead limb relieving itself of an air pocket.

"You guys remember Morgan," someone might say, "that fat hardware salesman whose heart finally caved in under three inches of greasy bacon fat? Well, damned if I hadn't just finished juicin' him when the old boy sat straight up on the table. Must have been holding one hell of an air pocket in that cellulose gut of his. Almost made me drop my tuna fish sandwich right on the floor. Pass the potatoes, please."

I had never been in the basement of my aunt and uncle's mortuary. Then, one day, my aunt invited me to visit it. I followed close behind her as we descended the narrow staircase. My apprehension and dread mounted with every step. An image of mummylike corpses stacked in precarious piles flashed into my brain. I imagined myself, with my unique brand of clumsiness, bumping into a gauze-wrapped limb and causing hundreds of stiff, bloodless bodies to topple down from all directions, crushing me under their dead weight.

Then — relief. We entered a warm, carpeted room that smelled faintly of cigar smoke and mildew. All around me, six-inch-high platforms displayed beautiful, sleek containers of death. Each casket was as luxurious as a Mercedes, and down in this wet basement showroom, my uncle was the smooth salesman.

I had to stand on my toes to get a glimpse of the interiors of these expensive boxes. Their pillowy linings were made of shining white or pink satin trimmed in delicate lace. How comfortable they looked! For a moment, I forgot the real purpose of the boxes, and I wanted to crawl inside and feel the softness of a small satin headrest against my face. I picked out a small white casket for myself.

"Uncle Jim, when I die, can you put me in a princess casket like this one?"

But my aunt and uncle had disappeared around the corner. I followed them into the next room.

Under the cold blue fluorescent lights, two female corpses lay naked on large stainless-steel tables. I was seized by an urge to run back to the casket room.

My aunt approached the first body. Breathing carefully and trying not to let the shock show on my face, I followed her.

The corpse's skin was thin, almost translucent, a pasty gray hue spattered with blackish-burgundy age spots. Her breasts sloped outward to either side of her rib cage with an inert permanence, as if they had always been in this awkward position below her armpits. Her stomach displayed the characteristic bloat of the embalmed, coupled with two extra rolls of gelatinous, lumpy fat. I quickly

493

averted my eyes from the sparse mound of coarse gray pubic hair, feeling embarrassed for the old woman lying there naked among strangers. My eyes followed the long highways of purple varicose veins that ran down her heavy legs.

So this is death.

I touched her cool arm, and it was as heavy and stiff as a sturdy piece of firewood. It was at that moment that all my fear subsided. The thing in front of me was no longer an evil, frightening mummy or zombie, but a hollow shell, no more a person than the stainless-steel table it lay upon.

I painted each cyanotic fingernail with peach-colored polish and watched silently as my aunt carefully styled the gray mass of hair. I applied peach powder to the corpse's pale face, and with the addition of rouge and lipstick she was transformed into something that reminded me of a mannequin I had once seen in a Sears window.

Dressing a dead person is no easy task. The body weighs twice as much as it did in life and absolutely nothing bends. I watched my uncle hoist this stiff woman so a modest slip could be pulled to her waist. The angle at which he raised the torso was just enough to release a last small dribble of urine out of the woman's bladder and onto the table and my aunt's skirt. We all laughed.

Later that day, I spoke to my parents with unusual urgency. I asked my father if, in the event of my death, I could be cremated.

He looked at me with an earnest expression, and said, "Of course you can, if that's what you really want." In that reply I heard the tone of a professional man who had reassured countless

494

anguished strangers about their final wishes. I also heard a concerned father who had just heard his daughter make her first major decision about life and death.

"Yes, Dad." I said. "That's what I really want."

HOLLIE CALDWELL CAMPANELLA
*Klamath Falls, Oregon*

# DREAMS

# 4:05 A.M.

I sleep soundly most of the time and seldom need an alarm clock to wake up in the morning. My dreams are usually about work, and I try to forget them as quickly as possible. The dreams I do want to remember I usually can't. Only a few times in my life have I had a nightmare.

The dream started simply. I was driving a truck down the Kansas Turnpike. I have never driven a truck, and although I lived in Kansas City at the time, I had never been on the Kansas Turnpike. It was night in the dream, and I could see only my hands on the steering wheel and what was illuminated by the truck's headlights. Suddenly in front of me, shining in the headlights, was a human arm. Horrified, I swerved to keep from hitting it as I frantically tried to step on the brake, but I couldn't slow the truck, and as soon as I got around one body part, another appeared up ahead. The farther I went, the more body parts I saw. They kept coming up at me, faster and faster, until I finally hit one with a grisly thump. A moment later, I sat up in bed screaming.

I realized that I was having a nightmare. I took a deep breath and looked at the clock, more to reassure myself than to find out the time. It was 4:05 A.M.

I enjoyed my Saturday and forgot about the dream. Sunday, I bought the weekend paper and read it in my usual leisurely fashion. Near the end of the first section there was a two-paragraph article about a truck driver who had run over a body lying on the Kansas Turnpike. The accident had occurred on Saturday, at 4:05 A.M.

MATTHEW MENARY
*Burlingame, California*

# In the Middle of the Night

In 1946 my father bought a small grocery store in a suburb of Cincinnati. The store was open six days a week from 7:00 A.M. to 6:00 P.M. and he was there almost all the time, so he had a real feel for the place. He knew all the equipment in the store very well.

One night in the late 1950s, my mother woke up to find my father dressed, with his hat and coat on. When she asked him what he was doing, he said, "There's something wrong at the store," and with that he left. Later he would tell her that he had been awakened by a loud popping sound and that he had instinctively known that something had happened at the store.

The store was about a mile from the house, but my father hadn't been gone more than a minute or two when the phone rang and the caller said, "Is Max there?" My mother told him that he was out of the house and asked who was calling. The caller identified himself as one of the local policemen and said, "There's water running out under the back door of the store." She told him that my father was on his way.

The back room was filled with water-cooled refrigeration equipment, and the freeze plug on one of the shut-off valves had popped in the middle of the night. Somehow, my father had heard the sound and knew that he had to do something about it.

STEVE HARPER
*Fayetteville, North Carolina*

# BLOOD

In the summer of 1972, I went home to visit my parents in Burnsville, Minnesota, for a couple of weeks. I slept downstairs in the basement. Every now and then, a fourteen-year-old boy named Matthew would come to mow the lawn. Early one morning, as I was sleeping in, I heard him outside cutting the grass. I paid no attention and went back to sleep.

I dreamt that I was in the upstairs bathroom, standing in front of the sink and looking at my face in the mirror. It looked like my face, but at the same time there was something odd about it. I could see my black hair, my blue eyes, my mustache, but the shape of my face was different. I looked down at the sink, where the water was running in a counterclockwise circle down the drain. I held my hands under the water and started scrubbing my hands with soap. Again, I looked at the face that wasn't my face. There was something different about it, but it didn't really trouble me.

I went on scrubbing my hands, but my left thumb hurt. The pain was fairly intense, and I wondered what I had done to make it hurt so badly. It felt as though it were sprained.

Then I looked down at the sink again, and there was blood running into the water, going round and round in that counterclockwise circle. "What's going on?" I said to myself. Blood was gushing from my thumb, pouring out from the fatty part just below the knuckle, then running down my arm and dripping off my elbow into the sink. I grabbed my throbbing hand and said to myself, "What did you do, Jim? What did you do, Jim?"

I heard a voice calling out to me. "Jim! Jim!" I woke up and realized that it was my mother calling me from the top of the stairs. She told me to come quickly. I threw on some clothes and rushed up to her. Matthew had hurt himself cutting the grass, she said, and she wanted me to go to the bathroom to help him.

Still half asleep, I walked into the bathroom and was astonished to see Matthew standing in front of the mirror and holding his left hand over the sink. Blood was pouring out from a gash between his thumb and first finger. The blood was running down his arm and into the water, going round and round as it flowed down the drain.

JAMES SHARPSTEEN
*Minneapolis, Minnesota*

# THE INTERPRETATION OF DREAMS

I was a late-in-life child and never knew my father's parents. They both died before I was born.

My sister, who was twenty years older than I was, began dabbling with dream interpretation as a hobby. One day, when I was eighteen, she asked me to recall a dream for her, and she would tell me what it meant.

The only thing that came to mind was a recurring dream I had been having since I was about ten years old. I told her I had the dream about once every two or three months and that the dream became longer and clearer each time I had it.

In the dream, I explained, I'm sitting in the passenger seat of a red car, driving through a field. I never see who is driving the car. We come across a house sitting on a beautiful green pasture. We pull up the gravel driveway. There is a white, two-story house with cement steps that have started to sink into the earth on one side. There are two steps leading to the porch, and on the porch there is an old swing.

Upon entering the house, I see a dining room to my left (which I never entered), a staircase in front of me (which I never climbed), and a room to my right. The room appears to be something of a sitting room, and the color that I remember is burgundy. There is an old gossip bench and a rolltop desk, with a photograph of one of my sisters crouching down behind an old pickup truck. I can see beyond the burgundy room to the kitchen in the back of the house, and I can see out the back window. I notice an old clothesline, although there are no clothes drying on it.

As I told this story to my sister, I began to notice that she was staring at me, stunned. When I asked her what the dream meant, she didn't speak for a few moments. Finally she said, "That was our grandmother's house. You just described our grandmother's house perfectly, down to the picture on the rolltop desk."

My grandmother died three years before I was born. Immediately after her death, the house was torn down.

V. FERGUSON-STEWART
*Indianapolis, Indiana*

# HALF-BALL

When I was nine years old, back in the early '50s, my brothers and I spent most of our free time playing a game we called "half-ball." You start with a hollow rubber ball (preferably a white pimple ball with a star on top) and cut it in half. Since our "field" was the tiny backyard of our two-family house in Boston, we pitched underhand, and fast pitching was not allowed.

But even throwing slowly, we could make that ball dance. If you cupped it properly, the ball would catch the air and fall down and away — or even up and in. It felt wonderful to see the ball move rapidly away from the batter, to watch him fan the air with the sawed-off hockey stick we used for a bat.

Scoring was determined by how high up on the three-story house you managed to hit the ball — although we always lied to our grandmother, who lived on the first floor, and told her that we weren't trying to hit the house. The first floor was a single, the second floor was a double, and so on.

One summer day, I was up on the second story porch watching my older brother play a game with his friends. These were the big guys — boys in their midteens — and we younger kids were generally relegated to fetching the ball when they played.

My job was to retrieve balls that were hit onto the second-story porch, including those that rolled off the porch and got caught in the rain gutter that went around it. We were constantly jumping over the railing, grabbing hold of one of the spindles, and leaning over to knock the ball out of the gutter.

I did this many times that morning, but then something happened. One of the spindles in the railing was loose, and it came off in my hand. My weight carried me over the side, and there I was, falling to the ground, heading toward the wooden stairs and the concrete walk about twelve feet below.

But the strange thing was that I had no idea that it was happening. I had gone into another world. Even as I fell, I remember thinking that I must have been dreaming.

I started reviewing everything I had done that morning, going over each activity slowly and carefully, trying to decide whether I had dreamed it or not. In the end, I calmly came to the conclusion that I was not, in fact, dreaming. Before I could do anything about it, I hit the ground.

All this couldn't have taken more than a second, but it felt like ten minutes to me.

My right shoulder landed on the concrete walk. My buttocks hit the wooden stairs, which caused an odd-looking straight-line bruise. Luckily, my head just missed the concrete.

My mother insisted that I go to the hospital, but nothing was broken. The doctor said that I had escaped serious injury because I thought I was dreaming. My body had been relaxed during the fall, he told me, and I had "bounced" when I hit the ground.

At the time, I didn't think much about it. I was glad that I hadn't been hurt badly, and that was all. But now I look back on it in wonder. Why did I think I was dreaming? Did my subconscious mind "know" that I would be protected if my conscious mind was occupied with the idea that the fall might not actually be happening? If my mind could do that, could it move my body in such a way as to change where I landed? Was it luck, or was it something else that kept my head from hitting the concrete?

JACK EDMONSTON
*East Sandwich, Massachusetts*

# FRIDAY NIGHT

When I was in college, I lived in a wing of a dorm where everyone was very friendly and got along well. The atmosphere was casual, and we used to walk into each other's rooms unannounced. The guy in the room next to ours, Andy, had a fridge and a TV, rare commodities in dorms back in 1972. He generously allowed us to use them whenever we wanted.

It was a quiet Friday night in October. I spent the evening studying, turned in early, and slept well. At one point during the night, I woke from a strange and vivid dream. In it, I saw myself leaving my room and going next door to get a soda from Andy's fridge. When I entered the room, I saw several people sitting around on the beds and chairs. One of them, sitting in the middle of the room with his head down, was Andy's brother, a shy, obese man I had met only once about a year before. I also recognized Andy, Andy's girlfriend, and four other students from our wing. They all had their heads down and seemed despondent. When I asked them what was wrong, they all looked up at me, except for Andy's brother. A moment later, they turned their eyes away again and looked down at the floor in silence.

I didn't think about this dream again until the middle of the afternoon the next day, when I decided to go next door and grab a soda from Andy's

510

fridge. When I entered the room, there were several people sitting around in the same positions I had seen in my dream. The only difference was that Andy's brother was not in the chair in the middle of the room. When I asked what was going on, I received the same silent and awkward glances I had been met with in my dream. I asked again, and Andy averted his eyes. His girlfriend looked up, her face all red from crying. "Andy's brother had a horrible accident this morning," she said. "He was driving a couple and their two little children somewhere, and he went off the road. The children were both killed."

I left the room stunned. As I walked back to my own room, I kept rehearsing the timing of the dream and the accident. Over and over, I said to myself that the dream had happened on Friday night and that today was Saturday. I kept saying it because I didn't want to make a mistake. I wanted to be sure that I wouldn't start wondering years later if I had reversed the two events in my mind. Memory sometimes works like that, and I wanted to make certain that the dream had come first.

STEVE HODGMAN
*Bedford, New Hampshire*

# FARRELL

My second cousin's name was Farrell. He suffered from uncontrollable epilepsy and lived in a small brown room at the back of his mother's house. There was little hope for epileptics in those days, and he never held a job. Twice a week he walked a block and a half to the Bluegrass Grill and bought a strawberry pie. Other than that, he seldom left the house.

When I was young, I saw Farrell only once a year. On Christmas day, we would all pile into the Plymouth and drive to his mother's house to give them a fruitcake. Farrell would come out of his room and try, embarrassingly hard, to make polite conversation with us. More often than not, he would wind up telling enormously long stories. They must have seemed witty to him, since he guffawed a lot as he told them, but I could barely follow what he was saying, and my mind would wander. At a certain point, I would begin watching the door, praying that we would get out of there soon. Finally, my father would clap both hands on his knees and stand up saying, "Well, we've got many more stops tonight. Merry Christmas!" And then, in a rush of coats and hats and long woolen scarves collected from the horsehair sofa in the front room, we would be gone for another year.

As I grew older, I paid less and less attention to

Farrell's stories. They washed right over me, with no more effect than the blare of the television his mother kept running the whole length of our visit. Farrell's voice became just one more noise to be endured until that blessed clap on the knees that signaled my salvation for another year.

Eventually, the visits stopped. I went to college, graduated, and came back, but there didn't seem to be the same need to deliver fruitcakes anymore. Without the visit, Farrell disappeared from my world. He was a childhood memory for me now rather than a living human being.

It therefore came as a great surprise when I was startled awake one night from a terrifying nightmare. In the dream, Farrell was standing across a wide street from me. With an exaggerated motion of the arm, he was beckoning me to cross the four lanes of traffic that separated us. His expression was utterly blank, but I knew that he wanted to tell me something of great importance. Again and again, I stepped into the road to try to reach him.

Each time, however, the traffic picked up. Horns blared, and trucks and cars and great yellow buses hurtled between us. My path was blocked, and I couldn't get to him. I woke with a start.

The next morning, my father called to tell me that Farrell had unexpectedly died that night.

I think I can come to terms with the idea that something of Farrell reached out to me at the moment of his death. But why couldn't I cross the road? I'd like to think that there is a chasm between the living and the dead, a gulf that mortal flesh cannot cross, not even in sleep. Perhaps that is why I was prevented from hearing that last story he wanted to tell me. But it may be that on those endless visits, so long ago, I learned too well how to ignore another human being, a man living out his life in a brown room at the back of his mother's house.

STEW SCHNEIDER
*Ashland, Kentucky*

# "JILL"

I met Ali through the Internet one summer, and we had talked almost daily online ever since. Our topics of discussion ranged from school (she was a high-school junior, I a senior), to theater, to the writings we shared on an e-mail writing group.

One night this past summer, Ali sent me an e-mail outlining her plans for suicide. Her life had gotten to be too much, she said, and then she went on to describe what she was planning to wear on the night she drove her car off the road. I immediately messaged her and tried to talk her out of it. Even though she had begged me not to tell anyone, I contacted her best friend, hoping that she would be able to help.

I spent a good three hours in conversation with Ali. I had been suicidal myself once, and writing back and forth to her was a tiring and traumatic experience for me. Finally, I had no choice but to leave her in the hands of her friend and go to sleep.

As I was falling asleep, I got a mental picture of Ali driving her car off the road. To comfort myself, I placed a mental picture of myself in front of the car, holding up my hands and trying to stop her. The image stayed with me as I fell asleep. If only I could have that effect on her in the real world, I thought.

Her suicide note had given the date when she was planning to kill herself. That day came, and I

515

was relieved to find out that she was still around. She made no mention of it, but a week later I found a fictionalized account of it in a message she sent for our e-mail writing group. In the story, she changed my name to "Jill" and made it sound as though I were living near her in Florida rather than talking to her online from Virginia.

However, the real shock came when she described a dream she'd had on the night we'd had our three-hour conversation. In the dream, she had been on the point of driving herself off the road when, out of nowhere, "Jill" jumped in front of the car and tried to stop her. The dream had woken her up, and the shock and fear, she said, had been enough to make her reconsider her thoughts of suicide.

KARA HUSSON
*Williamsburg, Virginia*

# D-DAY

During World War II, my older New York cousin, Morty, was drafted into the army. After completing basic training, he was sent to medical school in South Dakota. In 1944, unbeknownst to my California family, Morty's entire class was taken out of school, placed on a ship, and sent to serve as infantry in the coming invasion of Europe.

About a month after D-day, my mother came to the breakfast table and told my father, brother, and me that she had had a disturbing dream. In it her father, years dead, had come to her and beckoned her to follow. He led her across a devastated battlefield, pocked by shell craters, clouded in drifting smoke. Suddenly, he held up his hand and said, "You cannot go farther; remain here and wait for me," and he disappeared into the smoke ahead. Soon he reemerged and said, "It's Morty. He's badly wounded, but he'll be all right." This was the end of the dream.

My mother was very upset by the dream, but she didn't write or telephone Morty's family.

A few months later, we received a letter from Morty's mother telling us that he had been badly wounded in Normandy, but that he was going to be all right (her words).

At our urging my mother wrote to ask when Morty had been wounded. Although we cannot be absolutely certain of its accuracy, the best estimate his family could make (and they knew nothing of the dream) was that Morty had been wounded on the morning of the day on which my mother had her dream.

You will appreciate that midmorning in Normandy would be just after midnight in California, given the nine-hour time difference.

I, myself, do not believe in clairvoyance or psychic phenomena, so I do not welcome experiences like this, which require explanations beyond what physics or neurophysiology provide. But, as the English might say, there it is.

RICHARD R. ROSMAN
*Berkeley, California*

# THE WALL

She was waiting for me when I entered the class-room. The white starched fan around her face stood out vividly against her flowing black habit and the jet-black beads hanging from her waist. She was a little French nun in her eighties with warm, dark eyes and a little mustache that trembled when she spoke.

"Fermez la porte, s'il vous plaît," she said to me, pointing to the door. Her accent was so thick in English that it was just as easy, or easier, to understand her in French.

It was the summer after my senior year in high school, and I had enrolled in an introductory French course at Barat College in Lake Forest, Illinois, a small Catholic college run by the Sisters of the Sacred Heart. I was the only student in the class, and so we made rapid progress. We talked in French most of the time, but we also used many gestures, and the hours we spent together were always punctuated by much gaiety and laughter. Whenever I pointed out an inconsistency in French grammar to her, she would look at me with amused eyes and answer in her very French accent, "My dear, why do you say in English box-boxes, ox-oxen? Now we will continue!"

One morning, I woke up with puffy eyes, and my neck and throat were very swollen. Even my mother, who summoned doctors only when you appeared to be at the point of death, decided that I should stay home from school. I lay in bed for days with a pounding headache and a very high fever. One night, I told my parents I was afraid that if I allowed myself to fall asleep, I would be gone in the morning. My mother paid no attention, but my father, who had to get up at 5:00 A.M. to commute to Chicago, sat up all night reading to me. I had no idea what he read, but in my delirium I saw myself standing on a tall stone wall that had almost split in two. I knew that if it split apart, my soul and body would be separated. My French teacher stood on the other side of the split, holding out her hand to me. I took it, stepped over the crack, and joined her. Afterward, I fell into a deep sleep and knew that I would be safe. The next morning, before he left for work, my father said to my mother, "You will get a doctor."

Lab tests determined that I had "mono," a newly recognized glandular fever. I was given antibiotics and slept and slept for most of the summer. One morning I awoke feeling renewed, refreshed, suddenly aware that birds were singing outside. I rushed to resume my French classes at Barat College with my dear teacher, but the nuns told me that she had died while I was gone. She had left this world on the same night she helped me over the wall.

VICKY JOHNSON
*Great Falls, Montana*

# HEAVEN

This happened to me when I was six years old. I'm now over seventy-five, but it's as fresh in my mind as if it happened just yesterday.

My sister Dotty was eight years older than I was, and she was responsible for taking care of me after school. She hated having to do this, but I loved going along with her when she visited her friends. One afternoon, Dotty had to go to another girl's apartment to do a homework assignment and dutifully dragged me to the building and up three flights of stairs. I knew that I was going to be bored. When they did homework in the kitchen, I was neglected in every way. The two of them would giggle and ignore me. They called me brat and pest and often teased me to tears.

On that particular afternoon, I had nothing to do. After all, I was only six years old. I tried to get their attention, but they were hard at work and wouldn't look over at me. So I decided to have a fit. I just lay down on the floor and started kicking my feet. I screamed, I banged, I made all the noise I could. The tenant in the apartment below couldn't tolerate the noise, and so she grabbed a stick and started banging on the ceiling. That frightened me, but I stubbornly continued to kick and scream. What a horrible noise I made. But my sister went on ignoring me, and she and her friend just laughed to show how little they cared about what I was doing. And the lady below, in her second-floor kitchen, kept banging up and screaming at the top of her lungs. Finally, I stopped crying — out of pure exhaustion — but the lady kept on banging against her ceiling. I could feel the vibrations in my body, and then I heard her scream: "I'm coming up! You'll be sorry when I get there!"

My sister and her friend panicked — and so did I. Dotty grabbed my hand, pulled me to the door, and opened it, listening to make sure that the woman wasn't on her way up to our landing. "Shut up," she said to me, and then she gave me a pinch on the arm to make sure I'd behave. I was so scared, I was whimpering, but she kept pinching my arm until I calmed down. As we stood there on the landing, listening for signs of the woman, I could feel Dotty's body shaking with fear. We couldn't leave the building by going down the stairs because that would have meant passing in front of the woman's door. Dotty was worried that she was waiting for us. The only way out was to go up the stairs.

She pulled me up to the fourth floor, to the fifth floor, to the sixth floor, and then we came to a steel door. Luckily for us, she was able to open it. We went out onto the roof of the building, but I didn't know this. I had never been on a roof before, and I didn't know where we were. I didn't know what this place was. I remember that we climbed over walls, running from one rooftop to another. Then Dotty stopped at another steel door and opened it and guided me down the stairs to safety.

We stepped out onto the sidewalk of this

strange block. I don't know why, not even to this day, but when our feet touched the sidewalk, I thought we'd gone to heaven. I imagined that we were in heaven. I looked around and was amazed to see children jumping rope, just like we did, and that everything looked the same — except how could that be when this was heaven? When we turned the corner, I could see stores, and people going into them and out of them carrying bundles, and I was amazed. "So this is what heaven looks like," I said to my sister, but she wasn't listening. Every new block was more exciting to me than the last. I figured we'd reached heaven by climbing up the stairs and crossing over the rooftops. I was so happy to be there, where children played like me. Then we turned one more corner, and we were on the block where we lived. "How did our street get up to heaven?" I asked my sister. But she didn't answer me. She just pulled me in through the door of our building and said, "Shut up."

I kept this experience to myself for many years. It was my secret. I truly believed that I'd been to heaven. Only I couldn't understand how I'd gotten there — or how I'd found the way back to my house. This happened in the Bronx. We lived on Vyse Avenue.

GRACE FICHTELBERG
*Ranchos de Taos, New Mexico*

# MY FATHER'S DREAM

Many years ago, my father had a dream about flying. It was so vivid to me that I told all my friends about it. As time went on, I repeated the story so often that I began to think of it as something that had happened to me.

My father was the manager of the camera department at Macy's. In the dream, he reached for the blue ballpoint pen in his breast pocket to jot something down on his memo pad. When he pressed the springy button on top of the pen, he rose up into the air. In no time at all, he was floating above the glass display cases and drifting toward the ceiling. He felt very pleased with himself, very happy.

Next, he pressed on the side-clip of the pen. With some models, that clip can make the point of the pen retract. To his astonishment, my father found himself moving forward in a straight line. By fiddling with the pen, he discovered that he could control the speed and direction of his flight; when he touched the clip again, he was able to go backward. He was elated, filled with a sense of enormous well-being. He began flitting around the store, and because he was so high up, no one could see what he was doing.

Emboldened by this new talent of his, he waved and smiled at some of his coworkers as he sailed over their departments — an airborne, mustachioed little man in a dark business suit and a clip-on bow tie. None of the shoppers noticed him as he dipped and dived above their heads. They were too busy looking at the merchandise in the store.

At breakfast the next morning, he told the family about the dream. He said it was a wonderful thing to be able to fly like that, to be powerful, free, and happy. Someone had once told him that dreams of flying were a sign of good mental health. He felt that his dream affirmed that theory.

I have thought about my father's dream many times over the years. What I liked most about it, perhaps, was the way he seemed to expand whenever he told the story, the way his face would light up as he described the joy and secret freedom of cruising along above his coworkers' heads.

My father is eighty-seven now, and he doesn't remember his dream of flight. It was just one of the hundreds of odd, uncatalogued dreams that visited him. He talked about it for a few weeks, and then he forgot all about it. But the smallest things impress a child, and his dream stuck to me. I felt its buoyancy, took it, and made it mine.

In my version, I rise up, pen in hand, and watch waves of sea grass, deep-brown furrowed fields, the Great Plains, and ferocious spring rivers pass below me as I sail through the air. I arc over shimmering African villages and vast expanses of bluish snow without feeling heat or cold. I see armies of emperor penguins on the curve of Antarctica waiting for spring like mute statues, and roiling masses of humanity crushing into subway stations. Despite the shifts in geography, my imaginary landscape is forever and always sunny, allowing me to track the wiggly shadow of my self as it speeds over the earth's pitted, craggy surface.

I think my father was right about the power of dream flight. While I can't say that these dreams are indicators of my own sound mental health, I do know that I awake from them well-rested, no matter how many miles I've traveled. I feel unrestrained, capable, and a tad sneaky. As if I had been flying on the sly.

MARY MCCALLUM
*Proctorsville, Vermont*

# PARALLEL LIVES

I have always envied people who can go back to the place where they grew up, who have a place they can call home.

For a while, I had such a place myself. It was in Mundelein, Illinois, in the section of town known as Oak Terrace, at 244 Elmwood. Built in the 1940s, the house stood on an acre of land surrounded by trees. The property abutted a man-made channel that led out to a small lake. Shortly after my parents' divorce, my mother asked me if it would be all right if she sold the house and moved us to Madison, Wisconsin, so that she could finish school. How could I say no, especially at the curious age of sixteen?

From that day on, I've felt a strong connection to my old house. For many years, I traveled back to it in my dreams almost every night.

As my life spun me farther and farther away from Oak Terrace, moving became habitual. I suppose I was looking for a place where I could feel roots sprouting. No matter where I landed, I always felt like a fallen limb on asphalt.

I moved to California to follow chance. I moved to Chicago to follow the birth of my sister Alexandra's twins, Joey and Izzy. I moved to Europe to get lost. I moved to Texas to follow a job. I moved to Colorado to follow my wife's career. No matter where I was living, the house stayed fresh in my mind through those vivid dreams. Strange people, familiar people, the occasional journey through the walls of the house into another dimension, where everything is opposite. Powerful dreams of standing over the burial spot of a favorite childhood pet while the house is consumed in flames. Falling in the grass, feeling the familiar coolness and smell of rotting willow leaves.

Occasionally, I would go back and visit the house, just to see what the owners had done with it. The first time I went, the family was just getting into their boat and heading out to the lake. I didn't want to intrude on them, so I got back into the car and drove out to the bridge at the end of the channel. When their boat passed under, I was standing on the outer edge, and the mother, father, and little boy were all looking out in the same direction. The little girl, however, who was lying at the bottom of the boat, was looking up. Our eyes met, and something surprised me and moved me about her gaze. We connected somehow, as if we had known each other for a lifetime or more.

A few years passed, and I found myself living in Austin, Texas. I had met my future wife, Melissa, on my travels, and she moved to Austin to be with me in September. On the night she arrived, there was a knock at the door. Melissa's dog, Luna, started wagging her tail and sniffing at the crack under the door. I looked out through the window but didn't see anyone. Suddenly, the door opened, and a large chocolate Lab walked in. The dog looked at me with an expression that seemed to say, "I'm home." Luna and this strange but friendly dog immediately began romping around together. When I checked the dog's collar, I was surprised to see that the address on the tag was 914 Jones Street, which was my address. The name on the other side of the tag was "Zoey." We liked the dog and eventually found out the cause of the confusion. After moving away, the previous tenant had neglected to change the address on her dog tags. The dog had broken loose and come back to her old house.

Exactly one year later, my wife and I went on a trip to Chicago. While we were there, I decided to show her the place in Mundelein. When we pulled up in front of the house, the father was outside. I explained that I had grown up there, and he very nicely asked me to come in so he could show me what he had done with the place. I was thrilled.

When he opened the door, out leaped a beautiful chocolate Lab. I asked how old she was, and the man said, "One year this month." Then I asked him what her name was, and the man said, "Zoey." My wife and I looked at each other.

We went inside. The house seemed so much smaller. The man's wife took me upstairs, and I was flooded with memories. On a shelf of toys, I noticed alphabet blocks linked together to form the names of her two children: Alexandra and Joey. Melissa and I looked at each other again.

Was this woman tuned to my dream channel? We were all so amazed that I started opening up to her. I told her that I dreamt about the house all the time and hoped that she didn't mind. She had always felt a presence in the house, she said, but no one had believed her.

I figured that her first child, Alexandra, had

been born around the time that my sister Alexandra had come to visit me. It had been an important and powerful visit for both of us, and we reconnected after years of living apart. The woman's son, Joey, had been born around the same time that my sister's Joey had been born. To top it all off, the family had picked out a chocolate Lab puppy and named her Zoey a month after a dog of the same breed with the same name had knocked on my door in Texas.

Someone once told me that synchronicity occurs when our personal angel tells us that we are in the right place at the right time. Bread crumbs to destiny.

TIMOTHY ACKERMAN
*Erie, Colorado*

# ANNA MAY

I grew up in a comfortable residential area in central North Carolina. Our neighborhood was modest, and most of us lived in small, older houses: hardworking, blue-collar fathers, busy housewives, and energetic children of all ages.

In one house, however, there lived a singular person with the name of Anna May Poteat. She was an elderly woman, and she had no family that any of us knew about. Some of the more imaginative children believed that she was a witch.

In truth, Anna May Poteat was a decent person who kept largely to herself. Every morning, she would shuffle down the short length of her driveway to collect her mail and newspaper, but the rest of the time she stayed inside her small, white-tiled house.

As a child, I was one of the few people in the neighborhood who came to know Anna May. The mothers on our street would give her homemade cakes and pies during holiday seasons, but I saw her on a regular basis. Once a week during the summers, I mowed her lawn. I was given three dollars for my labor.

Once I was finished with the lawn, however, Anna May would always engage me in conversation. I would stand in her parlor, sweating from the heat and humidity, breathing in the strange odors that permeated the house as I waited for her to give me my fee, and inevitably she would start talking about her favorite subject. I recall that her voice was frail with age, but it took on a certain youthful excitement whenever she pulled out her scrapbook to show me the proof of her most recent triumph. The scrapbook contained the chronicle of what she liked to call her "God-given gift."

The gift was the gift of prophecy. She claimed to have dreams that announced the deaths of famous people, and she kept a meticulous log of these dreams and the dates on which they occurred. She would jot down her recollections on a page in the scrapbook, and eventually, when the subject of the dream had died, she would clip that person's obituary from the newspaper and tape it onto the page beside her earlier comments. To her way of thinking, this was conclusive evidence that her dream had preceded the death of this or that famous politician or celebrity.

I remember that she showed me sections on Eisenhower, Marilyn Monroe, and Martin Luther King Jr. There were many other entries in the thick book, but the majority of the people were from earlier years, and I wasn't always familiar with their names. I suspected that she was quite proud of her gift, for she frequently kept me there for as long as an hour, flipping through the pages with arthritic fingers, recounting her old predictions with mounting excitement as she saw how accurate they had been, or else droning on sadly about the loss of heroic and inspirational folk.

I was barely a teenager at the time, and I remember being more interested in collecting my three dollars and making a gracious exit from her house. But more times than I can recall, I would sit beside Anna May Poteat in her small parlor, disguising my impatience and listening to her accounts. When I told my parents of Anna May's disclosures, they took the opportunity to educate me on the phenomenon of senility and senescence. They also reminded me of my duty to show her respect and good manners, regardless of her infirmity. I followed their instructions and continued to mow her yard, to endure her odd ruminations as politely as I could, and to collect my earnings.

Then, one summer afternoon, I showed up with my lawnmower at Anna May's house. As was my custom, I proceeded to mow her lawn. After I was done, I knocked at her door, but no one answered. That was peculiar. The knock had always signaled the moment for her to usher me into the house for iced tea and conversation. At dinner that evening, I told my parents of Anna May's failure to answer the door. My father seemed concerned, and to my surprise he went over to visit with Ms. Poteat later that evening. I soon learned that Anna May had fallen very ill.

That same night, both the police and an ambulance were called to her home. Anna May was comatose when they found her and very nearly dead. She was taken to the hospital, but she didn't live through the night.

In the days that followed, members of one of the local churches volunteered to clean out her house and pack up her belongings, which were then sent on to one of her relatives in Juneau, Alaska.

Two years later, when I was in high school, my parents told me what they had learned from a church member who had participated in the effort. Anna May Poteat's scrapbook had been found and read, and the people of the congregation had learned about her "God-given gift." In her last entries, she had apparently written down dreams of her own death. She had put them in her chronicle, sketching in some of the details of the dreams, and then, at the bottom of the page, she had added a footnote, reminding herself to leave money for my work.

JEFF RAPER
*Gibsonville, North Carolina*

# LONG TIME GONE

Jimmy died in 1968, but I didn't start mourning him until I found his name at the Vietnam Veterans Memorial Web site four years ago. I didn't expect that seeing it on a computer screen would hit me so hard, would hurt so much. Thirty years is a long time, seven years longer than Jimmy's life. But not long enough, it seems. I felt as if I had just gotten the news.

That night, I dreamt that I had a huge wound in my stomach. It was shaped like a crater that had been left by a mortar shell. The emergency-room doctor shook her head and said, "You need to do something about this right away, but you're going to have to find another doctor. I can't handle anything this big."

People who study dreams sometimes say that each character represents a different aspect of the dreamer's psyche. So, if I'm the doctor as well as the patient, I'm telling myself that it's taken me this long to face Jimmy's death because it's so big, and I'm going to need help.

For the next six months, I watched documentaries and movies and read about the Vietnam War — historical accounts, memoirs, oral histories, letters home, Internet newsgroup postings, confessions of bottomless rage and bitterness, lingering confusion and despair, even from men who had believed in the war.

535

One vet, who lives in southern Louisiana, dreads seeing the bayous abloom in spring, because that means that summer is coming, as steamy and oppressive as the tropical jungles of Southeast Asia. Summer thunderstorms sound like artillery, and, when lightning illuminates the darkness, he sees the faces and bodies of dead friends, just the way he has every summer for the past twenty-nine years.

"Once I thought I would eventually forget these terrible memories," he wrote to an Internet vets' newsgroup one night. "But I realize now that isn't going to happen."

Another former soldier, who lives in a middle-class suburban neighborhood, suffers flashbacks so vivid that he found himself one night "dressed in camouflage fatigues, my face painted black, in a strange yard, where I had just slit a dog's throat."

The Vietnam War isn't behind us at all; it's still inside us, like the deep, dark, bloody wound in my dream.

For months I went to sleep each night hoping for another kind of dream, one that would let me tell Jimmy good-bye. Then I called his sister Ann, one of my best friends in high school, and we talked for the first time in thirty years. It was one of the nicest things I'd done for myself in a long time. We spent an hour laughing and being disrespectful of our former teachers and classmates, just like way back when.

Ann has a son she named Jim who broke her heart not long ago by joining the Marine reserves. She told me Jimmy was scheduled for Christmas R & R the week he was killed but decided to spend the holidays with his men instead. Six days before Christmas, he was shot in the head and died instantly.

Isn't that what we all want to believe when someone dies?

The night I talked to Ann, I finally dreamed about Jimmy. He was just passing through, wearing khaki pants, a faded red knit shirt, and loafers, close enough to recognize, but too far away to touch or talk to. I kept looking at him, trying to get his attention but, hands in his pockets, he was lost in thought, staring straight ahead. It was twilight, and we were in a field that stretched to the horizon in every direction. He was alone, walking west toward the setting sun, and I was with a group of people going the other way.

Last June, Jimmy would have been fifty-four. Back in our hometown, I stood at his grave for the first time. It sits in the shade of a magnolia tree, a simple marble headstone among 43,000 exactly like it, within sight of an azure and emerald bay. I read the few words and numbers over and over, but if they were hiding any secrets or mysteries, I didn't find them.

LYNN DUVALL
*Birmingham, Alabama*

# MEDITATIONS

# SEWING LESSONS

I had my first sewing lessons as a young child, sitting on the floor and stitching scraps of fabric into tenuous little creations. Above me, at the dining room table, my mother made the sewing machine fly. Every now and then, she would interrupt her sewing to snip me apart from the thing to which I'd sewn myself, or to show me how to spit on one thread tail and slip it back through the needle's eye. My child stitches resembled Morse code meandering across the fabric.

Along with my mother's lessons came her stories — about how her mother could cut a man's suit pattern from a newspaper, and how, during the Depression, her own dresses were fashioned from flour sacks. I heard about a childhood filled with loss, about war, day-to-day survival, and my own birth. These stories were as natural as breathing, and I inhaled them the same way I inhaled the air.

By suppertime, finished or not, our sewing was put away to make room for a meal and the intrusions of family business. Next morning, out came the machine again and our projects continued.

My official sewing lessons began in a seventh-grade home-economics class. A semester of sewing and a semester of cooking were required to prepare girls for their future roles as wives and mothers. I was eager to begin my first challenge of early adolescence.

My teacher, Mrs. Kelso, was a plain, stern woman with brown curls arranged tightly around her head. I was sure she had no imagination, since she wore only two-piece suits she had sewn from equally plain material. "Classic," she called them.

The sewing technique Mrs. Kelso struggled to impress upon our prepubescent sensibilities had little in common with my mother's. Mom would spread fabric on the floor, lay out a pattern (if she had one), stick in some pins, cut, and sew. And a short time later, I would have a new dress.

Mrs. Kelso was by the book. Our first project — a passage rite, it seemed — was to sew snaps onto little squares of fabric. Each time we pulled the thread through the hole on the snap, we made a knot, pushing it close to the edge of the fastener with a thumbnail. My dingy knots didn't line up around the snap, so I had to repeat the exercise two more times. When I showed my mother what I'd learned, her response was, "Phooey, who's got time for that?"

Technique aside, the greatest difference between my two teachers was their philosophy of work. My mother whistled and clapped her hands. We sang "Sixteen Tons" with Tennessee Ernie Ford and marched in circles to a worn recording of "The Gollywog's Cakewalk." One of the rare times I saw my mother weep was to a recording of Gypsy violin music as she adjusted gathers on the bodice of my dress.

To Mrs. Kelso, sewing was a science — something you went to college to learn. She didn't allow singing, not even a radio. A smile seldom cracked her stern façade. I imagined her alone and childless, but was shocked to learn that she was neither.

When my class was finally judged fit for real sewing, Mrs. Kelso picked a foolproof A-line, V-neck jumper: no buttons, zippers, darts, or pizzazz. My mother helped me choose a lovely gray flannel for my jumper. I could hardly wait to cut into it.

Before we were allowed to remove fabric from sack, Mrs. Kelso made us read the entire pattern instruction sheet and tested us on pattern terms. Finally, we spread our fabric on big tables, pinned the pattern pieces exactly as the layout instructions showed, and cut along the solid lines, making little triangle bump-outs at the notches. (My mother never bothered with notches.) With dressmaker's carbon and tracing wheel, we were to mark every sewing line on the pattern. I tried and tried to mark the lines onto my flannel until my tracing wheel cut through the paper and the seam allowances fell away from the pattern. When I reported this frustration to my mother, she pointed to the ruled markings on the sewing machine's throat plate, told me to pick one, follow it, and forget about tracing wheels.

Mrs. Kelso made us hem the jumper to a length below our knees. The horrible outcome of this effort was evident in the mirror: I resembled a skinny chicken in a flour-sack dress. I don't remember my grade.

I brought my jumper home, vowing never to wear it. My mother salvaged the outfit by raising the hem to 1965 standards, adjusting the side seams to fit my slim body, and buying a pink crepe blouse with long ties that wrapped into a bow under my chin.

By the end of the semester with Mrs. Kelso, I didn't want to be a wife or mother. But by the time I was twenty-one, I was both and I didn't have time for most of what Mrs. Kelso had taught me. But my mother's lessons helped me to work quickly through each project. I learned to match my effort to the amount of baby spit-up that was likely to embellish the little bibs and shirts I made. While I sewed, I sang and clapped my hands and played with my son. Pink Floyd replaced Tennessee Ernie Ford. Instead of sewing, my son built Lego castles at my feet. As he grew, my stories were replaced by his reading from the latest Star Trek or Piers Anthony novel.

Later, when time wasn't so precious and perfection could be justified by the cost of fine fabric, I recalled Mrs. Kelso's lessons — and the lessons of other women. The knots anchoring my snaps lined up like soldiers. I found that notches were very useful.

Now my mother — eighty this year — calls long-distance to get my advice on making a dust ruffle for her bed or a rain hat for her five-pound dog. I think this is her way of telling me that I, at last, have something to teach her.

DONNA M. BRONNER
*Santa Teresa, New Mexico*

# SUNDAY DRIVE

The path between my cousin's house and ours is a long stretch of industrial bleakness that we travel back and forth every Sunday. From my perspective, the succession of steel mills, metal die casters, and diesel-truck fueling stations runs by like a movie framed in the side-view window. I imagine what goes on behind those walls. I picture middle-aged men with hairy backs bent over some mechanical contraption, looking over bifocals, cigarettes wedged to one side of their mouths, a half-inch-long ash suspended in air by some force of gravity. The hits play on the AM radio; I'm hoping they will play my favorite of the moment, "Build Me Up Buttercup" by the Foundations. We pass vacant lots surrounded by chain-link fence and barbed wire. We talk to each other in Italian but I'm not saying all that much. I'm allowed the luxury of being in my own little world. The summer air is hot and muggy but the windows are down and the wind feels good blowing through my hair. The city reservoir, famous for its foul odor and huge rats, runs along this same path, paralleled by railroad tracks that intersect at a certain point and cross right in front of us. The warning signal sounds, and the cross guard goes down. Now we have some fun wondering if it will be a short one or a long one. We have waited for as long as fifteen minutes. The disc jockey is talking really fast during the beginning of

"Tighten Up" by Archie Bell and the Drells. I hate it when they do that. Why don't they just let the song play? My Grandma talks about what we might eat tonight. Maybe polenta. Maybe pasta. Pasta I hope. The caboose goes by, and the cross guard comes up. This one wasn't so long. My uncle skips first gear, going right to second and on into third.

But I'm not really thinking about all this. It's only in the periphery, barely noticed. What's on my mind right now are the comics I was reading over at my cousin's. He's older, and some of them go back to even before I could read. He has hundreds of them, and I beg him to pull them out every time I visit. He doesn't always feel like pulling out the old ones, or maybe he just likes to see me suffer. Today I was reading some more recent issues. Captain America is dead, or so they think. He only faked his death to throw off the agents of Hydra. They're in for a real surprise. The artist, Steranko, who also draws Nick Fury, Agent of S.H.I.E.L.D., has a style that reminds me of the old gangster movies I like to watch on Saturday afternoons. I read some current issues of the Avengers. There is a new villain called The Vision, but he's not really a villain because right now his mind is under someone else's control. He's an android, which means his body is made up of synthetic parts. He has strange powers, like being able to control the density of his body. It can become diamond hard or he can break down his molecular structure so he can walk through walls. Some of the comics reprint stories from way back in the 1940s, and I like to imagine myself as one of those kids who looked like the Bowery Boys, kicking around the Lower East Side, cashing in my empty pop bottles to buy a copy of *The Human Torch* or *Sub-Mariner* at the local drugstore. The '40s Torch was in a comic I read today, fighting some giant monster who was terrorizing Coney Island. This Torch is an android created by a scientist, unlike the current Human Torch, Johnny Storm of the Fantastic Four, whose power is the result of exposure to cosmic rays. But what I learned today is that The Vision's body used to be the body of the '40s Torch. One and the same. Somewhere along the line the original body died but was later revived in an altered form by another scientist. I don't have all the details, but I'll get to the bottom of it. While I read, my cousin sits on the couch watching a Western on TV and listening to the ball game. My Grandma is in the kitchen having coffee and visiting with my great-aunt and -uncle. My uncle never comes in. He just drops us off and picks us up later.

We're almost home. We've passed the industrial section and now see people hanging around on the streets and in front of their houses. Women wear wet towels around their necks as they fan themselves and drink lemonade. The men listen to baseball and drink Falstaff beer. Kids ride bikes and play stickball. A group of them are gathering around a fire hydrant. Sounds like we're going to have pasta, and I know we still have some watermelon in the refrigerator. I like to eat it at night, sitting in the dark by the back screen door so I can listen to the crickets and watch the fireflies. Sometimes we sit in the dark by the front screen door and wait for the ding-ding of the Mr.

Softee ice-cream truck.

Before I go to bed I'll pull out my own comic book collection. I don't have many, but the ones I do have I treasure and read over and over. I keep all of them in one box in case there is a tornado and we have to go downstairs and get underneath the sink. A tornado will never catch us by surprise, since the warning siren is located right in our alleyway; when it goes off you can't even hear yourself think. Among the most treasured comics I have are the first two I bought at the drugstore with my soda deposit return money, *Daredevil* #35 and *Spiderman* #54. Then there is *Hulk* #105 and *Fantastic Four* #76, which my Grandma bought me after I accidentally cut my hand on a piece of glass and had to go to the hospital. My uncle can't stand the superheroes, but we both like *MAD* and the characters from Harvey, like Richie Rich and Hot Stuff.

Grandma probably doesn't care much for the comics, but she's happy I have something to occupy my mind, and she encourages my drawing. We watched the Disney special where they show the animators at work. It looks like a good steady job. She knows drawing is a skill you can use.

My uncle used to draw in his notebooks, which I'm not supposed to look at. There are characters who are always carrying boxes around, and it looks like they are building something. Right now, I think he is more into weight lifting and karate, though he did go out and buy the new Beatles album last week. He bought a new record player at the same time and set it up on the kitchen table. I sat there watching the apple spin around as the

548

opening jet-plane sound of "Back in the U.S.S.R." started off the record. The whole album was great and sounded like something from another world. He has every Beatles album so far.

We're finally home. It's not really that long of a drive, but I wouldn't want to walk it. My Grandma goes for the water hose right away and gives the backyard a good dousing. She works hard at keeping up the yard. We have a fig tree that's been there since before me and has never produced a fig, but she still takes care of it and covers it up every winter. Once she found a baby squirrel that had fallen from a tree. The poor thing couldn't have been more than a couple of days old, in a fetal position, eyes still closed. She brought it in hoping to nurse it through the early stages. For about two weeks we gathered around the little box set up in the kitchen. My grandma watched over it, using a medicine dropper for feeding. Every day we checked on it lying there, wrapped in a blanket, little hands moving around, and every once in a while its eyes would open and look up at us. But alas it wasn't enough. We did all that we could do. We buried it in the backyard.

When we have dinner, we always end up talking nonsense and breaking each other up. Some language we've developed amongst ourselves. Maybe it's just the humorous sound of some Italian phrases. Something sets it off and then my Grandma starts laughing and my uncle and I catch it, and before you know it we're all red-faced and our stomachs are hurting from laughing so hard and we can't even remember what it was we were laughing about. But it feels pretty good afterward.

Before bed my Grandma will watch *Mutual of Omaha* or *Jacques Cousteau*. My uncle will be downstairs lifting weights, and I'll be immersed in my comics again. Through the night fans will help us sleep in the sweltering Midwest heat. There is one in my Grandma's room and one in the room I share with my uncle. Come September we won't need the fans anymore, but it will be hard to fall asleep without that whirring sound for a couple of weeks.

In the morning I'll be awakened by the Sealtest truck pulling into the alleyway and unloading crates of milk at the grocery store. I'll hear the faint sound of voices and the clanging of hand trucks. I'm in a halfway dream state, and from the kitchen comes another episode of *Chicken Man* as pancake batter hits the skillet.

BOB AYERS
*Seattle, Washington*

# MAYONNAISE SANDWICHES

Patty ate tape. She carried around one of those red-and-green Scotch-tape dispensers — the metal kind with the serrated edge — and every now and then would pop a piece into her mouth. I attributed her pale skin to that delicacy, and wondered how the tape was able to traverse the miles of intestine we had read about in *Scholastic Science*, the weekly newssheet Sister Edward made us subscribe to and read from every Thursday afternoon to break up the archaic lab experiments we, or rather she, demonstrated, flanked by Bunsen burners, pipettes, and crotchety nine-volt batteries, in a vain, nationwide, knee-jerk response to supplant Sputnik; the same Sister Edward, or "Stir" Edward, the truncation used when, leaning forward in the wood-and-wrought-iron desks bolted in tandem to the floor, we vied for our fifteen minutes of fame as we arced our propped-up hands 130 degrees in front of her great stone face to signify our readiness to regurgitate some trivium if called upon; the same Sister Edward, ornamented with half a dozen rubber bands on each wrist, who held a marksmanship medal for knuckle accuracy at three yards with a twelve-inch ruler, and who, like Merlin, kept, among other trinkets, a handkerchief up her sleeve. Patty may have been partial to tape, but my pièce de résistance was mayonnaise sandwiches, ideally accompanied on their journey to the center of the torso by a slug of Ovaltine, which, decades before the cyanide-laced Tylenol scare sent American companies scrambling for ingenious devices to outwit disgruntled, axe-grinding former employees as well as garden-variety sick tickets, used a waxed paper seal that had to be broken to get to the brown crystals, and which, if sent with a fifty-cent piece taped to a square of cardboard to some storefront address in Battlecreek, Michigan, displayed at the end of Captain Midnight's Sunday morning black-and-white half hour, entitled the sender to one plastic decoder ring.

THOMAS CORRADO
*Voorheesville, New York*

# SEASIDE

I don't know where I got the idea. I just knew that this birthday was supposed to be different somehow. It wasn't that I didn't have friends who wanted to celebrate with me. It wasn't that I was away from my family. It wasn't even that I had just broken up with that man. All I knew was that I wanted to drive away. I wanted to honor myself alone and separately. So, on my twenty-fifth birthday, I took a wad of cash out of my cash jar, got in my car, and drove away. I had explained to everybody that it wasn't personal. I was just going away for my birthday. That was where my explanation ended.

When the fateful morning arrived, I found myself with the strangest feeling of exhilaration. I actually woke up feeling good. After I got the cash and climbed into the car, the feeling only got better. Just driving down the road and seeing buildings I'd never seen before made me want to smile. Everything seemed exciting and full of potential. Then I saw a sign that said "Nena's Restaurant." My mother's nickname is Nena, so I took a right and landed on the beach. I had no clue what part of the coast I was on or when it would end. I noticed the seagulls, the spray off the top of the waves. The world seemed strangely in focus, but I hadn't known it was out of focus.

I found my car stopping at this peculiar-looking

cobblestoned row of shops right off the water. It was the only trace of civilization I had seen in miles. My car parked itself in front of a little bed-and-breakfast and I opened the door. I don't remember why, but I walked in and asked them how much it would cost for a room. It didn't matter what the price was; I was staying. A woman in a paisley suit walked me up a flight of pristine peach stairs with clean, white walls and showed me my room. I saw a wooden four-poster bed covered with lace throw pillows. There was a welcoming fireplace and a patio with the same view of the water I'd been following for miles. The claw-foot tub had an old-fashioned curtain ring on top of it. The fridge was full of drinks and the coffeepot was preset to brew in the morning. I thanked the woman and waited for her to go.

I pulled my CDs out of my bags, then my incense and my cigarettes. I just sat there for a while letting the room sink into my pores. Its energy was so foreign and perfect that I just wanted to feel it, every twinge of it. I ran my fingers over the soaps in the tub and flung myself on the bed. I was free, I was perfectly, unbelievably free, and I knew beyond all questioning and second thoughts that I was supposed to be there.

I ventured down the stairs and explored the little nook beside the sea that was mine for the day. I went and bought a sandwich and a bathing suit and felt the sun on my face. I talked to strangers and read the literature on the walls; I smelled the bakeries and tasted the salt on my lips. Somewhere in between lunch and the sun going down, I took a paperback out of my bag and read for a while on the beach. As the sun went down and the well-manicured beach dwellers trailed into the restaurants, I stayed. I watched the sun start its downward trek and the sky begin its dance of color. My hands were wrapped around my knees, and the soft, warm, white sand pushed in between my toes. I got up and went toward the water, longing for the feel of the spray against my body. As I walked over, I felt that my body was becoming part of the planet. It was as if some part of me remembered that I was just one person on this globe and that I belonged here. All of a sudden, I was part of the ocean and the sunset and the moonrise, and my body wanted to dance. And I did. I started running and playing in the water, and jumping and splashing and sliding and twirling and cartwheeling and dunking myself and not caring who was watching or even if anyone was. I sauntered and skipped and cantered. I lay in the water and let it rush over me; I felt myself being sucked back out to sea. I was so free. And I was safe.

When I was finally worn out and the sky grew dark, I returned to my room. The room was waiting for me, and I obliged. I didn't go out for dinner. Eating the rest of my salami sandwich and reading my book about love: this was what I longed for. I took a bath and lit some more incense. In between each chapter of the book, I would find myself smoking on the lawn chair on the patio. On these breaks, I would think the strongest thoughts. I remembered that no man could make me happy or unhappy. I remembered the stars and all that they represent. I remembered that I had always longed to be friends with my mother. I felt pulled down by no one and nothing. Everything seemed perfect and in alignment and achievable. I didn't want to go to sleep. I didn't want the feeling to stop. For the whole night, all I did was read and smoke and look up at the perfect night sky and know that I was okay. The feeling was the best feeling I'd ever had. It wasn't attached to any other person or object, and it couldn't be taken away. It was mine and it came from a place that would never run dry. I had never felt like this before; nothing had ever come close.

When I finally slept, it was only for about two hours. I woke up and my feeling was still there; it hadn't left me while I was asleep. I walked around the bed-and-breakfast and found a wooden ladder that led up to a glass window in the ceiling. Climbing up, I found a set of lawn furniture and tables on the roof. All the chairs were at the perfect angle to watch the sun as it lifted itself above the ocean. I sat. It seemed that the chairs had been waiting for me. The sleep was still in my eyes. I was in my pajamas, the pinks and blues and yellows washed over my head. I just closed my eyes. I just felt it.

I was gone for only twenty-four hours. When my car finally drove me home that afternoon, I knew that something had clicked over inside me. It has never quite clicked back since. It was only twenty-four hours.

TANYA COLLINS
*Oxnard, California*

# AFTER A LONG WINTER

Washington, D.C.

Up earlier than usual. The air is calling. Spring air is different from winter air. Tree branches are serrated with red-bud teeth. Later, they grow chartreuse fuzz, making pale green auras in the sun. Summer leaves will be dark, shading, but spring leaves let the light through. Spring trees glow in the daytime, spreading translucent canopies.

The birds are out, racketing their news from bush to branch. Cats are still curled up on fire escapes. They are in no hurry to get about in the brisk morning air. They know it will warm up later. They are watching the birds. They can wait.

The air is clear, clean, cool. The smells are tiny smells, little whiffs of green, a ribbon of brown mud, the blue smell of the sky. Midday is mild enough for shirtsleeves. I eat my lunch outside, sitting on a warm brick wall. The breeze lifts my hair and riffles the edge of my skirt. I have to squint. Everything tastes better.

Until today, I had been too huddled in my winter coat to notice the quiet coming of flowers. Suddenly, daffodils smile in my face, parrot tulips wave their beaky petals, and fragrant white blossoms are pinned to dogwood trees like bows in a young girl's hair.

The evening is soft, I need my thin jacket. It's

still light out when I walk home from the Metro. I could walk for hours. Like a kid playing street games with her friends, I don't want to go in.

When I went to work this morning, I left my windows open. Spring came in through the screens while I was gone. It's as if I had used a big silver key and rolled back the roof like the lid on a sardine can. The indoors smell like the outdoors. It will be like lying down in the grass to sleep. The sheets are cool. The quilt is warm. The light fades outside my windows. This weekend, I think I'll wash my car.

EILEEN O'HARA
San Francisco, California

# MARTINI WITH A TWIST

There's no finer martini in Washington State than the one served in the bar at the old Roosevelt Hotel in Seattle. One sip of this sultry solvent is at once as cold as winter rain and as dry as the desert itself. One sip, and your past and future collide in one crystallized moment that is now.

Above all, the martini is cold. Not just cold. Siberian cold. Hypothermic. There is no ice in evidence, but the idea of ice is embedded in every sweet swallow. How could something so cold impart such warmth? That is the irony and magic and mystery that define the martini.

The glass is important. And that's just one thing this bartender gets right. There is nothing that beats the classic funnel shape. You want to tip your glass and ease your palate into the shallow end of the pool, not plunge it instantly into the depths of the diving well. The rich aroma of vermouth should suggest its presence, not drown you with overly oppressive vermouthiness.

Shape, yes. But also size. And this libation liberator gets that right, too. Big. It declares boldly: Yes, I am a martini. Not a wine spritzer. Not a Bloody Mary. Not a daiquiri. An adventurer, a climber, a bon vivant. Halfway through the second double, I can out-Bond Bond. I find myself demanding that the barkeep shake, not stir, my libation.

Part of the appeal of the V-shaped vessel is the perfect house it creates for the olive, the garnish of choice. Gently inclined sides provide the ideal sliding board. There it lies. Sexily lounging in the pit of the pendulum, leaning to one side, then the other, as the glass is raised. A single pimiento-leg exposed, dangling in the drink.

After the plastic sword that has pierced through the rubbery green of its salty, chewy, suit has been removed, the vodka-drenched olive reaches its destination.

Ambrosia.

Martinis are not chatty. A conversation lubricated with a martini is significant, enhanced by a catalyst that at once lowers your inhibitions and heightens your sense of irony and pathos. Martinis are subtle. Introspective. Reflective.

They are Mahler and twilight and the dark side of jazz. A deep look into the eyes of just one who is listening. At once spiritual, physical, ritual, and unique. You are one and none and all. A swallow away from understanding and transformation. Actor, rebel, dreamer.

Where martinis are selective and thoughtful, beer is verbose and unedited. Microbrewed for maximum-volume discussion accompanied by broad gestures and wild exaggeration. Beer is showy and full of jokes and vaudeville. Lawyers, salesmen, sports enthusiasts.

Beer is Bartók. It's tympani and wild action and dramatic crescendos. Beer is for crowds and joke telling and sweeping stories with predictable punch lines and big belly laughs. It is huge and boisterous. Powerboats.

Martinis are philosophical. Thoughtful. Progressive. Ironically twisted. Mimes. Knowing smiles. Sailboats. All the simple complexity of life rises to the surface of vodka and vermouth. You become. You live. You are.

Strained. And clean. And brilliant. Martinis are brutally honest. No coloring. No flavoring. No additives. No head. No froth. Only as good as the worst ingredient. A cheap vermouth defines the vodka; a bargain vodka defines the vermouth. You are the company you keep.

A good martini enhances what you experience in the moment. Beer exaggerates what you were in the past.

You can drink a martini alone, but you are never alone when you drink one. The essence of the people and the generations and the countries that have preceded you are distilled in every sip. Stir well with melancholy blues piano and a bittersweet saxophone and you have a drink in your hand that no one has ever sipped before, no one will ever sip again, and everyone has sipped from the beginning of time.

Martinis are tied to place and people. Whether you travel from coast to coast in North America or around the world, wherever you find a bottle of gin or vodka and dry vermouth, you will find a bar that touts their martini as the best in the city or the state or the country or the world.

They are all telling the truth.

Your experience. Your enjoyment. Your memory is inextricably linked — not just to the sensation of the satiating sauce as it splashes over your palate — but is entwined forever with the rich histories of the people and the land where the drink was born and lived and breathed.

In a vodka martini, you inhale the pain of the Russian peasant along with the stoic remorse of a Russian czar. You are bound together in your humanity, in your triumphs, in your defeats, in your belief in this transparent elixir, in your desire to be free and prosperous and loved.

Sharing a martini is an invitation to explore the intimacy of the icy island that only you inhabit. Every sip thaws the iceberg until, gradually, imperceptibly, a glacial coating melts away and releases the lush tropical paradise beneath.

At once you are aware of your profound aloneness and your undeniable connectedness. Coursing through your veins is the lifeblood of every martini drinker who has preceded you. Together, you are born and live and grow old and die. Along the journey you gain and lose the family and friends and love that made life bearable and unbearable.

If you thirst for knowledge, look no further than the bottom of your glass. Stir your dreams gently, and your thoughts and imagination will take you beyond your fondest wishes and hopes.

A good martini is the culmination of all the decisions of your life. Epiphany explodes when you discover that what seems new and revolutionary in the moment has actually resided in you all along, lying dormant, waiting for the perfect martini.

DEDE RYAN
*Boise, Idaho*

# NOWHERE

Morning in the west of Texas, almost to New Mexico, and the road begins to wind. It seems that this last forty miles has been endless. I am going down a steep grade, other cars pushing from behind, but it's much like being at the same point I was an hour ago.

The road is rolling by; doing seventy-five has become habitual. I have been doing this more than I want, but out of necessity, and now the overall loss of stability has reached an edge. Some of the road trips involved work for the company, some were personal, and some were very much the most important thing I did. It is not an active doing. The car does the work, and the product of miles of road is the only outcome.

When one returns from these escapades away from the familiar, the returning does not give a sense of completion. Especially hard on a mindful activity of being are the essential stops for food, fuel, and rest. But, often, these things are forgotten, as the miles must be covered. . . .

And now, with the rain having passed, the last two hundred miles of rain-drenched and almost submerged road being crossed, I have sensed the futility of this movement. I have no way to know what anyone else might think of me here, in this partial moment, but I know because someone is aware of my passing — because someone's thoughts are with me.

That's when I hear the manifestation of that outside inner awareness of me. It starts both above and between the crossing I am in. It is a noise that intercedes in my noisy reverie of road. It whistles through the night, the tonal balance coming in focus, and then departs. The noise is loud, invasive, and just as quickly a receding reminder that I am nowhere.

JOHN HOWZE
*El Paso, Texas*

# WHERE IN THE WORLD IS ERA ROSE RODOSTA?

It's a beautiful name, and I think of it often. Era Rose Rodosta. Her sad brown eyes with the blank stare, long ash-brown pigtails, stoic silence, and the persistently sniffling nose. Her life was already purgatory, and we set out to make it hell. She lived with old grandparents who had strange accents. No one knew where her parents were, and no one thought to find out. Probably just as well. We would only have used the information to badger her.

We attended Gundlach Grade School in St. Louis. We were all white and pure and sure about who and what was acceptable. Woe to anyone with the most minor difference. I remember curly-redheaded Stanley. He was proudly Jewish, and that was the problem. If only he had been a bit more . . . well, modest about his difference. Then, of course, there was little Cilia Kay, that foolish girl who dared to be born with one green eye and one brown. To top it off, she had the misfortune to be poorer than the rest of us, and lived above a shabby donut shop run by her parents. Every morning, we joked about what variety of donut we smelled emanating from her clothes, which always reeked with their daily infusion of grease. But most of all I remember Era Rose.

As we meandered to school from our modest

homes and apartments, we passed a small, obviously poor black section. This is almost too painful to speak of, but the inhabitants of that neighborhood were our morning entertainment. We pushed and shoved to position ourselves on the house side of the sidewalk; that way we were sure to see better. One family often sat on the porch, all munching from the same box of cereal. Everything we saw was "less." Paint-less, screen-less, and grass-less. It was also less fair, less nice, and less affluent. We giggled at the unusual hair-dos; we stared but never spoke or smiled. But even more clearly than this recurring view, I remember Era Rose.

Era Rose was such an easy target. She never fought back. She stood firm and remained distant and disengaged. Some things got through her armor though, because I would see an occasional tear. I was raised to know better, so I remained at the fringe of the taunting crowd. My gut feeling was, "She's interesting," but I never had the courage to seek her out. My brain could not even engage the argument.

She wore tacky hand-me-downs. Faded plaid with a let-down hem, droopy socks, and, always, the sniffling nose. Now I know that I was jealous of Era Rose. She was better than I was at what I loved most: drawing. It was my claim to fame at school, yet inside me I knew that she was more talented. More importantly, she drew for herself. She drew all the time, beautifully and naturally. Her faces had natural lines and creases that I envied but couldn't duplicate. My school day wasn't complete if it didn't include an envious peek at her notebook full of wonderful, creative images. I would try to copy her work, not understanding the impossibility of that task. She appeared in my consciousness as a suffering, fascinating being somewhere around fourth grade and stayed in my peripheral vision through freshman year at Beaumont High School.

By ninth grade she was morphing. The sniffling stopped. Her legs became long, and she was becoming thin and curvaceous — all hidden under those still-horrible clothes. Every now and then, she did a thing or two with her hair, and even applied occasional lipstick. She was enveloped in velvet skin, and her ash-brown hair was heavy and shiny. I noticed her name on the roster of art clubs I was too busy to join; then one day I saw her leave an art room actually walking and talking with someone. Her mouth was nearer to a smile than I had ever observed. No one really paid her much notice that sophomore year, but now I have a sense of the monarch drying its wings before flight. It was forty-three years ago when I had that last sighting. I moved on, to St. Louis County and Normandy High School, but when I look back, so often I remember Era Rose.

What became of this girl with the beautiful name? At impulsive moments, I've dug through phone books. No luck. I have a hope so intense that it is out of proportion; a hope that she is living well, that good was given in extra measure for all those years so devoid of happiness. Era Rose, ever the girl I never befriended.

CAROLYN BRASHER
*Wentzville, Missouri*

# PETER

Peter and I were seventeen. We were both students at a boarding school in northern Michigan. I was drawn to him because I found him nonthreatening, easy to talk to, and yet passionate. He was slightly built. Blond with intense blue eyes, he walked slightly hunched, peering intensely through round wire frames at a time when everyone else wore horn-rims. He wanted to be a writer.

One snowy evening we sat across from each other at dinner. Peter looked at me, considering. Finally he said, "Think of a number between one and ten." An odd request, but then Peter was odd. He won a national poetry competition that year and had celebrated by wearing a tuxedo to class. So I complied. I imagined a theater screen with a radiant number two splashed across it. Peter bowed his head toward me, tipping it slightly sideways. "Two?" he said after a moment. We tried three more times. Each time, Peter guessed correctly. I was astonished. I asked him if we could do the same thing with numbers between one and twenty. It took a bit longer, but for several minutes Peter continued to identify every number dancing across the stage of my mind.

"How do you *do* that?" I asked. He told me he could only do it with certan people, that he went through the numbers consecutively in his own mind until one of them "stuck." Intrigued, I asked

568

if he'd ever tried to intuit objects instead of numbers. He said that he hadn't. "Look," I directed, "I'm going to imagine an object in this cafeteria and you tell me what it is." Peter agreed, although he seemed hesitant. We sat in the large dining hall, I with my eyes closed, Peter with his head bowed and tilted. After about twenty seconds, his head came up. "The milk machine?" Yes! We did it twice more. Each time, his tentative words matched themselves to the images in my mind.

Peter was getting a headache. But I was excited and kept pushing him further. "Okay, I'm going to imagine that I'm *doing* something . . . some kind of activity. You tell me what it is." Peter reluctantly agreed. I sat back and visualized myself in the shower, the water rushing against my face and chest, my fingers rhythmically working the shampoo into my hair. It took about a minute, but Peter finally raised his head. He asked if I'd been washing my clothes. Granted, the reception was not perfect. But he seemed to have made out the essentials: the water, the white suds, the act of cleansing. On our next and final attempt, I visualized myself sitting at my desk typing, my fingers stabbing at the keys. Again, after a minute, he asked if I was writing a letter. The keys, the letters, the process of arranging words . . . I was convinced now that he had somehow *seen* it.

After dinner, we walked through the snow. I was reeling, but Peter had become quiet and pensive. A student came out of a building near us and walked past briskly. "He's anxious around me. . . . I make him nervous," Peter said. He told me that feelings and thoughts did not come to him sepa-

569

rately but together, all of a piece.

Later that night, as I turned down the dormitory hall to Peter's room, Peter was already in his doorway, waiting. We sat in his room listening to Barbra Streisand. He seemed awkward and uncomfortable. I had the sense that things had suddenly changed between us. "We can't be friends anymore," he said finally, embarrassment infecting his smile. It was obvious then that there was something painful to Peter about his gift. Somehow, by getting close to it, I had become part of that pain. Confused, I could only honor his request.

In the twenty-five years since that night, I continue to extract its meaning in the shifting light of my own life. Although I've gone on to become an academic, a trained skeptic, my training has not eroded the conviction that what I experienced that night was real. There are facts that, although they transcend our ability to know or understand them objectively, are facts nonetheless. I've cautiously shared this story in academic circles, where the metaphysical is often met with glazed stares. "He was likely reading your facial expressions or some other cue," they assert. I realize that you can believe something without having to understand it.

I saw the Amazing Kreskin, a self-described "thought reader," years ago on the Johnny Carson show. For fifteen minutes, he revealed people's thoughts, found hidden objects, and planted suggestions. But that was not what impressed me. What I was captured by was his apparent love, love for what he was doing and, more importantly, for the people he was doing it with. I had always regarded Peter's abilities as a curse. After all, who would choose to live his life defenselessly awash in the fear, hate, and envy of other souls? But here was Kreskin, swimming real-time in a river of human thought and emotion and coming up with joy. I realized that Peter's pain was not about being confronted with an objective picture of the human soul. It was about *him*.

I've made several attempts to find Peter, always without luck. I wonder how he's fared. I wonder if he has ever used his gift (they say that every great therapist has this ability to some degree). Or did he continue to run from it? Mostly, though, I hope that he, like Kreskin, has learned to see the good.

MARK GOVER
*Lansing, Michigan*

# EARLY ARITHMETIC

Sometimes I went with my mother to the street of stores. Really there were hardly any stores there, there was hardly anything in the place where our store once stood, and now there is nothing. Only a highway where cars streak madly on their way, the endless rushing past of the cars in the place where I walked with my mother. I put my hand in hers and over us I see the drifting branches of the trees and hear the leaves in their green murmuring, a canopy over us as we go along, and the travel agent looks up from where he sits on a straight-backed chair reading the Hungarian newspaper *Nepszava*, looks up to wave at us, in his window the picture of an ocean liner, faded blue and red, no one we know ever goes on an ocean liner, but still the picture is there, a reminder of possibility that can visit us at any time. My mother carries her purse she calls her satchel, always have a clean handkerchief whenever you go any place, she tells me. We are going to buy what she calls "rat cheese" and I think it must be the favorite of the rats. But it is for the cheese sandwiches my father sells along with coffee and newspapers, the *Daily Mirror* and the *Daily News*, the *Bridgeport Post* and the Hungarian paper — no one ever reads the *New York Times*. "Candy store owner," says my father when I ask him what to tell the teachers when they ask for information for the school records. But that is not all he sells, that is not all we are.

"And where is your father's business?" the teacher asks. They want the numbers, the exact address for the records they say will follow us throughout our lives. But I can never keep the numbers in my head. The corner of Cherry and Pine is what I tell them because it is words that I can remember. And I love to say the words together, cherry and pine, cool northern forests where we have never been and cherry like the Smith Brothers' cough drops in the candy case, red and sweet but not as good as black licorice with the taste of darkness on your tongue and not as good as HB cough drops, "Hospital Brand" I read on the box because I am always reading everything I see, words are like food and air to me. And my mother tells me to stop reading so much because it don't pay to be too smart. Look for where the blue Dodge is parked, I could tell the teachers. He drives it forward every morning, I hear his steps clumping down the back stairs, resenting this interruption of my dreams. The early morning hours are the best, he tells me. Look for the blue car of my father and there you will find the place of soda water and jujubes in the candy case I have dusted with the rags of old undershirts he gives me. Jujubes with the taste of perfume, like jewels that stick in your teeth, and I just got your teeth fixed says my mother, only she pronounces it teet, which is without the *th* sound the teachers have told me is so important. I could tell them I don't know the address but find my way there every afternoon, like a sleepwalker going under the railroad tracks and then past the clanking factories until I see before me the green faded awning with our name in white block letters, the stone step of my father's store and the wooden screen door with holes for the flies to fly through. But this is not what they want of me. It is the numbers I can never remember. I can't count back to give change the way he showed me. "Don't let the kid near the register," the customers tell my father. How can I add up the dimes when the thin face of the man pictured there is everything we will never be; someone who has power over us, I can tell just by the look of him there, polished and thin. The customers slap their change onto the counter and I see the buffalo on the nickel, his head bent toward the grass, I can feel it under my feet as I am transported to his place of prairies, open land for miles where I can feel the strength of the sun and the buffalo ignores me, like the customers, their heads bent to their coffee and newspapers, intent and separate in their places at the counter. I try not to disturb them as I sweep unobtrusively around their feet the way my father showed me. Numbers are what I need if I am to succeed in the world, that is something everyone knows. But no one ever mentions the real life of the numbers that I see before me so clearly. No one ever mentions this in school. How I see the numbers as they go.

One with his power who dares to start off the long line of the numbers in their march. But he is alone. O one with no one to go with him. What good is all his power if he is alone? Not like lucky two, part of a pair, not odd, but even. Dangerous three with X rays of electricity flashing around him. Flash Gordon death rays to kill even Ming the Malevolent Ruler of the Universe. Three like

Richie Swenson, who sets fire to the wastepaper baskets and gets expelled so we will not have the danger of burning up. Four eyes he calls me. What's new four eyes he says. Richie Swenson, expelled and free like the buffalo to roam the streets, will never be like four. Fat and comfortable and safe. Five is a red convertible. And six is downtrodden, has to work overtime. Seven is infinite sorrow, of that I am sure. The sorrow of the world, heavy on your shoulders, old overcoat of sorrow you can't shrug off. I wish I didn't have my knowledge of the sorrow that is seven. I wish I could cast it off, but it is with me forever, knowledge of the infinite sorrow of the world that is contained in the number seven. Eight is reliable and dull, will never even know of seven's power. Nine is very smart but it doesn't matter; nine can never be happy. And ten rules them all, lives on a hill in the better part of town.

How can I add or subtract them? Meddle in their lives? If Johnny has ten apples and Jimmy takes two, how many will Johnny have then? O Johnny, how did you get so many apples in the first place? Johnny in your big house with all of your apples that come to you so easily. Jimmy down and out. No apples in the family. What of the perfume of the apples? They are lined up on the windowsill in the attic room where my aunt sleeps. Green and golden delicious are their names, she has them lined up because she says it is a wonderful thing to sleep in a room that smells of apples. In the attic room, I read all of the stories in her citizenship book one after the other. "Mabel, listen to this child read," says the note the second-grade teacher gives me to take to the fifth. I keep failing arithmetic. She must be stupid, everyone says. I believe them all.

SANDRA WALLER
*New York, New York*

# REFLECTIONS ON A HUBCAP

It was autumn in the northwest. Memories of the weekend with my old friend Keith, at his place in Seattle, had left me feeling warm and satisfied. Now, after several hours of driving, I had adapted to the rhythms of the journey home. The comfortable vibration of my solid car, with its fat rubber tires humming beneath me, the golden light illuminating the scenery along this sparsely traveled stretch of highway, and the soft, almost subliminal sound of the radio contributed to my wistful mood. Lost in this reverie, I was gradually drawn into a pleasant state of awareness in which I felt particularly alert and receptive. An intriguing state of anticipation followed.

I focused on an approaching road sign and felt a dim sense of recognition as I read the name of the upcoming town. It was a distinctive and beautiful name, and I remembered it as the place to which another friend, Shawnee, had intended to relocate the last time I had seen her, several years ago.

The exit was a short distance ahead, and I found myself gliding onto the exit ramp. It was a Sunday afternoon, and the streets were quiet. I drove the length of the main street imagining what it would be like to surprise my friend with a visit. Within a few minutes, I understood that this was exactly the kind of place to which Shawnee would be attracted. An abundance of graceful old trees

577

shaded the sidewalks, and small groups of people were gathered informally, enjoying the warm afternoon together.

Upon spotting a phone booth, I pulled over and searched the directory for clues as to my friend's address or business location, but found neither. Surprisingly, the feeling of anticipation I had been feeling intensified. I interpreted this as encouragement to continue my search and spent another two hours peering into the windows of professional buildings, driving the residential neighborhoods looking for Shawnee's distinctive old vehicle, and asking local townspeople if they knew her. None of these efforts seemed to be bringing me closer to my friend.

At last, recognizing that evening was approaching, I resigned myself to the futility of my search. After a final, disappointing loop through town, I pulled onto the ramp that would lead me back to the highway. As I picked up speed, I heard a strange rattling sound coming from the passenger side of the car. Before I could determine its origin, I was startled by the sharp metallic sound of a hubcap falling off and careening down the hard pavement. I applied the brakes and guided the car onto the shoulder of the narrow roadway keeping my eye on the hubcap as it bounced wildly into the distance. I got out of the car and walked briskly to where I had observed the hubcap entering the high brown grass. I stepped into the fragrant overgrowth and, after a few minutes of searching, saw the silvery dish near the bottom of a steep incline. I struggled down the embankment into a hollow that would not have been visible from the road and stooped to collect the dusty cap.

At that moment, I heard the sputter of an engine in the distance. I looked up to see an old red jeep coming toward me out of the dense pine forest. My eyes moistened and my heart pounded when I recognized the driver of that jeep. It was Shawnee. Our eyes met through the streaked windshield as she approached the hollow where I was crouched, holding on to the dented hubcap.

For a moment my attention was drawn to the reflection of this eerie scene as it unfolded on the convex surface of the hubcap. On this expanded plane, I saw myself and the shadowy embankment behind me stretching and merging disproportionately in the perimeter of the disc with the scene around and before me. The sound of the engine grew louder, and the vehicle itself appeared on the shiny surface. At the top of this little dome of activity were the vivid reddish hues of the twilight sky.

Within this strange new dimension it seemed possible, for an instant, that I could comprehend the incredible convergence of events that I was witnessing. I strained to understand, but before I was able to awaken to the challenge, my senses were occupied by the presence of the rusty jeep shuddering to a stop in a cloud of dust a few feet from me. I sprang to my feet and pulled my astonished friend out of her seat for a long overdue and decidedly mystical reunion.

ROGER BRINKERHOFF
*Galilee, Pennsylvania*

# HOMELESS IN PRESCOTT, ARIZONA

Last spring I made a major life change, and I wasn't suffering from a midlife crisis. At fifty-seven I'm way beyond that. I decided I could not wait eight more years to retire, and I could not be a legal secretary for eight more years. I quit my job, sold my house, furnishings, and car, gave my cat to my neighbor, and moved to Prescott, Arizona, a community of thirty thousand, nestled in the Bradshaw Mountains with a fine library, community college, and a beautiful town square. I invested the proceeds from selling everything and I now receive $315 a month in interest income. That is what I live off of.

I am anonymous. I am not on any government programs. I do not receive any kind of welfare, not even food stamps. I do not eat at the Salvation Army. I do not take handouts. I am not dependent on anyone.

My base is downtown Prescott, where everything I need is within a radius of a mile and a half — easy walking. To go farther afield, I take a bus that makes a circuit of the city each hour and costs three dollars for a day pass. I have a post-office box — cost, forty dollars a year. The library is connected to the Internet, and I have an e-mail address. My storage space costs twenty-seven dollars a month, and I have access to it twenty-four hours a day. I store my clothes, cosmetic and hygiene supplies, a few kitchen items, and paperwork there. I rent a secluded corner of a backyard a block from my storage area for twenty-five dollars a month. This is my bedroom, complete with arctic tent, sleeping bag, mattress, and lantern. I wear a sturdy pack with a water bottle, flashlight, and Walkman, toiletries and rain gear.

Yavapai College has an Olympic-size pool and a women's locker room. I take college classes and have access to these facilities; cost, thirty-five dollars a month. I go there every morning to perform my "toilet" and shower. I go to the Laundromat with a small load of clothes whenever I need to; cost, fifteen dollars a month. Looking presentable is the most important aspect of my new lifestyle. When I go to the library, no one can guess I'm homeless. The library is my living room. I sit in a comfortable chair and read. I listen to beautiful music through the stereo system. I communicate with my daughter via e-mail and type letters on the word processor. I stay dry when it's wet outside. Unfortunately, the library does not have a television, but I've found a student lounge at the college that does. Most of the time I can watch *The News Hour*, *Masterpiece Theater*, and *Mystery*. To further satisfy my cultural needs, I attend dress rehearsals at the local amateur theater company, free of charge.

Eating inexpensively and nutritiously is my biggest challenge. My budget allows me to spend two hundred dollars a month for food. I have a Coleman burner and an old-fashioned percolator.

I go to my storage space every morning and make coffee, pour it into my thermos, load my backpack, go to the park, and find a sunny spot to enjoy my coffee and listen to *Morning Edition* on my Walkman. The park is my backyard. It's a beautiful place to hang out when the weather is clement. I can lie on the grass and read and nap. The mature trees provide welcome shade when it's warm.

My new lifestyle has been comfortable and enjoyable so far because the weather in Prescott during the spring, summer, and fall has been delightful, though it did snow Easter weekend. But I was prepared. I have a parka, boots, and gloves, all warm and waterproof.

Back to eating. The Jack in the Box has four items that cost one dollar — Breakfast Jack, Jumbo Jack, a chicken sandwich, and two beef tacos. After I enjoy my coffee in the park, I have a Breakfast Jack. There's a nutrition program at the adult center where I can eat a hearty lunch for two dollars. For dinner, back to the Jack in the Box. I buy fresh fruit and veggies at Albertson's. Once in a while I go to the Pizza Hut — all you can eat for $4.49. When I return to my storage space in the evening, I make popcorn on my Coleman burner. I only drink water and coffee; other beverages are too expensive.

I've discovered another way to have a different eating experience and to combine it with a cultural evening. There's an art gallery downtown, and the openings of the new shows are announced in the newspaper. Two weeks ago I put on my dress and panty hose, went to the opening, enjoyed eating the snacks, and admired the paintings.

I've let my hair grow long, and I tie it back in a ponytail like I did in grade school. I no longer color it. I like the gray. I do not shave my legs or underarms and do not polish my fingernails, wear mascara, foundation, blush, or lipstick. The natural look costs nothing.

I love going to college. This fall, I'm taking ceramics, chorale, and cultural anthropology — for enrichment, not for credit. I love reading all the books I want to but never had enough time for. I also have time to do absolutely nothing.

Of course there are negatives. I miss my friends from back home. Claudette, who works at the library, befriended me. She was a feature writer for the local newspaper and is adept at getting information from people. Eventually, I told her who I was and how I live. She never pressures me to live differently, and I know she's there for me if I need her.

I also miss my Simon cat. I keep hoping that a cat will come my way, particularly before winter sets in. It would be nice to sleep and snuggle with a furry body.

I hope I can survive the winter. I've been told that Prescott can have lots of snow and long stretches of freezing temperatures. I don't know what I'll do if I get sick. I'm generally an optimist, but I do worry. Pray for me.

B.C.
*Prescott, Arizona*

583

# BEING THERE

*For the first seven years of my life (1953–1960) I lived on a small five-acre farm in rural southeastern Michigan. My father worked at a tool-and-die shop twenty-five miles away, but he and my mother preferred to live in the country, what they considered "the good life." The following is a recollection of one particular summer evening during that time.*

I am standing in my summer pajamas, the lightest of cotton. The top buttons up to a flat lapel collar that lies open at my neck, like a sport shirt my grandfather might have worn. The bottoms are held up by an elastic waistband that I tug and release, snapping it gently against my clean body, fresh from a bath on a Saturday evening in June. A faint breeze curls through the baggy openings of the pajamas and swirls over me like a soft electric charge. I feel weightless.

My father has just finished cutting the grass. I hear the crunch of gravel and the rattly echo of the mower's hard wheels as he pushes them over the driveway and into the gray cinder-block garage. He is wearing what he always wears in my childhood memories of him in the summer: a white V-neck T-shirt and baggy gray work pants. His hair is black and cut flat on top. He is a lean six-footer with neck and arms browned and freckled by the sun, his left arm more so because of the way he angles it out of the window of the car whenever he is driving. Parking the mower marks the end of his labor for the week. In my memory he is smiling that jaunty off-to-the-side smile, one I could never confuse with anyone else's.

Sounds drowned by the roar of the mower begin to return: the cooing of an evening dove, muted by a hazy stillness, drifts on the air. I look in the direction of the cooing but see only a field of knee-deep grass surrounded by a boggy woods. From their already darkening depths comes the steady croaking drone of frogs, invisible but as present as the cool grass beneath my feet.

My mother is sitting in an old metal lawn chair holding a white-haired baby, my brother Pat. She wears a breezy summer housedress, one that she made herself, and she is singing softly, a song about sitting on top of the world and the street where you live and a yellow bird.

I smell lilac blossoms, the freshly cut grass, cow manure, Ivory soap.

I hear the rhythmic squeak of the rope swing as my sister Marianne glides back and forth under the massive cedar tree in the front yard, her red-blond hair and nightgown flowing together like flags in the wind.

My sister Sharon, in her pajamas, sits on the edge of the porch, petting a black-and-white kitten.

The tractor is parked in front of the garage. My brother Mike has climbed up into the seat and is holding on to the steering wheel. He thinks he's a big man driving down the road. Mike's hair is like mine. Mom has given us our summer haircuts with the electric clippers so that what we have left is more like suede than hair. My brother Kevin is standing a few feet away, feeding handfuls of grass to Jerry, our spotted pony. Kevin has the suede look, too. He and Mike are both wearing their pajamas.

I have other memories of the farm, memories that seem to be there for some obvious reason: they might be dramatic or humorous or frightening. But my pajama night memory is different. In it, I am simply standing barefoot on the lawn. I remember the dove, the rope swing, my mother and father, sisters and brothers, the barn, the lilacs, the woods — all bathed in the diffuse radiance of fading summer light.

TIM CLANCY
*Marquette, Michigan*

# AN AVERAGE SADNESS

It is with small shame that I move to turn on the radio today. Radio is the friend I usually neglect; the friend I only think to call upon when life has turned sad and desperate. I always return to it flushed with guilt — but it is always waiting for me; it is always ready to take me back.

When I first lived alone, I listened, like so many, each day: when I awoke in the mornings, and again in the evenings, when I returned from work. While I waited out the siege of my first New York summer, radio's sounds were the only ones I could tolerate.

And so, when my first relationship went bad, I found myself in an apartment steeped in brown, and again I turned to radio. The taste of yucca, which I fried for the first time in that tiny kitchen, the smell of smoke-saturated curtains and Murphy's Oil Soap, the interviews, the news reports, the long recitation of member stations in the Berkshires — these are bound to each other and to me, they are the taste, the smell, the sodden air of that isolation.

Radio was made for the lonely, after all, the displaced and the out of touch. Unlike television — which stares stubbornly in a single direction, which demands the attendance of the whole battered body — radio is everywhere. Single people need radio, for only it can fill the enormous empty spaces that even their smallest apartments harbor. It does not spite us for our distraction, but tactfully begins from the moment we switch it on.

Its sound is our guardian angel; ubiquitous but unassuming. We move about our business while radio patiently follows. Its persistence soothes even our most sudden and sharp-edged isolations, softens the spaces between our souls and the ever-distant walls.

In these ways, radio is forgiving, and the lonely are in need of forgiveness.

Last spring it seemed my whole life abandoned me — a needed job fell through, my relationship failed. I took the first, smallest, dingiest apartment that offered itself. I didn't have the patience, or the courage, to look further. I switched perfumes. I listened to the radio. And words started to drop in on me without warning.

As I shivered in the rush of possibility, my comforts and routines wrestled away from me; I became aware of the air nearest to me. This air knew my skin, it was warm with my own voice. Sheltered, I grew still. I lifted plain and shining words from the cold that braced my insides. They swam to me, they offered themselves to my net.

For months I lived like this, avoiding new friendships, neglecting the few that had survived my prior couplehood. I postponed getting a new job, preferring to subsist on coffee, on toast, on the sun that would brave my filthy windows. These days were indulgent and untenable — I would have to find work, I would have to revive old friendships, I would have to form new ones. The harvest would fall off.

Though I cried myself to sleep each night, this time was as sweet and as thick as any I ever lived. Each moment I distilled and drank off at my leisure; each day I reaffirmed my greed for my own uninterrupted time, and only radio was invited.

I grew strong, alone like that. But slowly, practicality ended my respite. I moved in with a friend, I took a job. I fell in love.

Falling in love is like painting yourself into a corner. Thrilled by the color you've laid down around you, you forget about freedom shrinking at your back. Neglected, my river slowed, my catches grew meager. I stopped listening to the radio. I once again began to think of time alone as something to spend or will away, rather than something I could stretch myself across.

And now, now that I have forgotten, things prepare themselves to fall away again — another love will leave; I will take an apartment by myself. I feel the air turn crisp, the walls edge farther from my body.

Shivering, nervous, I turn on the radio, for the first time in months. Paul Auster is reading a story about a girl who lost her father, who dragged a Christmas tree down the streets of a midnight Brooklyn. He is asking us for our stories.

There are conditions: that they be both brief and true.

But I have no deaths, no travels worth repeating. I have no strokes of wild fortune or incredible tragedy. I have only an average sadness. Worse, I have been unable to write for weeks now, my mind riddled instead by imminent departures, imminent change.

Then it strikes me: this moment is the friendly hand of solitude. The radio is inviting me back, back to the rooms it will fill with its voice of warmest flannel, back to the warm light of time spent alone.

I have recognized the invitation only as I have written these lines. That is my story, complete with the climax that is now.

Sometimes it is good fortune to be abandoned. While we are looking after our losses, our selves may slip back inside.

AMENI ROZSA
*Williamstown, Massachusetts*

# INDEX OF AUTHORS

Garrett, Mary Ann, 288
Gibson, Tim, 472
Goff, Beth Twiggar, 253
Gonzalez, G. A., 466
Goodman, Lion, 316
Gover, Mark, 568
Graves, Don, 97

Hagen, Erica, 281
Hale, Steve, 387
Hall, Bruce Edward, 308
Halpern, Jeanne W., 345
Hardman, Olga, 454
Harper, Steve, 501
Hayden, Lucy, 127
Heffelbower, Holly A., 226
Helmantoler, Bill, 352
Hodgman, Steve, 510
Hoke, Jerry, 87
Howze, John, 563
Hsu, Martha Russell, 169
Hudin, Barbara, 116
Huffman, Yale, 30
Humiston, Paul K., 298
Husson, Kara, 515
Hustvedt, Lloyd, 366

Isler, Saul, 278

Jackson, Simonette, 33
Johnson, Marie, 114
Johnson, Vicky, 519

Keith, John, 119